CHARACTER
COUNTS

CHARACTER COUNTS

The Creation and Building
of The Vanguard Group

John C. Bogle

McGRAW-HILL

New York   Chicago   San Francisco   Lisbon   London   Madrid   Mexico City
Milan   New Delhi   San Juan   Seoul   Singapore   Sydney   Toronto

McGraw-Hill

A Division of The McGraw·Hill Companies

1 2 3 4 5 6 7 8 9 0 AGM/AGM 0 9 8 7 6 5 4 3 2

ISBN 0-07-139115-0

This book was set in New Caledonia by North Market Street Graphics.

Printed and bound by Quebecor World/Martinsburg.

McGraw-Hill books are available at special quantity discounts to use as premiums and sales promotions, or for use in corporate training programs. For more information, please write to the Director of Special Sales, Professional Publishing, McGraw-Hill, Two Penn Plaza, New York, NY 10121-2298. Or contact your local bookstore.

This publication is designed to provide accurate and authoritative information in regard to the subject matter covered. It is sold with the understanding that neither the author nor the publisher is engaged in rendering legal, accounting, or other professional service. If legal advice or other expert assistance is required, the services of a competent professional person should be sought.
—*From a Declaration of Principles jointly adopted by a Committee of the American Bar Association and a Committee of Publishers.*

 This book is printed on recycled, acid-free paper containing a minimum of 50% recycled, de-inked fiber.

To my beloved wife, Eve, who patiently, lovingly, and energetically holds our family together and accepts my commitment to the mission of assuring that the millions of human beings who depend on their mutual fund investments get a fair shake.

*To the finest crew in the history of the mutual fund industry, which has the strength of purpose, the guts, the conviction, the spiritual staying power, and, above all, the character to build a future worthy of our past.**

---

*See reference on page 209.

The only history worth reading is that written at the time it treats, the history of what was done and seen, heard out of the mouths of the men who did and saw.

— John Ruskin

"That is the true test of a brilliant theory," says a member of the Nobel Economics Prize committee. "What first is thought to be wrong is later shown to be obvious." People see the world as they are trained to see it, and resist contrary explanations. That's what makes innovation unwelcome and discovery almost impossible.

— *New York Times* editorial, 1985

I find the great thing in this world is not so much where we stand, as in what direction we are moving: To reach the port of heaven, we must sail sometimes with the wind and sometimes against it—but we must sail, and not drift, nor lie at anchor.

— Oliver Wendell Holmes

CONTENTS

CONTENTS

Contents

xi

INTRODUCTION

As THE autumn of 1974 began, a company named *Vanguard* would shortly come into existence. Just twenty-seven years later, as 2001 drew to a close, that company had become one of the largest financial institutions on the face of the globe.

Beginning with $1.4 billion of investor capital under management, The Vanguard Group of Investment Companies now manages $530 billion for more than 15 million investors, sited largely in the United States but also scattered all over the world. What is more, the 25 percent compound annual growth rate that the firm has achieved has, against all odds, been sustained at a remarkably steady rate—21 percent per year from 1974 through 1984, 29 percent from 1984 through 1994, and even 23 percent since then. While the turbulence in the world economy, the burst in the stock market bubble as the twentieth century ended, and the staggering impact of the September 11, 2001, terrorist bombings in the United States—vividly exemplified by the utter obliteration of the proud towers of New York City's World Trade Center—have markedly slowed the growth rate of the investor capital managed at Vanguard, the firm continues to thrive.

What accounts for this remarkable record of growth? Certainly the great boom in the financial markets that began in 1982—a period that saw the Dow-Jones Industrial Average rise from 770 to 11,700 in January 2000, before tumbling to 9,600 in the late summer of 2001— played a major role. The impact of that long boom, magnified by the rise to preeminence of stock funds, bond funds, and money market funds as the investments of choice on balance sheets of American families, has carried the assets of the U.S. mutual fund industry, $36 billion when Vanguard began, to $6.0 *trillion* today.

In such an environment, to be sure, few asset management firms have failed to prosper. But the industry's growth rate has been but a fraction of Vanguard's. More than one-half of Vanguard's growth has come at the expense of its rivals in the mutual fund industry. With a 1981 market share of less than 2 percent of mutual fund assets—the fourteenth-largest firm in a dwindling industry—Vanguard now holds an 8.2 percent share. Our firm is now the second-largest firm in a vibrant industry, and it is slowly closing in on the industry asset leader.

But what accounts for Vanguard's growth is something more than booming financial markets and a burgeoning mutual fund industry. That something is that we have marched to a different drummer. Our indisputably successful drive to become the world's lowest-cost provider of financial services was the sine qua non. It led to our record of innovation, most notably the creation of the industry's first index funds, structured bond funds, and tax-managed funds. And our unprecedented decision to abandon our dealer distribution network and offer shares to investors without sales loads also set us apart from most of our rivals.

But our rise to leadership goes even deeper than that, to the very *character* that undergirded all those business decisions: the ethical standards, the moral values, and the investment principles to which the firm has adhered since its creation. Only you, the reader, can judge how many enterprises you have encountered of which it can be said: *This is a company that stands for something.* Something bigger than mere commercial success, something more important than growth at any price . . . something called character.

A Company That Stands for Something

A company that stands for something. I believe you can say that of Vanguard. What we stand for, if I were to pick a single word, is: *stewardship.* The loyal stewardship of the assets entrusted to us by millions of investors; placing the interests of our fund shareholders paramount; holding long-term investment values and strategies above speculation and marketing opportunism; and assuring that shareholders receive their fair share of the returns earned in the financial markets. *A company that is of the shareholder, by the shareholder, and for the shareholder.*

It is Vanguard's unique *mutualized* structure that is the foundation of most of our principles and values. Other fund managers operate their mutual funds under contracts that generate substantial management fees, and on which the managers earn generous profits. Vanguard is owned by its shareholders and operates at cost. Other fund groups view their shareholders as *customers,* there to buy their *products.* Vanguard views its shareholders as *owners,* there to receive our *services.* Vanguard, then, is an enterprise with a singular character, reflected in the particular moral qualities, ethical standards, and principles that drive the conduct of our affairs.

Character counts. That is the message I seek to convey in this book. The way I intend to convey this message is *not* in the form of conventional corporate history, in a chronological, step-by-step, event-by-event fashion. For I fear such an approach would *describe,* rather than *explain,* Vanguard's growth. The march of events would overwhelm the underlying character that shaped those events. What is more, I fear that my retrospective view of the events of our history might, however inadvertently, alter their original reality. *So, I shall tell most of the story when it happened, as it happened.*

It is easy to tell the Vanguard story in this way. For over the past quarter century, I have spoken regularly to our crew, the word I've used since the outset to describe our staff, about our mission—first at our asset milestone celebrations, beginning with billion-dollar increases, then larger thresholds; then each midyear and at each year's end; and finally at our twenty-fifth anniversary and at the fifty-year mark of my career in the mutual fund industry. All told, forty-two speeches are included in this book.

Four Purposes

I gave those speeches primarily for four purposes:

1. *To celebrate:* Savoring what we had accomplished, for just a moment in a day that was always busy and sometimes chaotic, and expressing appreciation to the members of our crew for their work in the greater good for Vanguard and our clients.
2. *To communicate:* Presenting a chronicle of The Vanguard Group's history and traditions, going all the way back to the founding of Wellington Fund—the first fund in what would come to be called "The Vanguard Group"—in 1928. And commenting about the march of events at Vanguard, in the financial markets, in the marketing of financial services, and in the mutual fund industry, always attempting to highlight the important differences between the

way we do business, and the way so many of our rivals do. Since any company exists as a continuum, it responds to each new challenge based on the totality of its past experiences. My intention was to convey both *a sense of history* and *a sense of who we are.*

3. *To inculcate:* Pounding home the importance of a solid system of human and ethical values in the modern business enterprise: Integrity, discipline, honesty, quality, ambition, loyalty, competition, creativity, innovation, cooperation, continuity, even a sense of humor—in all, the *character* of our company. Maintaining these values may well be more important measures of success than such conventional business standards as our billions of dollars in assets, our market share, or our productivity.

4. *To elevate:* Raising the context of our mission by seasoning my talks with quotations from some of the great (and less great) persons of history: John Maynard Keynes, Grantland Rice, Marcus Aurelius, Lord Horatio Nelson, Thomas Paine, Longfellow, Tennyson, Shakespeare, Archimedes, Frank Sinatra, Carl Sandburg, Queen Victoria, Robert Frost, Rudyard Kipling, Joseph Schumpeter, even Isaiah and Ecclesiastes. As we considered the worthy mission that Vanguard had set for itself, I wanted to elevate our mundane work with a grand—not, I hope, grandiose—perspective.

Publishing these speeches today has some wonderful benefits. First, now they are, well, *published*—preserved not only for today's crew members and shareowners but for future generations. Second, they represent history not in neat retrospect but in the messy way in which history is actually experienced—truly, *a living history.* And third—although this may prove to be a vain hope—the speeches and accompanying text may inspire those idealists out there who still believe (or persuade those who can be persuaded to believe) that it is possible to create a firm that can succeed in a competitive, dog-eat-dog business, all the while holding to a stern set of values and standards. To build, as it were, a firm that is both a *commercial* and an *artistic* success. To validate, finally, this one great premise about creating a company and building it to a position of industry leadership in the right way: *Character counts.*

John C. Bogle

Part I

THE FORMATIVE YEARS, 1974–1979

I GAVE THE FIRST of my speeches to our crew when we reached our $3 billion milestone, on September 19, 1980. Because the events that led up to that milestone are a vital phase of our history, I want to tell you, in my own words of today, of the genesis of Vanguard, how it was created, and what we accomplished in our formative years.

Vanguard was incorporated on September 24, 1974. When we began operations on May 1, 1975, we employed twenty-eight crew members, largely engaged in legal, accounting, and processing activities. The 50 percent market decline that began in early 1973 was just weeks from its nadir. We had formed a company to administer just $1.4 billion of mutual fund assets, assets that were draining away, week after week, as more fund shares were liquidated by existing shareholders than were being purchased by new shareholders. It might have seemed an inopportune time to begin a new business, but I don't recall ever being discouraged, nor do I recall any signs of concern among the crew of our tiny enterprise.

It's fair to say that the ideas that make up Vanguard's intellectual foundation—the rock on which we stand—go back to an extraordinary piece of luck that arose twenty-five years earlier, and it led to the 140-page senior thesis that I researched and wrote at Princeton University in 1950 and 1951. I entitled it "The Economic Role of the Investment Company," and our founding ideas were, at least arguably, expressed right there. The introduction to my thesis baldly asserts that "the prime responsibility of mutual funds must always be to their share-

	Total Net Assets[1]	Net Cash Flow[1]	% Change in Assets	Number of Funds	Crew Members	Expense Ratio (%)	Stock Funds	Balanced Funds	Bond Funds	Money Funds	Stocks	Bonds	Bills
								% of Fund Assets In:			Annual Return[2] (%)		
1974	1,457	−52		11	28	0.73	42	55	3	0	−3.2	7.6	2.6
1975	1,781	−56	22.2	12	47	0.66	47	51	2	0	37.1	12.3	6.0
1976	2,049	−128	15.0	15	97	0.60	49	48	3	0	23.8	15.6	5.1
1977	1,849	−90	−9.8	17	99	0.61	50	45	4	1	−7.2	3.0	5.5
1978	1,919	49	3.8	17	106	0.62	51	40	6	3	6.5	1.4	7.4
1979	2,380	278	24.0	17	133	0.58	52	30	10	8	18.4	1.9	10.3
Cumulative	1		10.3[3]								13.1	7.9	6.9

[1] Figures are in $ millions
[2] Stocks: Standard and Poor's 500 Index
  Bonds: Lehman Bros. Aggregate Bond Index
  Bills: 90-day Treasury-bill
[3] Annual Rate

holders." The conclusion demands that funds must *serve*—"serve both individual and institutional investors, . . . serve them in the most efficient, honest, and economical way possible." And the intervening text urges funds to reduce sales charges and management fees, to exercise their responsibility for corporate citizenship, to refrain from excessive claims of management ability, and to "make no claim to superiority over the market averages."

Today, it's easy for me to make two diametrically opposed statements about those prescriptions and proscriptions: (1) They represent the mindless prattle of an idealistic, immature college student, unwise in the ways of the world; and (2) they represent a carefully thought out philosophy and a remarkably prescient design for the firm I would found twenty-three years later. Fuzzy ideals or practical ideas? Some of each? You'll have to decide after you hear the story.

The Beginning

That original piece of luck from which all else would follow was an article on the mutual fund industry in the December 1949 issue of *Fortune* magazine, which I happened upon in the reading room of Princeton's then brand new Firestone Library. My thesis led me directly into a career in this industry, for it was read by Walter L. Morgan, a fellow Princetonian, legendary fund pioneer, and founder in 1928 of Wellington Fund. While its assets in mid-1951 were but $150 million, it was one of the larger funds in the industry. When I graduated, Mr. Morgan hired me.

With few experienced executives in the Wellington Management organization, my ascent was rapid. Early in 1965, at age thirty-five, I was named executive vice president, becoming Mr. Morgan's obvious successor. He told me to "do whatever it takes" to fix the firm's problems— notably (1) an overreliance on a single, highly conservative balanced (stock and bond) fund; (2) the lack of an aggressive equity fund during that booming "go-go" era in the stock market; (3) a paucity of investment management talent at the firm; and (4) a complete dependence on the mutual fund business.

Lady Luck, or so it seemed at the time, favored me again. Brash, overconfident, and impetuous, I found a way to solve all four problems in one fell swoop early in 1966, and I was able to merge Wellington Management Company with Thordike, Doran, Paine and Lewis, Inc., an aggressive equity manager located in Boston. With the merger, we

3

added their go-go Ivest Fund to our "product line" (as I *used to* refer to it); we acquired the talents of their four founders, a remarkable group of highly talented (or so I was convinced at the time) young money managers known as the "whiz kids"; and we brought their burgeoning private investment counsel business into the fold. In the merger, however, I relinquished too much of the voting control of Wellington Management Company for my own good.

Success, Then Failure

The merger was an extraordinary success. But only until the end of the go-go era—an era in the stock market eerily reminiscent of the boom and bust in technology and Internet stocks during the stock market bubble of the late 1990s and into early 2000. The subsequent onset of a great market crash—from the 1973 high to the 1974 low, stock prices tumbled nearly 50 percent—was itself perhaps a precursor of the precipitous 75 percent drop in the NASDAQ market from its mid-March 2000 high to its level as autumn 2001 began. In that earlier decline, our firm's aggressive equity funds tumbled even more than the market, and, sadly, even the conservative Wellington Fund (which my new partners had made more aggressive than ever before in its history) fell sharply. The aura of omnipotence surrounding our managers vanished, and money began to pour out of our funds. Our funds suffered a run of net liquidations that was to persist for eighty long months, until mid-1978. Bad times always put pressure on tenuous partnerships, and at the company's board meeting in Valley Forge on January 24, 1974, in the midst of the bear market, my four partners banded together to fire me as chief executive of Wellington Management Company.

I had experienced my first major failure. But when a door closed— slammed!—a window opened, another lucky break. Here's how it happened: The board meeting of the Wellington funds—the collective name we used to identify those mutual funds that were managed by Wellington Management Company—was held in New York the very next day, January 25. It was there that I proposed the implementation of a plan I had actually described to the entire senior management staff of Wellington Management Company in 1971. My plan would have "mutualized" the funds, by having them purchase all of the stock of both the management owners and public stockholders of the management company. Then, the company would be owned by the funds themselves and operated at cost, serving solely the interest of the fund shareholders, at last bereft of the inevitable conflict of interest involved when *two* masters must be served—a structure that was then, and with Vanguard's exception now remains, the universal case in the mutual fund industry. While my rivals also served on the fund boards, they were in the minority, and I hoped to pull off this remarkable reversal of fortune quickly.

One-Third of a Loaf: Better Than None?

Alas, cautious corporate directors are likely to break neither old precedent nor new ground, and the fund board deadlocked. So I urged upon the directors a new structure that would give the funds themselves a dedicated voice of advocacy, manifested in a staff of their own, and the ability to establish an arm's-length relationship with Wellington Management, the funds' investment adviser and share distributor. Our job would be to assure that the new organization would serve solely the interests of the fund shareholders.

That argument finally carried the day. In mid-August, after seven months of tedious, stressful negotiations, the fund board agreed to retain me as a full-time fund president, in charge only of administration—accounting, legal, shareholder recordkeeping, and so on—but to oversee the continuing relationship with Wellington as fund adviser and fund marketer. It was a victory of sorts, but, I feared, a Pyrrhic victory.

Why? Because success in the fund field is *not* driven by how well the funds are administered. Though their affairs must be supervised and controlled with dedication, skill, and precision, success is determined by what kinds of funds are created, by whether superior investment returns are attained, and by how—and how effectively—the funds are marketed and distributed. We had been given one-third of the fund loaf, as it were, but it was the least important third. It was the other two-thirds that would make us or break us. Yet we were formally prohibited from performing the critical functions of portfolio supervision and distribution. Nonetheless, we were permitted by the board to create a new administrative company and provide a new corporate identifier for it.

And it was here, despite that gloomy start, that a bright star quickly shone on us: The name "Vanguard." In early September 1974, as I was contemplating a name for our new enterprise, Lady Luck struck yet again. A dealer in antique prints happened by my office. I bought from him four prints showing various naval battles of Great Britain during the Napoleonic Wars era. He gave me the book from which they had been removed, and I happened upon the text describing the Battle of the Nile, at which Lord Nelson, while losing scarcely a British ship, had demolished Napoleon's French fleet. Right before my eyes was Nelson's dispatch to the admiralty, announcing the glorious victory and praising his crew. At the top, he had written the name and location of his flagship: *"Vanguard, off the mouth of the Nile."* I knew immediately that I had found the name for my new enterprise!

Strategy Follows Structure

As 1974 drew to a close, what was in place was a tiny company with a staff of but twenty-eight, responsible for only the administration—nothing more—of $1 billion-plus of mutual fund assets; a brand-new name, albeit one with a proud nautical tradition; and a *mutual* structure without precedent in the industry—a structure in which the funds would be operated not in the interest of their managers but solely in the best interests of their shareholders. The foundation of Vanguard's character was built on the quintessential rock of this structure. While these might seem rather meager credentials, that structure set in motion all that was to follow, for, as I have often said about Vanguard's mission: *Strategy follows structure.*

And so strategy would follow structure in Vanguard's case. Consider what logically follows when mutual funds are owned and controlled by their own shareholders. First, a passionate desire to serve shareholders with integrity, candor, fairness, and honor. *Treat your clients as your owners, simply because they are your owners.* Second, importantly, a focus on the management of existing assets, not on the gathering of new assets by the marketing of shares. Third, the creation of funds that reflect enduring investment principles rather than transitory investment fads. Fourth, a high level of economy and efficiency, operating at bare-bones levels of cost and negotiating at arm's-length the terms of our contracts with external advisers and distributors. For the less we spend, the higher the returns—dollar for dollar—for our shareholder-owners.

While we had the *structure*, however, we could not control the *strategy*. I had realized all along that the narrow mandate that precluded our engaging in portfolio management and distribution services would give Vanguard insufficient power to control its destiny.

While a third of a loaf was better than none, I concluded that we should promptly set about seizing the other two-thirds. And with remarkable speed, we did just that. Within less than two years after we began operations, we had begun to manage our first fund and had taken over control of all the distribution. In retrospect, going so far so fast must have involved a heavy measure of determination. It also involved a generous dose of opportunism, spiced by what might be described as a touch of disingenuousness.

The Index Fund

Our entry into fund management was paradoxical: *the world's first index mutual fund.* Originally dubbed "First Index Investment Trust" and now named "Vanguard 500 Index Fund" and modeled on the Standard & Poor's 500 Stock Index, it represented a 180-degree departure from the traditional actively managed fund. The index fund was an idea hinted at in my thesis fully twenty-five years earlier. (Remember, funds "can make no claim to superiority over the market averages.") My experience at Wellington Fund, to say nothing of the sorry aftermath of my brief liaison with the whiz-kid money managers whom I'd brought in as partners, had disabused me of the notion that certain money managers had some God-given lock on superior investment returns.

I backed up my own hard-won experience with some statistics that I had produced by hand in mid-1975, showing that during the prior twenty-five years the annual return of the average mutual fund had fallen 1.5 percent short of the return of the Standard & Poor's 500 Index (9.5 versus 11 percent). And I buttressed my case for indexing with strong financial journal articles by Massachusetts Institute of Technology professor and Nobel Laureate Paul Samuelson ("Challenge to Judgment") and Greenwich Research founder Charles D. Ellis ("The Loser's Game"), both of whom applauded the indexing concept.

When I proposed the index fund, the directors viewed it with a jaundiced eye. But I produced my own research, showed them the articles, and assured them that—since the fund was not actively managed and thus did not require traditional stock-picking and portfolio supervision—we would not be exceeding Vanguard's narrow administrative mandate. Sound logic or not, the directors agreed, and, just four months after Vanguard began operations, they approved our entry into the field of, well, investment management. On December 30, 1975, the world's first index mutual fund was incorporated. It took the winter and spring to persuade a reluctant group of Wall Street investment bankers to manage the public offering, but as the date for the underwriting approached, their initial $150 million target began to melt away. They finally raised $11.4 million. On August 29, 1976, our index fund began operations. *We had started the world's first index mutual fund.*

The Final Third of the Loaf

Taking over distribution came swiftly thereafter. Given our structure, I had no doubt that Vanguard could fairly quickly reach a level of unit operating costs (that is, mutual fund expense ratios) that was the lowest in the world, a stamp of character that would become our mantra. But how valuable an asset would the low-cost provider status be when investors still had to pay a sales commission—then nearly 9 percent of the amount invested in the fund—when they bought their shares? Yet Wellington Fund shares had been distributed through broker-dealers in that manner for nearly a half century. And no-load funds were the exception rather than the rule.

Ever the frugal Scot, however, I had always had an affinity for the no-load business. What is more, as I pondered the future, it was easy to recognize some obvious trends: The American population was growing. As productivity grew, family wealth would grow. With growing wealth, higher education would rise in importance, enhancing public interest in economics and finance. With more information and more knowledge, millions of families would become more aware of the benefits of low costs, and they would develop the confidence to make their own decisions. Every one of those patently obvious ideas pointed to the same place: *For a firm with our simple investment principles and rock-bottom costs, a no-load distribution network was the logical choice.* I concluded that we had no recourse but to take over our distribution and marketing activities, and promptly eliminate all sales loads.

It wouldn't be easy. While most of our directors shared my sympathy for a no-load system, all were aware that it could be seen to abrogate our charter restriction. They also were properly concerned about whether we had the skills to make it work (the no-load business was then but a small part of the fund business) and whether angry brokers, having sold Wellington shares, wouldn't persuade their clients to redeem them,

8

leaving our firm in a risky no-man's-land. But determination carried the day, and we persuaded them that the opportunities vastly outweighed the risks. With another dose of opportunism and another hint of disingenuousness, we also persuaded our directors that we weren't becoming a distributor. *We were simply eliminating distribution.*

Eliminating all sales loads and abandoning our lifelong dealer network—another decision without precedent in mutual fund history—would bring to Vanguard the control of our distribution system. Together with our role in managing the index fund investment portfolio, we had essentially completed the move to become a full-service mutual fund complex. By the narrow margin of just two votes, the board approved the proposal on February 8, 1977. Our mutualization was now substantially complete.

The First Mover

While the term did not exist in 1974, in its own modest way Vanguard had become a "first mover." And it was our character—rooted in the very structure that logically demanded that we focus solely on the interest of shareholders—that carried the day. From the express objective of becoming the world's lowest-cost provider of financial services, everything else would follow. Of course we recognized—as our competitors must also have recognized—that there are powerful odds against beating the financial markets themselves. After all, *before* the deduction of the costs of the financial intermediaries, for all investors as a group, beating the markets is a zero-sum game. *After* the costs of all those intermediaries who provide financial services are deducted, therefore, beating the market becomes a loser's game.

Those costs—all of those management fees, sales charges, marketing costs, brokerage commissions, opportunity costs, and operating expenses—are considerable in the mutual fund industry. Together, they amount to more than 2.5 percent per year, or nearly 25 percent of the stock market's historical annual rate of return. So the gap between *market* return and *investor* return is, and must be, wide. As a result, the odds against any particular equity mutual fund gaining a significant edge over the market in the very long run are, by my reckoning, something like fifty to one. *Thus, the honest steward who charges least, wins most.* But not for himself; for those investors who entrust their assets to his care. It is not all that complicated.

9

Quickly, Another Major Innovation

While investment costs *always* matter, they matter most where they are at once very large, compounded over time, and directly proportionate to the value of the services provided. *Each of these characteristics applies directly to the mutual fund industry.* Once we had assumed responsibility for distribution, the ramifications of this simple insight resounded even more powerfully. Immediately after we started operations in May 1975, we had formed one of the early money market funds, and our low costs were already differentiating us from the herd. By their nature, money market funds are obliged to own high-quality, limited-maturity certificates of deposit, commercial paper, and U.S. Treasury bills. As a result, the expense ratio difference accounts for upwards of 98 percent of the difference in yield. If money market funds best exemplify the principle that *lower costs are directly associated with higher returns,* we thought, why not carry that principle through to bond funds?

Why not indeed? When Congress passed a law enabling the creation of municipal bond mutual funds in 1976, a great opportunity presented itself. By early 1977 most of our competitors had offered them, largely *with* sales charges. Clearly, a no-load municipal bond fund would serve investors more cost-efficiently. Equally clearly, being the low-cost provider would further enhance the returns our investors would earn. And even as I had come to believe that precious few stock managers could outguess the stock market, so I had come to believe that precious few bond managers could consistently outguess the bond market, accurately forecasting the direction and level of interest rates. Yet our high-cost peers were, in effect, offering "managed" bond funds that purported to do exactly that—an implicit promise that could not possibly be fulfilled.

Here arose a simple insight, in its own way as obvious as the index fund. Why not depart from the crowd, I thought, forming not a *single* tax-exempt bond fund that was *managed,* but a *three-tier* bond fund, one in which a narrow range of maturities would be set for each series: one, *long-term;* two, *short-term;* and three—you guessed it!—*intermediate-term.* There would be no speculating on interest rates. Further, there would be no compromising on quality; each portfolio would hold only top-grade bonds. None would carry sales charges; all would soon operate at the lowest costs in the field.

On September 1, 1977, our new municipal bond fund introduced this simple three-tier structure—so similar in character to our own stock index fund—to the mutual fund industry. We retained Citibank as investment adviser, our first use of a firm other than Wellington Management Company to perform such services. Our innovative fund was to prove equally important in changing the way investors would think about bond investing. *We had changed the rules of the game.* The three-tier structure would gradually become the industry standard, not only for municipal bond funds, but for corporate bond funds and U.S. government bond funds as well. We were well on the way toward establishing our credentials as the industry's bond fund leader.

Business As Usual?

It would be nice to be able to say that, amid all of this innovation, it was "business as usual" for Vanguard during its formative years. But that was hardly the case. We still had a business to run, and as we readied the firm for the future there was no shortage of challenge, change, and progress. In 1976, we assumed responsibility for shareholder record-keeping duties, the better to prepare ourselves to provide service excellence to our shareholders in a new environment in which they would interface directly with us, rather than with the stockbrokers who had distributed our funds' shares during the previous fifty years. In 1977, to help with this task, we began our first use of a toll-free 800 telephone number, which soon became the most widely accepted means of shareholder communication in the direct marketing segment of the mutual fund industry.

We were busy on the investment side of the business too, and 1978 was a landmark year. We won a competition to acquire Allstate Enterprises Stock Fund, merging it into W.L. Morgan Growth Fund, nearly tripling its assets. Facing limited success in marketing our index fund in its early years, we merged our Exeter Fund into First Index Investment Trust, nearly tripling its assets as well. In both cases, we achieved significant economies of scale for the funds' shareholders. But the most significant change was restructuring the investment program of Wellington Fund, substantially narrowing the range of asset allocations (common stocks would be required to constitute between 60 and 70 percent of assets). We also directed Wellington Management, the fund's adviser, to shift the equity portfolio emphasis from growth stocks to value stocks, with the goal of reducing the fund's risk and increasing its dividend income. Wellington Fund's assets had tumbled from $2 billion in 1965 to below $500 million in 1974, and the time for corrective action was long overdue.

Nineteen seventy-eight ended with a bang. Just before year-end, we introduced two of the industry's first high-yield bond funds, offering higher yields along with a commensurate reduction in investment quality. The high-yield municipal fund would be run by Citibank, the high-yield corporate fund by Wellington. Neither fund, however, would join the "junk bond" group, which soon became popular; both were held to higher credit quality standards. But with their sparse expense ratios, the two new funds could nonetheless deliver fully competitive net yields.

Survival First, Celebration Later

In those early years of 1974 through 1979, amid the frenzy of competition and innovation—of creating an unprecedented corporate structure and making an unprecedented departure from the traditional distribution system; of converting an administrative company into a full-bodied mutual fund complex; of dealing with cash outflows, month after month—we were nonetheless able to grow a bit. Why? First, because the stock market slowly began to recover from its near-50 percent decline from the 1973 high to the 1974 low. The Dow-Jones Industrial Average rose from a low of 577 in 1974 to 839 by the end of the 1970s. Burned by the earlier stock market decline, however, investors began to look to bonds, and our bond funds gained recognition. And in an environment of soaring short-term interest rates, our money market fund assets began to burgeon, part of a huge new industry component that miraculously appeared just in time to provide a powerful additional weapon. Money funds enabled the mutual fund industry to become a vigorous competitor, not only for the *investments* of America's families, but for their *savings*. Nonetheless, Vanguard remained a tiny company, fighting for its life.

Our assets crept upward, from $1.4 billion at the outset to $2 billion in mid-1976, only to fall back to $1.7 billion in October 1977, then recovering by March 1979, when we crossed the $2 billion mark again, this time for good. But we ignored that evanescent milestone. After all, we'd been there before. Wellington Fund alone had reached the $2 billion mark in 1965, and at the stock market's 1973 peak the total assets of all the then-Wellington funds—later to become the Vanguard funds—totaled $2.8 billion. With assets at $2.4 billion as 1979 came to a close, a $3 billion milestone celebration would have to wait.

Not only was there no occasion to celebrate in those early years, we were all too busy to think much about celebrating. The task, above all, was survival. What is more, there seemed little need for me to make speeches about what we were doing, why we were doing it, and how we were doing. Our crew was tiny, and everyone knew what was going on. Of course, as our responsibilities grew, our line of funds grew, and our asset base expanded, our crew grew too—from 28 members to 133. We were all located on a couple of floors in a small Valley Forge building into which we'd moved, as part of Wellington Management Company, years earlier.

Furthermore, we didn't pioneer for pioneering's sake nor innovate for innovation's sake, nor did we break precedent after precedent merely for the sake of smashing industry icons. *We did the things we did because we thought they were right for investors, and we knew they would work.* We also knew that, since the central nature of our ethic was economy of operations, our rivals were unlikely to copy that strategy, or at least unlikely to copy it with very much enthusiasm. But most of all, we did what we did because it was consistent with the principles and values of our new firm, consistent, if you will, with our corporate character. And of this we were certain: *Character would count.*

Zest, Alacrity, and Accomplishment

In retrospect, of course, I wish that I had given more speeches to our crew in the early years. For I would then have more than memories, however clear, to recount those early days. But in mid-2001, I gave a speech that included a quote that took me way back to the early, happy, rough-and-tumble era when our small band of crew members was implementing our ideas, fighting the daily battles that would one day turn the tide so that the struggling creation of 1974 would start to grow, to gain traction, and to begin its march to industry leadership.

The thrill of building the new enterprise gave our crew a special zest. We battled joyfully, and we accomplished things with remarkable alacrity. Only seven months elapsed from our creation in 1974 to our start of operations in 1975; only four months more until the index fund was approved and eleven months until it was offered; only five more months until we had taken over distribution, completing our transition to becoming a full-line mutual fund complex; less then six months more for the novel municipal bond fund triad. We had built our foundation in less than three years. I'll never forget the feverish pace nor the extraordinary effort of our crew, which had grown to just 133 members as 1979 ended. How did we get it all done? *Together.*

It was a productive, exciting time. And it was the time we placed on Vanguard the stamp of character that shaped every move we made. In that 2001 speech, here's the way I described it:

> **That era constituted the formative era in our history. For those of you here tonight who were unfortunate enough *not* to have shared in the chaotic excitement surrounding the creation and conversion of Vanguard, you have my pity. The words that Shakespeare attributed to Henry V at the Battle of Agincourt on October 25, 1415—Saint Crispin's Day, nearly six centuries ago—express my emotions far better than could any words of mine:**
>
>> *We few, we happy few, we band of brothers,*
>> *For he today who shed his blood with me*
>> *Shall be my brother . . .*
>> *And gentlemen in England now a-bed*
>> *Shall think themselves accursed they were not here*
>> *And hold their manhoods cheap while any speaks*
>> *That fought with us upon Saint Crispin's day.*
>
> **And so what I say in retrospect to that original band of brothers—and sisters too—in those crucial battles in the opening chapter of Vanguard's history, I reiterate to you tonight: Thanks for fighting with us, and at my side.**

The Early Years in Retrospect

As I look back on Vanguard's formative years, it is obvious now what a blessing it was to have started the new firm at the very bottom of a bear market. Stocks had nowhere to go but up, and the equity market delivered a healthy 13.1 percent annual return from our inception through 1979. Bond returns, strong in the early years, were terrible in the later years. But the total bond market never actually experienced a down year (the rising interest payments more than offset the price declines) and the bond market return averaged a healthy 7.9 percent annually during the period. And the rise in the Treasury bill return from 2.6

percent to 10.3 percent set the stage for the coming boom in money market funds.

As 1979 ended, we were, in a sense, at the end of the beginning. Our assets had grown to $2.4 billion. Cash outflows of $320 million in 1974–77 had turned to inflows of $330 million in 1978–79. Following ample precedent, we had quickly moved into the money market arena. Breaking brand-new ground, we had formed the world's first index fund, the first three-tier bond fund, a pair of the first high-yield bond funds, and restructured the investment policies of Wellington Fund, our flagship for fifty years.

Little did we know how vital those pioneering decisions would be. Today our index fund is the world's largest mutual fund, and our municipal bond funds are now that industry segment's largest aggregation. Our high-yield corporate fund too is the largest in its field. While we were only one among many firms to quickly identify the merit of the money market fund, our money funds now compose the fourth-largest group in its field. The restructuring of Wellington Fund proved almost prescient. Its performance rapidly improved, and today, with $21 billion of assets, it is again the largest balanced fund in the world. Each of those funds represented a strategy that followed our structure. Each made the most of our low-cost mandate. Each was a manifestation of the Vanguard character, already firmly established as the 1980s were about to begin.

Part II

THE COMPANY TAKES OFF, 1980–1985

*T*HE 1980–1985 ERA would prove to be a truly remarkable period in the financial markets. At the outset, stocks continued their recovery, with the Dow-Jones Industrials rising from 820 to 1,016 in April 1981, only to tumble to 777 by mid-1982, as interest rates soared to unprecedented levels. The Federal Reserve had decided to put an end to the hyperinflation that had carried the Consumer Price Index to an astounding 12.5 percent increase in 1980, its second consecutive double-digit annual increase. The yield on ten-year U.S. Treasury bonds, which had averaged 7.1 percent during the 1970s, soared from 10.4 percent as 1980 began to 15.3 percent by mid-1981. Then, as the Fed's tight money policies set the economy aright, the Treasury bond interest rate fell to 10.7 percent and stocks took off, beginning the greatest, most enduring bull market of all time. In these topsy-turvy markets, even gold got into the act. The price of an ounce of gold leaped from $150 in the mid-1970s to a high of $660 in March of 1982, only to tumble to $310 by the spring of 1982.

When 1980 began, little did we know that we were facing such a volatile, and ultimately hugely rewarding, period for investing. Nor did we realize that our first billion-dollar milestone—$3 billion—was less than nine months away. The major building blocks of our future—our character, our structure, and our new equity, bond, and money market funds—had been put in place. *We had built it.* With no marketing force to drive our growth, we would just have to watch and wait, and see: *Would they come?*

At the close of business on the day of our first milestone, September 19, 1980, I gathered our small crew in an open area, brought out a pillow embossed with a profile of Lord Nelson's flagship HMS *Victory*—sister flagship to HMS *Vanguard*—and gave my milestone

	Total Net Assets[1]	Net Cash Flow[1]	% Change in Assets	Number of Funds	Crew Members	Expense Ratio (%)	Stock Funds	Balanced Funds	Bond Funds	Money Funds	Stocks	Bonds	Bills
							% of Fund Assets In:				Annual Return (%)		
1980	3,026	343	27.1	20	200	0.59	50	24	12	14	32.4	2.7	11.9
1981	4,110	1,108	35.8	22	300	0.59	40	15	9	36	-4.9	6.2	15.0
1982	5,617	1,064	36.7	23	400	0.61	38	11	16	35	21.5	32.6	11.3
1983	7,258	1,086	29.2	26	430	0.60	46	10	21	23	22.5	8.4	8.9
1984	9,925	2,462	36.7	33	700	0.54	46	7	22	25	6.3	15.1	10.0
1985	16,511	4,953	66.4	37	900	0.51	45	7	31	17	31.7	22.1	7.8
Cumulative	11,016		38.1								17.4	14.1	10.8

[1] Figures are in $ millions

speech, "A Time to Dance." I then held up the *Victory* pillow, the symbolism of which, I'm sure, was lost on no one. Then we all went back to work. Other than its brevity (the shortest of the entire forty-two speech series!), there seemed little remarkable about it. But the final excerpt from a poem by Robinson Jeffers turned out to be prescient to a fault: *The stone strength of our past—what we had just put in place—had indeed lent us the wings on which we have steadily flown through the ensuing twenty-one years.*

The next billion-dollar milestones—and the attendant speeches— came ever more swiftly: Exactly one year to $4 billion; eleven more months to $5 billion; three-plus months to $6 billion; seven months to $7 billion; nine months to $8 billion, six months to $9 billion, and only five more months to $10 billion. The pace of growth was beyond belief. In a bit more than four years, our assets had increased fourfold. Our confidence was building by the day, and the lengthy tradition-based, statistic-laced speech that I gave on February 21, 1985, was entitled "Vanguard and Victory." At that point, we decided the billion-by-billion pattern was getting out of hand. We began to celebrate at each $5 billion multiple, an implicit vote of confidence in our future growth. That confidence was rewarded in a flash. A mere ten months later, on October 31, 1985, we crossed the $15 billion mark, the culmination, as the title of my celebratory speech suggested, of our "Impossible Dream."

More Pioneering

In 1980, we pioneered the ultrashort maturity municipal bond fund (the fifth tier of our original three-tier fund), soon transformed into an early tax-exempt money market fund. During the same year, we formed the first GNMA fund to be directly marketed to investors, now by far the largest in its field. We took our first global step in 1981 and formed our international growth fund, selecting an outstanding London-based investment manager. In 1985, we created the first modern-day "fund of funds"—STAR Fund, holding a balance among Vanguard stock, bond, and money market funds. While *Forbes* magazine dubbed it "the worst idea in years," it is today by far the largest fund of its kind, with an outstanding record of performance.

On the conventional fund front, we formed Trustees' Commingled Equity Fund in 1980, retaining Batterymarch Financial Management as adviser, our first use of a non-Wellington equity manager. It quickly became one of our largest funds, but it ultimately was merged into

Vanguard Quantitative Portfolios in 1998. In 1984, we retained an exceptional new adviser, Primecap Management, placing its name on a new equity fund in late 1984. With just a handshake, we trusted them to do the investing, and they trusted us to do the administration and marketing. It worked. Primecap Fund has emerged as one of a handful of truly blue-ribbon funds in the industry, with assets now at nearly $20 billion. The secret? Investment professionals, sound strategy, solid stock selection, and long-term focus—in a word, *character.*

Among these hits, alas, there were some errors. One was our decision to offer sector funds. In 1984, probably too imbued with competitive zeal, I followed Fidelity's leading-edge sector funds with our own limited number (five) and improved design (I thought). Two of our portfolios—Service Economy and Technology—worked poorly and were given a decent burial in 1994.* Two did nicely—Precious Metals and Energy—but only within their generally lack-luster groups. In a sense, the fifth of the series made up for the failings of its siblings. The Health Care Fund, brilliantly managed by Wellington, has served its investors well in a booming market sector. Now at $17 billion of assets, it is the largest specialty fund in the industry.

Bringing Fixed-Income In-House

But perhaps the major event of the period was the decision to have Vanguard assume the responsibility for providing portfolio supervision for the assets of our municipal bond and money market funds. I had long been aching to expand our investment management mandate beyond our still-small index fund. As 1980 ended, the rapidly growing assets of our fixed income funds topped $700 million, at last giving us the critical mass we needed to establish our own investment team. It was time to act. I believed we could better control the funds' investment policies, enhance their returns, and reduce their expenses, and in August the Board approved my plan to establish the Vanguard Fixed Income Group. In mid-November, with $1.7 billion under management, the group began operating. Within a year, we'd expanded its

---

* The Technology Fund had suffered both from poor performance and volatile cash flows. The decision to close it looked foolish during the tech fund bubble of the late 1990s, but, after the bubble burst, almost brilliant. Fund investors were willingly lured into pouring tens of billions of dollars into such funds as the bubble reached its peak in March 2000, only to see their investment, plummet.

mandate to include corporate and U.S. government bonds as well. By the end of 1985, Vanguard managed $6.1 billion of fund assets in-house, fully 37 percent of our asset base.

In addition to opening twenty new funds in the years 1980 through 1985—more than the seventeen Vanguard funds that existed as this chapter in our history began—we also took yet one more action without industry precedent. On May 15, 1985, concerned about the impact of a huge surge in their cash inflows, without advance notice we closed both our Windsor and Explorer funds to new investments. I described our strategy as "not wanting to kill the goose that laid the golden egg." We would not allow the funds to grow to such a large size that they could no longer meet their goals. Happily, both have continued to produce solid relative returns to this day. Despite considerable doubt in the financial community, the clones we created for them to fill the gap their closing left in our fund line—Windsor II and Explorer II, each run by a different adviser—quickly found acceptance. Ultimately, Explorer II was combined with its forerunner, but Windsor II has continued to give a fine account of itself, and is now far larger than its older namesake ($25 billion versus $17 billion).

What's in a Name?

What's in a name? Litigation in the early 1960s precluded our giving other funds in our family the Wellington name. So at first we followed a "British W" strategy: Wellington Fund, Windsor Fund, Wellesley Income Fund, Westminster Bond Fund, Warwick Municipal Bond Fund, and Whitehall Money Market Fund. The 1967 merger brought us Ivest Fund, and we formed Explorer, W.L. Morgan Growth Fund, and a few other funds that performed poorly, now consigned to the history books. At the outset, with Vanguard a brand-new name in the industry, having little public recognition and a fragile asset base, I was apprehensive about applying our corporate name to the funds.

But by early 1980, I was confident that we were not only at last on solid ground, but that we were about to take off. It was time to establish our name. We would add "Vanguard" to the names of all of our funds ("Vanguard Wellington," and so on) and began by asking shareholders of Whitehall, Warwick, Westminster, and First Index to approve the addition. And approve they did. The names of all of our funds were ultimately changed, and ever since May 1, 1980, every fund we've introduced has carried the proud name that popped up when I read that two-century-old book of British naval battles of the Napoleonic Wars era: HMS *Vanguard,* the battling flagship of the Nile.

The principal themes of my speeches in the years 1980 through 1985 consistently revolved around appreciation for our crew and their work. The ideas we put into Vanguard proved to be good ones, but no idea gets very far without implementation. *Courage for the deed, grace for the doing,* it might be said. And it was our crew that stroked the laboring oars. Inspired by their efforts, in 1984 we instituted a recognition program that each quarter acknowledged the special contributions by individual crew members; their dedication, diligence, teamwork, spirit, and cooperation—in all, their character. The award quickly became a tradition. For as long as I can remember, I have believed deeply that *even one person can make a difference,* and that was the motto we placed on our Award for Excellence. It has remained there ever since.

The Vanguard Partnership Plan

Recognition is good, but words without deeds ring hollow. "Talking the talk," as it is said today, is fine, but it doesn't go very far without "walking the walk," too. From the day Vanguard began, my goal was to develop a system of financial incentives that would let our crew members know how much we valued their services. Alas, that idea had to lie dormant until we had the resources to accomplish the goal. Until our asset base grew to substantial size, we would have to hold the lid on expenses as we strove to bring our expense ratios down in order to achieve our "low-cost provider" goal. It was slow going, but we had driven our initial expense ratio (operating expenses as a percentage of fund net assets) of 0.73 percent down by 16 percent to just 0.61 percent in 1982. But we still had a long way to go.

As I incessantly preached about our mission to become the low-cost provider, it became obvious that our crew members had the impression that our cost discipline was reflected in an inferior compensation program and that they were bearing the burden of our strategy. While our pay scale was in fact more-than-competitive and our benefits package remarkably generous, I knew we had to make each and every crew member a partner in sharing in the earnings we created for our fund investors, earnings that our crew had helped to create, just as soon as circumstances would permit.

By 1984 we had reduced our expense ratio from 0.61 percent to 0.54 percent, now 26 percent below the 1974 level. At last it was time to act. We expanded our Vanguard Partnership Plan—which provided annual payouts to our officers based on a small share of the actual cost savings we achieved for our shareholders each year, plus the value of the excess returns we earned vis à vis the performance of peer funds— to include the entire crew, an annual cash payout each June that could reach 30 percent of each crew member's annual compensation. In 1984, the total payout was less than $1 million. By the turn of the century, it had soared at least 100-fold. *Our crew members deserve it. They've earned every penny of it.*

Business As Usual?

Just as in our formative years, behind the scenes of both the investment drama—opening new funds, assuming new responsibilities for portfolio supervision, and putting the stamp of Vanguard's character and name on each of our funds—and the human drama—the programs for recognizing individual accomplishments and rewarding collective success—it was hardly "business as usual," during 1980 through 1985. This era witnessed the birth of the tax-deferred retirement plan in 1981—the Individual Retirement Account for individuals and the 401(k) plan for corporate thrift and retirement programs—a field that would come to represent nearly one-half of the mutual fund industry's now-enormous asset base. Once again, Vanguard was a pioneer in this wave. We promptly developed programs for our investors, added stable value investment contracts to our offerings, and formed Vanguard Fiduciary Trust Company to serve as trustee and custodian of our retirement accounts. And, in another move unrelated to all of this feverish activity, we entered the fast-growing discount brokerage field with a new unit to provide these services to our clients holding individual stocks and bonds.

Sometimes it seemed to me that everything was going on at once at Vanguard, and most of my speeches emphasized the magnitude of the task before us as well as—especially at the outset—caution about our growth. In effect, "Yes, we've reached another billion-dollar milestone, but it may fall away in tough times." In addition, I urged the crew to maintain our character and uphold our reputation, as well as to focus on our values and take pride in our traditions. More than once, I issued this stern warning, which I hope will never be disregarded at

Vanguard: *When an institution goes down, one condition may always be found. It forgot where it came from.*

A Vote of Confidence

I was confident that we would not forget where we came from, never more than on September 18, 1983, in my speech at the dedication of our brand-new building, the Vanguard Financial Center. It was located in Chesterbrook, a few miles from our original Wellington space, and we continued to carry our prized Valley Forge address. By then, our crew had grown more than tenfold to 400, and I had our character very much on my mind. My theme, "A Course Made Good Upon God's Ocean," was intended as a reminder to our crew members and their families that "our boat must be staunch and true" and our sailors on their "mettle, no less in command for all their reverences in the presence of a power mightier than [our] own."

The stage had been set for our growth eleven months earlier. In August 1982, the high interest rates that had restrained recovery in the financial markets following the stock market collapse of 1973 and 1974 abruptly reversed course. Stock and bond prices soared. Ever market sensitive, the fund industry boomed too. We grew even faster, and my early caution about our prospects was abandoned in favor of astonishment at the sheer size of our assets. In mid-1985, assets topped $15 billion, and I marveled at seeing us described in the press as "The *giant* Vanguard Group."

Our growth, of course, was not solely the result of our own doing. To all of our pioneering, building on our character, and bringing our crew members "on board" with our mission was added the most rewarding investment environment in any comparable period of previous financial market history—and, as it turned out, any subsequent period as well. During the six-year span, the annual return on stocks averaged 17.4 percent; the annual return on bonds averaged 14.1 percent; and the annual return on Treasury bills averaged 10.8 percent. I might have said, but I didn't, "We shall not see its like again."

Our astonishing annual growth rate of 38 percent during these golden years was to prove by far the highest we would ever enjoy. From the start of 1980 through the end of 1985, our assets had multiplied sevenfold, from $2.4 billion to $16.5 billion. But our asset *mix* had changed radically. At the outset, our common stock and balanced funds had represented 82 percent of assets; by the end, that figure had dropped to 52 percent, with bond and money market funds constituting the remaining 48 percent. The wisdom of our early focus on a full line of funds with a variety of policies, strategies, and objectives could hardly have been more clearly demonstrated.

Yes, half of our asset growth was driven by the fabulous returns in the financial markets. But the other half was driven by our rising share of mutual fund industry assets. After slipping to 1.7 percent in 1981, our market share nearly doubled to 3.3 percent of fund assets as 1985 ended, and we rose in industry ranking from number 14 to number 8. My confidence soared. In the closing words of my final speech of this era of remarkable growth, shortly after reaching the $15 billion milestone, I laid out this bold prediction, using the ship's motto of the HMS *Vanguard: We lead . . . and we will be leading the way for a long, long time to come.* And so it was to be.

A TIME TO DANCE

September 19, 1980

*E*CCLESIASTES TELLS US that there is "a time to mourn, and a time to dance; . . . a time to keep silence, and a time to speak." This occasion is a time to dance, and, I hope, an appropriate time to speak about what we have together accomplished.

On September 17, 1980, the total assets of The Vanguard Group of Investment Companies crossed the $3 billion mark. This truly awesome sum, of course, simply represents in dollar terms the huge responsibility that has been entrusted to our stewardship by nearly four hundred thousand individual and institutional investors. The achievement of this milestone can stand some historical perspective. It took thirty-one years—from 1928 to 1959—for Wellington Fund, the first Vanguard fund, to reach $1 billion. It took only six years more for the assets of the Vanguard Funds in the aggregate to reach $2 billion, in 1965. But we then fell back below that mark, not crossing $2 billion for good until March 1979.

It has therefore taken us fifteen years—or more ebulliently, just eighteen months—to get from the $2 billion mark to the $3 billion mark. It may be for good, or we may go above and below it from time to time. Just remember that we crossed the $2 billion mark not only in 1965 and 1979 but also in 1970, 1976, and 1978.

What this brief perspective makes clear is that we are in a business of challenge, economic sensitivity, market (both stock and bond) volatility, and extraordinary competitiveness. In short, we must not lose sight of the fact that we are in a cyclical business, well described, though that was not his intention, by the poet Robinson Jeffers:

All these tidal gatherings, growth and decay
Shining and darkening, are forever
Renewed, and the whole cycle, impenitently
Revolves, and all the past is future.

Are we, then, just victims of fate? Can we not control any of the circumstances that confront us? Of course we can! With skill in what we do, imagination in what we create, integrity in what we produce, judgment in the goals we set for ourselves, courage in times of peril, good humor in adversity, we *can* continue to build this enterprise in the future, as we have in days and years past.

We have been through a lot together. And I thank each of you personally for all you have done to give us the success that $3 billion of responsibility represents. Without our people, we are nothing. And I wish each of you every personal success as we work together in what we try to make a good environment, one that challenges your abilities, one that will give you the rewards that you seek.

So, the first $3 billion is behind us—at least for now. It is, in that sense, past. And we must turn to future milestones, however measured, and whatever they may be. The poet Jeffers had some words on this subject too, and let me close by reading them to you:

Lend me the stone strength of the past
And I will lend you
The wings of the future.

GROWTH HAS ITS SEASON

September 9, 1981

*T*HIS IS an exciting time to be in this business, both because it is changing so very rapidly and because the securities markets, bond and stock alike, are so incredibly volatile. I would like to make a few brief comments on each subject.

We are here today primarily to celebrate the $1 billion asset milestone that Vanguard Money Market Trust reached on August 31, even as our total assets soar toward $4 billion. More importantly, we are here to express symbolically our appreciation to each of you for your assistance in making these achievements possible. As the Vanguard veterans among you may recall, I am a bit nervous about making too much of these milestones. For while our $3 billion celebration just a year ago proved to be durable, our celebration of $2 billion proved to be transitory indeed. As our assets rose and fell, above and then below $2 billion, we could have celebrated it something like a dozen times.

Today, aggregate assets of all of the Vanguard Funds total $3.7 billion. With considerable momentum in our cash inflow from investors (now running over $100 million each month), it is only a matter of time—perhaps a very short period of time—until we cross the $4 billion milestone.* While looking ahead to this next milestone is a bit uncharacteristic for me (I am more superstitious than you would ever believe), it seems that it is in the cards for us, a rare situation indeed. But it is engendered by our being in a new business: the business of *saving,* not merely of *investing.* Our money market funds (taxable and

---

*The $4 billion milestone was achieved less than two months later, on October 30, 1981.

tax free), which represented just 4 percent of our asset base three years ago, now account for 35 percent of the total—more than $1 of every $3 under Vanguard's aegis.

The growth of Vanguard Money Market Trust, of course, has been both rapid *and* consistent. In truth, it has been astonishing, with assets rising from $50 million at year-end 1978, to $170 million in 1979, to $366 million in 1980, now reaching $1 billion with three months left to go—and, we hope, left to *grow*—in fiscal 1981. But, more importantly, this growth mirrors the accelerating pace of change in the mutual fund industry, which provides such a great challenge to Vanguard and to each one of us.

The Pace of Change

Let me give you just three examples of how the pace of change has increased:

- To reach the $1 billion mark, it took Wellington Fund thirty-one years, Windsor Fund twenty-three years, and Vanguard Money Market Trust just six years from its inception.
- Even to reach the $50 million mark took Wellington twenty years, Windsor two years, and Vanguard Money Market Trust three and one-half years. Yet Vanguard's new Federal Portfolio has reached $50 million of assets in just five weeks.
- Finally, as the flagship of the Vanguard fleet, Wellington was our largest fund for fifty-one years, through March 1979, and Windsor was largest for just two and one-half years, through early August 1981.

I have seen too much of this business to rashly predict how long Vanguard Money Market Trust will rule the seas, for it will depend in large measure on the accelerating pace of change, both in Vanguard and in our competitive environment, including the potential challenge posed by the new All-Savers certificates offered by the banking industry.

I hasten to note that, in the traditional mutual fund sense, Windsor—with its superb record over more than two decades—has in no sense relinquished its flagship role. But Vanguard Money Market Trust has really put us in a *new* business, a business of complexity, transaction activity, technology, and service that is anything but traditional. Largely because of Vanguard Money Market Trust, our administrative group now handles some 50,000 investor purchases each month, compared with less than 20,000 in 1970, 10,000 in 1979, and 5,000 in 1978. Our telephone group handles some 50,000 calls each month. Each month we mail our nearly 400,000 shareholder reports, dividends, and marketing packages. Our accounting group now copes with twenty-two separate fund portfolios, compared to just twelve in 1975. So many of you do so much in these and other areas that I want to reiterate our appreciation for your work, at a time when we must run so fast just to stay in the same place. In a way, I wish that I could tell you that the pace of change will slow, but I am inclined to doubt that it will.

For change has been with us always, and will be with us always. The change we face is no different from that of life itself. And I therefore present for your consideration a few profound words from Marcus Aurelius that we all might bear in mind:

> **Time is a sort of river of passing events, and strong is its current; no sooner is a thing brought to sight than it is swept by, and another takes its place, and this too will be swept away.**

These are, as I noted at the outset, difficult days for investors in funds that are *not* money market funds. Perhaps they make you as nervous and edgy as they make me, for—to continue the earlier nautical references—it is as if a cannonball were loose on the deck in a stormy sea. Doubtless, many of us are asked for advice as to what is the best course of action. Today, *no one* can be sure—to say nothing of even remotely confident—of answers to even the simplest of inquiries about investing. What is needed, I think, is to communicate a sense of perspective, reflecting once again the change that is with us always.

Growth Has Its Season

In this light, I have enjoyed rereading a few short paragraphs in the book *Being There*. While the words may seem amusing—even more so in the wonderful movie, which starred the late Peter Sellers—they are still worth thinking about. Let me quote Chauncey Gardiner ("Chance, the gardener," the Peter Sellers role), a sad man who has no name and no identity, and who has learned all that he knows from watching television and working in the garden. He is, by an accident of fate, talking to the president of the United States at a time like this one, when the economy is slowing and the stock market crashing. Here is how the story reads:

> **Chance shrank. He felt that the roots of his thoughts had been suddenly yanked out of their wet earth and thrust, tangled, into the unfriendly air. He stared at the carpet. Finally, he spoke: "In a garden," he said, "growth has its season. There are spring and summer, but there are also fall and winter. And then spring and summer again. As long as the roots are not severed, all is well and all will be well." He raised his eyes. . . . The President seemed quite pleased.**
>
> **"I must admit, Mr. Gardiner," the President said, "that what you've just said is one of the most refreshing and optimistic statements I've heard in a very, very long time." He rose and stood erect, with his back to the fireplace. "Many of us forget that nature and society are one! Yes, though we have tried to cut ourselves off from nature, we are still part of it. Like nature, our economic system remains, in the long run, stable and rational, and that's why we must not fear to be at its mercy." The President hesitated for a moment. . . . "We welcome the inevitable seasons of nature, yet we are upset by the seasons of our economy! How foolish of us!"**

Well, perhaps we *are* foolish, but it is difficult to be completely rational—to realize that growth indeed always has its season—when we find ourselves at this intersection of dynamic change and chaotic markets. I thank you again—each one of you—for helping us to deal with this paradoxical situation. I look forward to celebrating with you at Vanguard's next accomplishment, whatever it may be.

THE MORE GLORIOUS
THE TRIUMPH

August 26, 1982

WE ARE gathered here to celebrate a triumphant milestone for The Vanguard Group of Investment Companies: crossing the $5 billion mark in assets. As many of you know, these celebrations make me a bit apprehensive because as tough as it is to reach each milestone, it is an even greater challenge to remain above it and to go on to the next mark. For in our volatile and competitive business, past triumphs may be prologue to the future— or they may not.

The fates, however, have been kind to us on this occasion. In the three short days between the time of our $5 billion achievement, to this celebration of it, our assets have remained above this "magic number," and as of this moment, they are about $5.17 billion.

Let me put these figures into a past perspective that is, to me at least, rather frightening. When I came to work here, in the summer of 1951, our *total* assets, made up solely by Wellington Fund, were $170 million, almost precisely equal to our growth in the past three *days*. And the assets of the entire mutual fund industry at that time were $2.8 billion, only a bit more than *one-half* of Vanguard's present size. Even in inflation-adjusted dollars, we have come a long, long way.

Much of the credit for our success goes to our predecessors, for this firm was built on the earlier achievements of fine men. Most especially, I single out Walter L. Morgan—our founder in 1928, and my predecessor as chief executive officer—whose legacy to us includes the steadfastness, innovation, and integrity that today remain our hallmarks. But, no matter what our heritage, our astonishing growth and success in more recent years have also been built on the achievements of each of you in this hall. I have not the words to express my appreciation, so I simply say thank you, to each member of this fine Vanguard crew.

But I also echo the words of Lord Nelson, written about his crew after his victory at the Battle of the Nile, according to his biographer, "the most complete victory ever recorded on the sea," 184 years ago, on August 2, 1798. Writing aboard his flagship, the HMS *Vanguard*, he said:

The admiral most heartily congratulates the captains, officers, seamen, and marines of the squadron he has the honour to command, on the event of the late action; and he desires they will accept his most sincere and cordial thanks for their very gallant behaviour in this glorious battle.

In that spirit, I transmit those words to you.

Milestones

Our previous celebration of a milestone in total assets came just a year ago, on September 9, 1981, when Vanguard Money Market Trust reached the $1 billion level, and when total Vanguard assets were about to top $4 billion. Just a year earlier, we had held our $3 billion celebration. On that occasion, illustrating the fragility of our firm, I reminded you that we first crossed the $2 billion mark in 1965, but with fluctuating business conditions, we did not finally cross it for good until 1979, fourteen long years later. To move to $3 billion, then to $4 billion, and now to $5 billion—in just three more years—is, then, all the more remarkable.

Unlike most of our competitors—or perhaps any of them—our success has been built on two distinct pillars: the traditional mutual fund business and the burgeoning money market fund business. We have avoided an overdependence on either segment, and we now have a well-balanced book of business, comprising $2.8 billion in traditional funds and $2.2 billion in money market funds, a balance that should help us to better surmount the challenges ahead.

Looking at our traditional funds, we are in an excellent position. Our product line is clearly delineated, our investment performance outstanding, our services first rate, our marketing strategy developing. Perhaps our success is best suggested by two important milestones reached in 1982:

1. Windsor Fund, with the extraordinary record it has achieved under portfolio manager John B. Neff and his crew, has just reached the $1 billion milestone.

2. Our market share of no-load sales volume is currently at a record all-time high of 15 percent. This means that one of every six investors now purchasing no-load funds is selecting Vanguard.

Here, of course, our assets have been markedly enhanced by the soaring securities markets of the past week—in fairness, however, just as they were impaired by the market doldrums of the past decade. We will not soon again see a week like that, so we should revel in the table of our weekly price changes from last Sunday's *New York Times*. Perhaps it will prove a symbol of the return to grace of bonds and stocks alike.

Mutual Funds
Week Ended Friday, August 20, 1982

| | **Week's Range** | | | |
	HIGH	LOW	CLOSING BID	CHANGE FOR WEEK
Vanguard Group				
Explorer	21.61	20.74	21.61	+1.03
Index Trust	14.52	13.38	14.52	+1.17
GNMA	9.05	8.72	9.05	+0.39
Ivest Fund	10.97	10.28	10.97	+0.66
Morgan	8.88	8.25	8.88	+0.63
Muni. Hi. Yd.	8.39	8.15	8.39	+0.32
Muni Shrt.	15.15	15.10	15.15	+0.06
Muni. Int.	10.10	9.78	10.10	+0.39
Muni. Long	8.72	8.40	8.72	+0.40
Qual. Div. I	12.37	11.81	12.37	+0.63
Qual. Div. II	7.26	7.03	7.15	+0.14
Trst. Com.	26.01	24.22	26.01	+1.94
Wellesley	10.88	10.45	10.88	+0.53
Wellington	9.91	9.30	9.91	+0.68
IG Bond	7.82	7.60	7.82	+0.29
Hi. Yd. Bond	8.50	8.27	8.50	+0.32
Windsor	9.45	8.80	9.45	+0.70

SOURCE: This table appeared in the *New York Times* on Sunday, August 22, 1982.

The Vanguard money market funds are also steadily building market share, albeit in a more modest dimension, and reaching record-high levels. Having said that, I must acknowledge that the challenges to this segment of our business are more profound today than ever before. The sharp decline in interest rates, helpful as it is to our equity and bond funds, is a potentially negative factor for the money funds, to say nothing of the added competition from well-managed financial services firms who want their "piece of the action," and the almost certain development of comparable products by banks within the next few years. You should know that we have a series of active projects designed to help us meet these challenges, for we recognize that, to grow, we must innovate.

The Harder, the More Glorious

So we are blessed by living and working in interesting times, times that will test us all. And if we live in an environment far less demanding than "the times that try men's souls" that Thomas Paine described in 1776, his words nonetheless carry a message that is valid for us in these far easier days, two centuries later:

What we obtain too cheap, we esteem too lightly;
The harder the conflict, the more glorious the triumph.

Our own conflict in a fiercely competitive business has also been hard, our triumph therefore all the more glorious. To each of you, again, thank you for your help in achieving our triumphant growth. If we are to maintain this record in the years ahead—which will pose their own set of challenges, as yet only to be imagined—it will require of you the same kind of industry, the same kind of innovation, the same kind of dedication, the same spirit of service with which you have brought us to this $5 billion milestone.

Thank you again, each and every one of you, and Godspeed always.

THE FUTURE IS NOW

December 7, 1982

*E*XACTLY 100 DAYS AGO, we convened to celebrate Vanguard's crossing the $5 billion mark. Today, by growing at the rate of $10 million per day (in combined cash flow and market appreciation) since August 23, we have now reached the $6 billion mark. So again we convene, again we celebrate, again we thank you for your role in reaching this new Vanguard milestone, accomplished so incredibly soon after its predecessor.

It is probably absurd even to contemplate asset growth of $1 billion in just over three *months*. Particularly so when we realize that our first (and for many years, our sole) fund, Wellington Fund, reached the $1 billion asset milestone only after thirty-one long and challenging *years* (1928 to 1959).

At these increasingly frequent celebrations, I always warn you that, whatever the number of billions we happen to reach, we cannot be sure whether an asset level will endure, or whether it will be ephemeral and transitory. Nonetheless, that *concern*—perhaps even that *warning*—is more necessary today than ever before. There is a big industry out there—our nation's banking industry—that wants to get "its" money back. Starting December 14, by fair means or foul, banks will be spending their great energies and their not inconsiderable financial resources to take on the money market funds on a level playing field, as they seek to recoup the $200 billion of assets that has flowed into the money funds in the past three years. They are deadly serious about it.

I think it is fair to say that the competition for the savings dollar from America's financial institutions in 1983 will be more rugged, more heated, more intense than ever before in history. I also think it is fair to say that the generosity of the stock and bond markets in late

1982 is unlikely to be repeated, at least at the recent extravagant rate, throughout 1983.

The Battles Ahead

Thus, maintaining and enhancing the $6 billion in assets under Vanguard management at this moment is going to be difficult. But to *recognize* the challenges we face is not to *shirk* them. We have our own weapons and our own fleet to fight—and to win—the battles that lie before us.

Our weapons, of course, include our outstanding and successful mutual fund portfolios, now twenty-three in number. They include our systems and computer network. They include our state-of-the-art telephone facility. And they will soon include the modern office building (I hesitate to call it a "fort") in Chesterbrook, where, over the next three months, we will all be moving.

Our weapons, equally important, include our Vanguard structure. Owned by the funds themselves, The Vanguard Group operates on an "at-cost" basis, giving our shareholders lower expense ratios and therefore commensurately higher returns on their investments. One of its correlative strengths is being able to work at arm's length with external investment advisers, whose responsibility is neither to *operate* nor *control* the funds but rather to *manage* their portfolios, with a view toward the optimal accomplishment of each fund's investment objectives for its shareholders over the long term. This structure, in place for less than eight years, has already played a major role in our growth, and it will continue to do so.

Finally, our weapons include a distribution system that we operate independently and on our own. In our marketing efforts—both to individuals and to institutions—we are beholden to no army of outside sales staff. Rather, we depend on the investor to come directly to us. This system provides the great advantage of commission-free purchases by investors. Our change from a broker-dealer load system to a direct no-load system took place just a bit over five years ago. Abandoning in 1977 the broker-dealer network that had been our modus operandi for nearly fifty years—turning our back, as it were, on our past history—was a high-risk and irreversible decision, and it was one of the most crucial decisions Vanguard has had to make. But, as this celebration testifies, our strategy is working remarkably well, and, in just five years, our direct marketing system has become part of the fabric of this enterprise. It too is a potent weapon.

Weapons Are Never Enough

Weapons, however, even these powerful weapons, are never enough. There must also exist a crew of people who are organized, disciplined, trained, and enthusiastic. Of course, Vanguard has just such an army, represented by each of you in this room. Without you, there can be no victory. What you have accomplished for us already is impressive. But we must now ask for more: We ask for your dedication, your diligence, your contribution, your cooperation—in doing the tasks you do so well. Seamen and officers alike, we need your skills, more effectively performed, more productively used, than ever before.

The paradox of thanking you for the past while asking for still more in the future, has, I am sure, not escaped you. But we will succeed—whether measured by yet additional billions or measured by enhanced efficiency and productivity on a stable or even smaller asset base—only if we all devote every reasonable energy to working together in the common cause of making Vanguard successful, making Vanguard a hallmark of performance and service in the financial services field.

So $6 billion, looking back, is a monumental achievement for us all. But $6 billion, looking ahead, is a monumental challenge for us to maintain and to build. Without committed people, we will not meet that challenge. But, as I look at all of you here today, I am sure we *can* meet it . . . and we *will* meet it.

Thanks to each of you, then, for being part of Vanguard's proud past, our exciting present, and our challenging future. And heed these words from Henry Wadsworth Longfellow, who reminded us:

Look not mournfully into the past.
It comes not back again.
Wisely improve the present.
It is thine.
Go forth to meet the shadowy future,
Without fear,
And with a manly heart.

In even fewer words, Washington Redskins' coach George Allen said it this way: "The future is now."

THE NUMBER SEVEN

June 28, 1983

Seven is a number unique in human affairs.

Beginning in primitive civilizations 6,000 years ago or more, the passage of time was kept by the four phases of the moon, each phase being seven days in length. Of course, that is why we now have "weeks." And presumably that is where the mystic character of the number seven begins.

It next emerges in religion. In Genesis, the Creation takes seven days: "On the seventh day the Lord ended his work which he hath made." The Pharaoh dreams of seven years of plenty, followed by seven years of famine. In Proverbs, there are seven pillars of wisdom. In Revelation, the seventh seal, the seventh heaven. In the New Testament there are seven sacraments, seven gifts of the Holy Ghost, seven cardinal virtues, seven deadly sins, seven words on the Cross, seven golden candlesticks.

In addition to these spiritual sevens, there are temporal sevens as well—seven ancient planets, seven seas, seven colors of the rainbow, seven notes of the scale, seven hills of Rome, seven ages of man, seven wonders of the ancient world.

And in mathematics, seven is also special, a number that cannot be equally divided, that does not fit into any series—not 2-4-8, nor 3-6-9-12, nor 5-10-20. In truth, the number seven stands by itself.

So we have fundamental sevens, spiritual sevens, temporal sevens, and mathematical sevens. In the vast scope of these subjects, the number seven as it applies to Vanguard today can hardly be considered overwhelmingly significant. But it does seem worth taking just a moment in our busy lives to pause and recognize our own seven—$7 billion of assets—more for the magic of the number itself than for whatever modest importance it may have in the history of this small but exciting enterprise.

As you know, on June 23, 1983, the assets of the funds in The Vanguard Group of Investment Companies reached a record high of $7,011,016,369. To state the obvious, this is an awesome number. It is a marker of sorts, representing the achievement of another milestone for us, setting the scene for the rites of passage we celebrate on this afternoon late in June. But, in truth, it signifies far more.

What $7 Billion Means to Us

First, it signifies responsibility. It gives a precise dimension to the trust that has been placed in us by more than five hundred thousand shareholders. We have lived up to this trust—in integrity, in quality, in service, in performance, in character. But we must ever maintain these standards, else we need not concern ourselves with future milestones measured in eights or nines or tens.

Second, competitive fire. We are but one player in a game of incredible challenge and complexity. Our success in reaching $7 billion is a clear statement that we are a successful competitor holding our own—and often far more than that—in a field that includes many larger mutual fund complexes, as well as other financial services giants who seem anxious to joust with us. Perhaps they will regret it.

Third, accelerating change. Consider that it took thirty-one years to cross the $1 billion mark, six more years to cross $2 billion, fifteen more years to cross $3 billion, one more year to cross $4 billion, one *more* year to cross $5 billion, three more *months* to cross $6 billion, and now just seven more months to cross $7 billion. To summarize, it took fifty-two years, from 1928 to 1980, to reach $3 billion in assets but less than three more years to add another $4 billion. If that numerical sequence does not suggest accelerating change, I cannot imagine what would.

Finally, it represents a tribute to each of you here this afternoon. You are loyal, diligent, contributing members of the Vanguard crew of some 375 persons, without whom we would be nothing, or at least nothing worth talking about. So, on behalf of your directors, I take this opportunity to salute you—fellow officers, mates, yeomen, seamen, the whole crew. Thank you for everything.

The Fragility of Numbers

I need not remind you of the fragility of this $7 billion number. You have heard me reminisce that while we reached $2 billion in 1965, we seesawed up and down around that mark for fourteen long years, finally crossing it once and for all (at least that is my assumption) in 1979. And while we measure today's monthly cash *inflow* in amounts like $50 million or $100 million, during that earlier period we experienced eighty consecutive months of cash *outflow*. That ghastly period of attrition began in May 1971 and did not end until January 1978.

I shall never forget those dark and dismal years, and I suspect that neither shall those who served with us during that entire period. So a special note of thanks for the durability of these veterans: Mary Broadbent, Joseph Frattari, Ethel Harden, Timothy Joyce, Raymond Klapinsky, Charlotte Paul, Doris Poole, John Pyne, Olga Tosh, John Walton, and Karen West. All of you must have had some confidence that the HMS *Vanguard* could survive those stormy seas. I have to confess that, in the quiet of the captain's cabin, I was sometimes not so certain. In any event, it is a sobering reminder that this is a risky business.

When we celebrated $6 billion of assets, only last December, I issued a warning to you that that milestone might prove ephemeral and transitory, facing as we were the immediate challenge of bank competition for our money market fund assets. You could say that I wasn't much of a prophet. But I would prefer to say that we met that challenge and surmounted it because we measured up to the standards I described. We used effectively the weapons at our command—our outstanding line of twenty-five mutual fund portfolios, our network of computers and systems and telecommunications, and our splendid new headquarters building. Crucially, those weapons were effectively employed by our small but determined Vanguard crew, which more than fulfilled my request for "your dedication, your diligence, your contribution, your cooperation." Without all of you, we would not be celebrating today.

Obviously, a favorable securities market environment and a recovering economy could be credited for much of our asset growth thus far in 1983. But I have warned you before—and I warn you again—that "the markets giveth and the markets taketh away." And indeed, as I speak to you today, the stock market has "taketh away" enough in the sharp drop of the last three days to establish $7 billion not only as an objective met in the past but as a challenge to reach once again, in the days and weeks ahead. That challenge, in my view, will be easily surmounted again, given your support and loyalty.

So, perhaps the number seven is again showing its mystery and its magic, tantalizing us with feelings of achievement, while requiring us to strive anew to achieve, yet once again, and perhaps again, and then again. I do not believe, however, that we are facing seven years of famine (as we in fact did in 1971 through 1977). Equally certain is that it would not be wise to treat our recent accomplishments as a license to relax in seventh heaven. Rather, if we can practice the seven cardinal virtues, and not fall prey to the seven deadly sins, the good ship HMS *Vanguard* and her worthy crew can safely and soundly sail the seven seas, heading for the mysterious horizon that ever beckons.

A COURSE MADE GOOD
UPON GOD'S OCEAN

September 18, 1983

W E GATHER TOGETHER today
to dedicate the Vanguard Financial Center, a building that symbolizes
both our accomplishments of the past and our hopes for the future.
While this is a festive occasion, it seems appropriate to spend a moment
before the formal dedication to consider what our company is, and
what we stand for.

In a sense, The Vanguard Group of Investment Companies can be
easily described. And since we are most obviously a financial institution, we can describe it in numeric terms. A growing company, with
assets measured in the hundreds of thousands of dollars up to 1935, in
the millions to 1940, in the tens of millions to 1950, in the hundreds of
millions to 1960, and in the billions since then. A durable enterprise,
we will soon celebrate the fifty-fifth anniversary of Wellington Fund's
birth on December 28, 1928: a diversified mutual fund family, comprising twenty-five different investment portfolios. It is a large institution today, with more than $7 billion in net assets, representing the
trust placed in us by some 540,000 shareholder accounts.

But Vanguard cannot be truly defined by a series of naked numbers.
We are much more than that. We are an organization with the vital
spirit of a competitor, indeed, a fighter. We believe that personal
integrity and professional conduct are not only basic standards but, in
the long run, they are the only sound basis on which to build a durable
business. We believe in innovation, ever trying to build the proverbial
better mousetrap, and, more often than not, we expect that the intelligent investor will indeed beat a path to our door (or so Ralph Waldo

Emerson has assured us). We are engaged in "the Vanguard Experiment," to see if our unique form of organization—an *internally managed* fund complex—will provide a better way to serve investors' needs, in investment performance, in product quality, in operational efficiency.

A Power Mightier Than Our Own

Neither the preceding words nor the numbers that accompany them can fully illuminate our enterprise. And so I would like to take a moment to look at Vanguard in a larger context. To do so, let us think in nautical terms, visualizing our corporate symbol, the HMS *Vanguard* and her crew. I can find no better words than these to describe the challenge of our mission:

> Sailors know what some citizens have forgot in this latter day: that no purpose is achieved, nor any course made good upon God's ocean, until first you have trimmed your sails and set the helm to fit His winds and the set of His tide upon the deep.
>
> Keen is the mariner's eye to discern those telling signs upon the clouds, at the line 'twixt sky and water, or on the crest of waves where the spindrift blows, by which he might foretell the bluster or the calm, the weather God has in store for him.
>
> And if he is so fortunate as to find wind that blows from Heaven exactly in the direction he would go on earth, then easy and gay the skipper who can barrel down before that wind, all canvas set, rolling along upon the bosom of the blast.
>
> This has been America in these latter times; affluent and easy, not having to work very hard to run out her log: just cruising wing and wing, tide and breeze at her back, and the men lolling upon the deck. . . .
>
> But more often in this world it is a head wind that we face. Then, though the bearing of your destination be precisely the same, you have to tack—back and forth, back and forth—close-hauled; wind in your face, spray on your legs; fingers white upon the sheet, body tense against the bucking tiller; fine-tuning your lively lade to the majestic forces of splendid Creation; and so wresting from that opposing wind the destiny of your desire.
>
> That's when your boat must need be staunch and true, well braced and put together, and lithe like a living thing. And that is when the sailor too is on his mettle, no less in command for all his reverences in the presence of a power mightier than his own.

These evocative words were part of a sermon given by the Very Reverend Francis B. Sayre, Jr., dean of Washington Cathedral, to mark the occasion on July 4, 1976, when a parade of tall ships arrived in Newport in honor of the holiday. It is difficult for me not to associate Dean Sayre's words with Vanguard. Surely we have oft experienced affluent and easy times, tide and breeze at our back. But we also have struggled through arduous and perilous times, facing strong headwinds and high seas, when success seemed impossible, and when we had to wrest from that opposing wind each yard of progress toward the destiny of our desire.

The Challenges We Face

I suppose that Vanguard's future—and indeed the future life of each of us—will inevitably swing back and forth between favoring winds and head winds, between stormy seas and tranquil seas. Surely enough challenges exist to assure that we will live in interesting times. Globally, we must be concerned with world population, widespread poverty, the earth's finite resources, the threat of nuclear holocaust. Nationally, we must be concerned with the protection of our hard-won liberty, the integration of minority groups into the American system, a political process in which we too often seem to have lost the ability to govern ourselves, and a too-fragile economy that needs rebalancing, fresh approaches, and renewed vitality. And finally, in our own field of finance, we must be concerned with the ongoing revolution in the way that financial services are provided to consumers, the threats we face not only from existing competitors but also competitors that are new to us—notably banks and trust companies, endowed with far greater resources, and so-called financial department stores—and the continuing challenge to efficiently provide investment services of quality and value.

We also, of course, face challenges from within. While our heritage is long, today's Vanguard is a young and inexperienced organization. Half of our people were not with us as recently as 1981. We must ever reaffirm that heritage and reemphasize our values and traditions, our corporate culture if you will. We have become a large organization, growing from forty-seven crew members in 1975 to almost ten times that number today. With this growth, we run the risk that the procedures and policies and disciplines that are used by many a substantial enterprise will deprive us of the very characteristics that have been responsible for whatever success we have enjoyed thus far—creativity, innovation, flexibility, camaraderie, entrepreneurial spirit, even what one of our people described as "inspired intuition." We must never forsake those exciting and enjoyable characteristics, for they are, to me, what life is all about, and what Vanguard must stand for if we are to meet the challenges we face.

Sailing to Far Horizons

In the final analysis, of course, our future rests largely in our own hands. It is our people, you and I alike, who will share the responsibility for what Vanguard becomes. For I have a profound respect for what one individual can do, a confidence in a single person's ability to change things for the better. If none of us is Archimedes, who said, "Give me a lever, and I can move the earth," surely each of us—in big tasks or small—can be a positive force in the long voyage on which the good ship *Vanguard* is sailing, helping to make it a better, truer, finer ship as we set off for far horizons.

Ten years ago, on August 24, 1973, I spoke at the dedication of the Wellington Management Company building, just a few miles from here. Little did we know then that what we now call "Vanguard" was only a single-year-plus from its launching. Indeed, if it had not been for a handful of individuals—perhaps six or seven persons who were willing to take the road less traveled by—Vanguard would not exist today. In retrospect, the words I used at that dedication were perhaps prophetic. But the reason that I repeat them at this dedication today is that the idea they endeavor to express is eternal:

> **I believe that even one person can make a difference. Thus, I dedicate this building to the individuals in our company—the individuals who got us started fifty-five years ago, the individuals who work with us today, and the individuals who, God willing, will come forth to assure our future.**

If we each do our share, and if our sails are trimmed and our helm is set, we can indeed follow a course made good upon God's ocean in the years ahead.

WHICH AXIOM?

March 21, 1984

*I*T IS A BRIEF nine months since we gathered, on June 28, 1983, to celebrate Vanguard's $7 billion milestone. Yet here we are "on a roll," together again, in celebration of the $8 billion milestone. This tradition—in which we mark each $1 billion of trust that is added to our asset base—has come to include both a celebration and a brief commentary that is aimed at putting our success in perspective.

This eighth billion is different in an important sense from its three most recent antecedents. Figuratively speaking, there was a fresh and favoring breeze at our backs when the HMS *Vanguard* sailed from $4 billion to $5 billion, and then to $6 billion, and then to $7 billion. The securities markets were rising fairly steadily, with the Dow-Jones Industrial Average moving upward some 50 percent—from a level of 850 when we crossed $4 billion in October 1981 to nearly 1,250 when we crossed $7 billion last June. Since then, however, stock prices have receded—more substantially, I would argue, than the present level of 1,150 for the Dow would suggest—and bond prices have dropped too.

Thus, our rise from $7 billion to $8 billion has come with the wind in our faces. This time, we have had to fight the breeze, tacking to and fro, trying to move our ship along its intended course. I am proud of all of you for the character and enthusiasm you have demonstrated in this effort. In the final analysis, our success has come from the three critical qualities that have been Vanguard's hallmarks throughout our history:

Innovation
Competition
Cooperation

I would like to make just a few remarks on each of these qualities.

Innovation

Perhaps the most striking example of our innovation is this singular fact: Two Vanguard mutual funds that did not even exist a year ago (Vanguard Qualified Dividend Portfolio III and Trustees' Commingled Fund International)—I am not sure they were even gleams in their fathers' eyes—are now the best selling of Vanguard's twenty-six portfolios, accounting for nearly one-half of our regular fund volume this far in March. Together, their assets now total $275 million, or a full quarter of our $1 billion growth. In both cases, they are a manifestation of our ability to innovate—to create superior investment products, to anticipate sound needs in the marketplace, to be flexible in our marketing approach, and to act promptly and decisively. (I would be less than honest if I did not acknowledge that they also manifest more than a little bit of luck.)

But these two innovations tell only half the story. The remaining half is that two other new Vanguard mutual funds (the Naess and Thomas Special Fund and the Insured Portfolio of Vanguard Money Market Trust) introduced during the past year have *not* been successful—yet. And that fact gives living witness to one of the basic rules of innovation: "Be prepared to fail." I hasten to add that I am not conceding failure. Because there is another rule, in this marvelous industry where the creation and maintenance of new products costs so little in risk and promises so much in reward: "Be patient." If the product is sound—and Vanguard's products must unfailingly meet that test—its time will come.

Competition

Competition is the next Vanguard quality. And surely our competitive zeal has been critical to our success. Our institutional marketing people have sailed fearlessly into the merciless marketplace, and they have placed Vanguard "on the chart" with corporations and foundations and endowment funds, many of which barely knew what mutual funds were and had never before heard of Vanguard. Our retail marketing people have developed creative and aggressive advertising and literature programs, and they have provided first-rate person-to-person communications that together have made Vanguard a part of the investment programs of 165,000 new shareholders since the beginning of 1983.

Competition, of course, is the battle against competitors. And perhaps the best sign of our success has been our ability to build assets at a faster rate than that of our competitors. Let me quantify that statement: During 1983, only a single mutual fund complex in this entire industry increased in assets by a larger amount than did Vanguard. *Our growth outpaced every other competitor,* and we were surely the envy of most of them, many of whom suffered significant asset declines. In the following table are the figures for a dozen of the majors.

	Assets, Billions of Dollars	
	DEC. 31, 1983	**CHANGE FOR YEAR**
Fidelity	$19.7	+$2.1
Vanguard	*7.3*	*+1.7*
Capital Group	7.7	+1.5
American Capital	4.0	+1.5
Putnam	6.5	+1.1
IDS	8.9	+1.1
Lord Abbett	3.3	+0.8
Mass. Financial	5.0	+0.8
Stein Roe	2.4	+0.5
T. Rowe Price	8.3	+0.5
Scudder	2.8	+0.3
Delaware	2.4	−0.4
Dreyfus	18.1	−2.2

This success was born of our balanced product line (we were not overly dependent on money market fund assets), our excellent cash inflow, and our superior fund performance. But I shall not engage in further self-praise, reminded as I am of the four-letter answer to the crossword puzzle definition of "Came in second." It is: "lost."

Cooperation

Finally, the quality of cooperation played a major role in our success. I am proud of the members of this fine Vanguard crew. You have worked together to solve problems and to capitalize on opportunities. Many of you—in areas as diverse as fund accounting, client services, computer operations and programming, and mail distribution—are the unsung heroes and heroines of a period when failure would have been devastating to our growth momentum. Your willingness to serve others—fellow crew members and shareholders—for the greater good has been an inspiration.

While a true spirit of cooperation is easier to develop in a small organization than in a large one, we have, I think, kept it so far. To be sure, our twenty-eight-person staff when Vanguard began a decade ago is now more than *ten times* that number. But we can still have the personal approach—the human touch—with as much freedom and flexibility, and as little bureaucracy, as is realistically possible. We have good people working at Vanguard, people who like it here, people with enthusiasm and interest and concern. I see you at board meetings and staff meetings, at work here and in the field, in training and on the telephones, during the week and sometimes on weekends. I thank you again for your role in our success.

Success: Breeding Success? Or Failure?

Vanguard's growth, then, represents our ability to cooperate and inno-vate so that we can compete. And we have been an increasingly tough competitor. Our growth has itself engendered more growth, as the Vanguard name, concept, and performance has made an ever-widening impact in the marketplace, just like the ripples from a rock thrown into a pond. In short, we have benefited greatly from the axiom that "nothing succeeds like success."

But there is a second axiom that says: "Nothing fails like success." The history of our civilization is littered with examples of the poignant accuracy of this paradox. Certainly there have been countless nations, business enterprises, and individuals alike who at the very moment of their greatest triumph were planting the seeds of their own destruc-tion. Consider ancient Greece and the British Empire. Consider Ben-dix Corporation and Baldwin United. Consider the thirty-seventh president of the United States, who had to resign his office. Consider the thirty-sixth. Consider the thirty-ninth too. (It seems to happen to presidents a lot.)

Can it happen here? Of course it can. If Vanguard's success causes us to lose the very qualities that were responsible for that success, surely our future is not very bright. So we must maintain our strength in innovation—and not sacrifice our decisiveness, our flexibility, our entrepreneurial spirit. We must hone our competitive edge—and not relinquish our willingness to work hard, our enthusiasm for what we do, our fighting spirit. And we must above all work together coopera-tively—and simply not accept the stranglehold of red tape, the curse of corporate politics, and the impersonality of technology. We can fail, in short, if we forget one of the great lessons of civilization. As Carl Sand-burg put it:

> **When an institution goes down or a society perishes, one condi-tion may always be found: They forgot where they came from.**

There is, of course, another way to fail. It is to relax, to think we have some divine right to succeed, or some magic formula that guarantees our success, to engage in self-praise about our accomplishments while ignoring our problems. I do not share that attitude. Indeed, just a few days before our $8 billion milestone, I spent several hours with some of our officers for the sole purpose of discussing what we are doing badly and what we could do better at Vanguard. (The list was discouragingly long, for we are not paragons.) So let's accept this warning, in the form that it was put by the chairman of the Coca-Cola Company, quoted in an article in the *New York Times* several weeks ago:

> **There is a danger when a company is doing as well as we are, and that is, to think we can do no wrong.**

A Fable for Our Times

Finally, a fable. "Once upon a time," there was a great worldwide insurance company, the largest in Great Britain. It was called the Commercial Union (CU), and it was headquartered in London. From the pinnacle of success, a short decade ago, it has rapidly declined, and it now faces dissolution. How did it happen? Here is the story, edited only slightly, from the *Financial Times:*

> **CU's experience reflects the unprecedented challenges thrown up by the increasingly competitive structure of financial ser-**

vices. It is a story of computers and software, of insights into some parts of the future, thwarted by hopes that other parts will go on as they have in the past; of overoptimistic management, excited by the idea of enormous market opportunity but complacent about its dangers; finally, of a company which had some good ideas but simply could not afford to implement them in the huge and treacherous financial services marketplace. The saddest aspect of CU's debacle is that it was due in part to a correct recognition that the financial services business was changing rapidly and forever. The CU has experienced a decade of disasters, and the one-time flagship of Britain's most successful service industry will almost certainly be broken up or swallowed by a predator.

No, the CU will not "live happily ever after."

Let us learn from that snippet of history. Let us learn from Carl Sandburg and Coca-Cola. Let us learn from other civilizations and other companies. Let us never lose what brought us to $8 billion in the first place—and will soon, I am confident, bring us to $9 billion and then to the magic $10 billion. Let us not lose these three qualities that, to an important degree, define what Vanguard is:

> Innovation
> Competition
> Cooperation

The extent to which we can maintain these qualities will determine which of our two axioms will apply to Vanguard. At $8 billion, then, which axiom? Will it be "nothing succeeds like success"? Or will it be "nothing fails like success"?

It is up to us.

NINE AND TEN

September 24, 1984

NINE BILLION DOLLARS! Just for a moment, consider the awesome enormity of that sum. Because that is the total asset mark that The Vanguard Group of Investment Companies reached on September 13, 1984, and that we celebrate this evening. You must be getting used to these "billion-dollar blasts" by now, for this is the fifth one we have had in the past two years. Nonetheless, I urge you not to take them for granted because, as I will note later on, the mutual fund industry is a volatile, uncertain, and risky place to ply one's trade.

There is a purpose to these gatherings, and I want to state it straight out: It is to thank *you*—each and every one of you—for your work in helping us to reach, and to reach so quickly, yet another Vanguard milestone. The directors, the officers, and most assuredly, "the captain" deeply appreciate your contribution to our growth and success. We cannot express this appreciation adequately, nor individually, nor frequently enough. You have done your part in keeping the HMS *Vanguard* shipshape and flying like the wind; we try to do our part by making her a ship that has a spirit of camaraderie, of diligence, of caring, of fun—a good ship on which to crew. Together, we can make the voyages and fight the battles that will help to build a better world of financial services.

"Flying like the wind" indeed. It was only a bit more than two years ago—August 26, 1982—that we had our $5 billion celebration. As remarkable as that growth is, I believe even more remarkable is its diversity. For example:

- Vanguard Fixed Income Securities Fund was then a $100 million fund. Today, assets are $600 million—and growing.
- Vanguard Municipal Bond Fund was then a $550 million fund. Today, assets are $1.5 billion—and growing.
- Trustees' Commingled Equity Fund was then a $100 million fund. Today, assets are $550 million—and growing.
- Explorer Fund, then $50 million, is now nearly $300 million; the QDPs, then $50 million, are now $250 million; and Morgan Growth Fund, then $200 million, is now $450 million.
- And of course Windsor Fund, the flagship of our fleet, her course steered by the redoubtable John B. Neff, then $980 million, is now $2.2 billion—one of the two largest equity funds in the industry.

Paradoxically, perhaps our most notable accomplishment is in the fund with our only asset *decline:* Vanguard Money Market Trust assets, then $1.85 billion, are now $1.82 billion. But to essentially maintain our assets when the total assets of all money market funds have declined from $240 billion to $180 billion—the result of new competition from the banking industry—is surely worthy of favorable recognition.

So we have come a long way in the two brief years since the $5 billion milestone. Our number of shareholder accounts has increased from 450,000 to nearly 700,000. And with obviously important implications for our future growth, something like 200,000 of these accounts represent retirement plans growth, something like 200,000 of these accounts represent retirement plans [IRA, 401(k), 403(b), and Keogh] to which investors are regularly adding dollars. The leverage in such a business is enormous, for—provided only that we do our job in giving competitive performance and excellent service—the number of these accounts is certain to grow, the dollars in each certain to increase.

Let me speculate for just a moment on the impact of this leverage. Today, our retirement plan business alone—200,000 accounts having an average investment of $5,000—totals $1 billion, which is beautifully diversified, with about 30 percent in Windsor Fund, 25 percent in Vanguard Money Market Trust, 20 percent in Vanguard Fixed Income Securities Fund, 10 percent in Explorer, and the remaining 15 percent in our other funds. Let's assume that, thanks to our retail and institutional marketing efforts, a few years from now there are 300,000 such retirement accounts. And let's assume further that, thanks to additional contributions and good rates of return, the average account is then $10,000. With these assumptions, we can see today's $1 billion of assets tripling, to $3 billion. And this is only a single part of Vanguard's multifaceted business. So, the future looks bright.

Vanguard's Tenth Birthday

In this context, then, let us turn to the "ten" of my title. No, I am *not* thinking of ten *billion*. I have been around too long to take for granted *any* projections of growth. And I am superstitious enough to fear that even speculating about when and how we will reach the magic $10 billion milestone might put the hex on us, a curse of Sisyphean proportions. (Sisyphus, you may recall, was the mythological Greek who lived out his days rolling a huge stone up a mountain. Just before reaching the top, the stone would slip away and roll to the bottom. Thus, Sisyphus was destined to repeat his labors, over and over again, until the end of time.) I do not want to take the chance that the $10 billion milestone will be Vanguard's rolling rock.

Rather, the "ten" to which I have referred is Vanguard's tenth birthday. It is—how remarkable a coincidence—today! For The Vanguard Group was incorporated on September 24, 1974. To review how things were at that time should remind us just how risky and trying and unpredictable this wonderful business can be. On that date, the assets of our eleven mutual funds were $1.35 billion. These assets had precipitously declined from their record high of $2.6 billion at the end of 1972, the same level they had touched at the end of 1968. So we were looking at a six-year secular decline that had slashed our assets by nearly 50 percent.

Shareholders were leaving us in droves, and 1974 was our third year in a row of net capital outflow. And, little did we know, we were facing yet three *more* years of outflow—with the six-year total to reach nearly $600 million. The Dow-Jones average had plummeted from 1,067 in January 1973 to 600 in late September 1974. And I was busy writing an annual report letter to Ivest Fund shareholders trying to explain a two-year total return of *minus* 56 percent. Even Windsor was laboring, and 1973 was to mark its third consecutive year of subpar performance, well below the Standard & Poor's 500 Stock Index.

This baneful scenario was, of course, not enough to discourage an inveterate optimist like me. So we had to append a corporate upheaval (fondly known as "the bifurcation"), which had led, during the summer of 1974, to the decision to dissolve Wellington Management Company's traditional all-encompassing relationship—management and administration, investment advice, and marketing—with "The Wellington Group of Investment Companies," as it was then known. The fund directors determined to internalize the management function and set up a unique new structure under which the funds would be independently operated by their own staff. Wellington Management Company would serve as an external adviser and distributor under contracts negotiated at arm's length.

Selecting a New Name

Remaining, in the summer of 1974, was the matter of the name "Wellington." Which of the two corporate entities—the funds or the management company—would be entitled to it? The decision was made that the management company would keep the name. The funds would have to develop a new name by which to identify themselves as a group. To paraphrase Queen Victoria, "We were not amused" by the decision. Indeed, I was flabbergasted and appalled. But one of our directors, Charles D. Root, Jr., gave me the encouragement and confidence I needed when he said: "Jack, put it behind you. You can call the group anything you want. And then go out and make it the finest name in the whole damn mutual fund industry!"

And so the name was picked. In an old book of Napoleonic Wars era dispatches from British ship commanders, there was Lord Nelson, describing his miraculous victory at the Battle of the Nile, writing from the deck of his flagship, the HMS *Vanguard.* And the new company was incorporated on September 24, 1974. Thus ended a period of incredible challenge and change, and thus began the decade that closes on this very day. It was only a few weeks until that devastating bear market ended. It wasn't much longer until both our absolute *and* relative performance figures improved. Windsor roared back, and it would outpace the Standard & Poor's Index in ten of the next eleven years. And in Ivest's 1984 annual report, I have just described a two-year performance of *plus* 63 percent.

Indeed, our fund performance improved across the board, and a new era of productive cooperation between the funds and our advisers was ushered in. Within just a few years, capital outflow was superseded by capital inflow, as Vanguard assumed the additional responsibility for all marketing and product development for the funds early in 1977. And it was only a few more years until the innovations we had put into place came to fruition and firmly established that spirit of innovation which is now our hallmark.

I would hardly presume to conclude by saying that, yes, today Vanguard *is* "the finest name in the mutual fund industry." But looking at our $9 billion asset total and the base from whence we came ten years ago, we have surely come a long way. Even more important then these quantitative measures of our progress is the kind of company we have built—proud, integrity laden, dedicated to quality in all that we do. Our drive to be the finest—our search for excellence—is in any event not a final harbor, but an exciting voyage.

Thank you again for sharing this voyage with us.

VANGUARD AND VICTORY

February 21, 1985

STEEPED IN THE BRITISH naval tradition that has become part of the spirit of this enterprise, most of our crew know that the HMS *Vanguard* and HMS *Victory* were the two best-known flagships of Lord Horatio Nelson. Aboard the *Vanguard,* he commanded the fleet that destroyed Napoleon's French squadrons at the Battle of the Nile on August 2, 1798, "the most complete victory," according to his biographer, "ever recorded on the sea." Aboard the *Victory,* he led the British fleet at Cape Trafalgar on the southwest coast of Spain on October 20, 1805. There, in a dark and storm-tossed sea, at the very moment of his triumph, he died aboard his redoubtable final flagship, the victim of an enemy musketball. Thus are the *Vanguard* and the *Victory* forever linked in history.

There is, however, a small footnote to this linkage, of which few of you may be aware: A decade ago, when we sought a name for the new organization that would assume the responsibilities of Wellington Management Company for the direction and administration of what was then known as "The Wellington Group of Investment Companies," we considered the name "The Victory Group" as well as the name "The Vanguard Group." Both names were associated with the Napoleonic Wars era, in which the Duke of Wellington had made his mark; both began with the letter *V*; both were words with definitions that themselves set forth lofty goals—for *vanguard,* "leading the way," for *victory,* "triumph over the enemy."

I believe we made the right choice of name. But it is exciting for me to recollect that footnote to our history on this salubrious occasion. Because the reaching of this magnificent milestone—$10 billion of assets—for The Vanguard Group of Investment Companies links *vanguard* with *victory* in a very real sense. It is not just the ringing strains of Beethoven's Fifth Symphony, whose "Dot-dot-dot-dash" notes—played at the start of our celebration today—match the Morse Code symbol for V, and came to symbolize V for *victory* for the Allies in Europe during the darkest days of World War II. Nor is it just the victory pillow, embroidered with Nelson's flagship, which reposes in my office but has frequently been raised high at our celebrations of asset milestones and other Vanguard triumphs.

Leading the Way

No, the connection between *vanguard* and *victory* is more than historical linkage, more than an inspiring symphony, and surely more than a pillow held high. Rather, it is an acknowledgment that to truly lead the way, we must triumph in a never-ending series of tough battles with formidable competitors. In a competitive world, and in one of the most competitive industries in that world, we must demonstrate that Vanguard's unique concept—a truly mutual structure that places stewardship, simple investment principles, and fair dealing as our highest values—will enable us to meet unsparing standards of investment performance, client service, and cost efficiency. Only by doing so can we produce victories over our competitors, and, much more importantly, victories that enrich the long-run well-being of our clients. That is our challenge.

The $10 billion milestone—our first foray into double-digit billions—is in itself a victory. We have been heading for this goal, in a sense, for a decade: At the end of 1974, the assets of The Vanguard Group were less than $1.5 billion; we crossed $2 billion for good in 1979; and then we really started to grow in earnest:

September 17, 1980 . . . $3 billion
October 31, 1981 . . . $4 billion
August 23, 1982 . . . $5 billion
December 7, 1982 . . . $6 billion
June 23, 1983 . . . $7 billion
March 15, 1984 . . . $8 billion
September 13, 1984 . . . $9 billion
January 7, 1985 . . . $10 billion

From September 1980 to January 1985, then we have grown from $3 billion to $10 billion. That is a compound *annual* growth rate equal to 30 percent. Surely it ranks Vanguard as one of the fastest-growing enterprises among all of America's financial and industrial firms. And even that astonishing 30 percent growth rate seems to be accelerating. Indeed, our growth in the few short weeks since reaching the $10 billion milestone on January 7, 1985, is by far the most remarkable of all, as these two examples illustrate:

1. Assets topped $11 billion on February 4, 1985, less than a month after we reached $10 billion. This is the first occasion on which we have crossed a second billion-dollar mark before we had the celebration for the first!
2. Today, our assets total $11.52 billion. The $1.52 billion increase since January 7, 1985, is larger than our total assets ($1.45 billion) when Vanguard began ten years ago.

Outpacing Our Rivals

Our growth has benefited greatly from industrywide blessings, in particular the invention of the money market fund in 1974, the inflation in our economy in the late 1970s, and the end of the bear market in bonds and the beginning of a great bull market in stocks in the summer of 1982. But all of our competitors enjoyed this same vibrantly healthy environment, yet we have been able to surpass their growth, often by considerable magnitudes. For example, let us examine Vanguard's rank among the major investment company complexes:

- In 1979, we ranked eighth among the twenty-five largest (assets of $1 billion or more) fund complexes.
- By the end of 1982, we moved up to seventh, passing Massachusetts Financial Services and Putnam, both of Boston. (Kemper Financial Services, in the meanwhile, moved ahead of us.)
- In the first quarter of 1984, we moved up to sixth, passing Capital Group of Los Angeles.
- In the third quarter of 1984, we ranked fifth, passing T. Rowe Price of Baltimore.
- And in the fourth quarter of 1984, we ranked fourth, passing IDS of Minneapolis.

We have grown, then, faster than our competitors, all of whom were working in the same environment as we were. All of us were engaged in constant competition "on a level playing field," but, far more often than not, it has been Vanguard that has enjoyed the fruits of victory.

How did we earn these victories? Perhaps the best answer is "together." Whether talking about Vanguard's initial crew of 28 in 1974, or today's crew of 700, we have all worked together to do the job. It has never been easy, for there are no easy victories. But we have set our minds to the tasks, spent our time (often including long hours and weekends) to do the very best we could. And we have, I think, maintained a spirit of goodwill—indeed, good humor—no matter how tough the challenge. For on a ship of battle, all members of the crew must play their role—no matter how big or small—and must do their duty—no matter how arduous—for failure by a single seaman may well cause the demise of the entire enterprise.

Struggling with Victory

Today, we are struggling with the fruits of our victories. Net cash flow invested in the Vanguard Funds in January and February—the past two months alone—will total more than $1.2 billion, the second best "year" in our history. Unbelievable! Why this incredible demand for our Vanguard Funds? I believe it is as simple as this: We have served the investor well. The record says that we have indeed reached high standards of performance, of quality service, of cost efficiency. We have put together an outstanding and distinctive "product line" of investment company portfolios—now thirty-four in number—and, thanks in important measure to our marketing effectiveness, investors are "beating a path to our door." And with this dollar inflow has come volumes of transactions in dimensions that no one could have imagined just a few short years ago. For example:

- We handled 285,000 total transactions in January, compared to monthly averages of 199,000 in 1984 and 17,000 in 1978. That is a seventeenfold increase in six years.
- We enjoyed 150,000 investor purchase transactions in January, compared with monthly averages of 108,000 in 1984 and 5,000 in 1978, a thirtyfold increase in six years.
- We processed 60,000 check-writing transactions in January, compared with a monthly average of 40,000 last year. In 1978, we were not even in the checking account business.

- We opened 30,000 new shareholder accounts in January, compared to monthly averages of 11,000 in 1984 and perhaps 1,500 in 1978. In 1978, in fact, we closed more accounts than we opened.
- January new-account figures include 12,000 individual retirement accounts, compared with a monthly average of 3,500 in 1984 and, of course, none at all in 1978. And since April's IRAs are normally three times January's, we must be prepared for another 36,000 accounts in a single month!
- We answered some 175,000 phone calls in January, compared to monthly averages of 85,000 in 1984 and 2,000 in 1978. In short, a month of phone calls in 1978 would have accounted for only two hours of 1985 volume.

To state what is obvious to all of you who help to sail this ship, we nearly choked on these January volumes. We were simply not ready for them. We had not planned adequately for them, although I acknowledge that volume increases of 50 to 100 percent in a month's time are not easy to plan for. We have had to operate in a crisis environment, and I can only say that the way you all have worked together to sail Vanguard through the tempest is a tribute to your dedication: I thank you for your Herculean efforts. I wish that I could promise you that the days of stress and strain are over, but I fear that, despite our best efforts, it will take some months to deal effectively with the challenges that we face. Together, we can do the job.

Success: Breeding Success? Or Failure?

When I spoke at our $8 billion celebration eleven months ago to the day, I talked about the profound risk that the axiom "nothing *succeeds* like success" could be transmogrified into "nothing *fails* like success" for Vanguard. I mused on the fact that "great nations and great business enterprises alike, at the moment of their greatest triumph, were planting the seeds of their own destruction." How prophetic these words sound today. What I had in mind was the risk that we would fail by forgetting the very values that had engendered our success—innovation, competition, and cooperation. Perhaps if I had been a bit wiser, I would have also touched on the risk we could face in being nearly throttled by the volumes we strived to create—the gourmand, as it were, choked by his own feast.

Well, we *are* working on solutions. We at last have the telephone lines we require, and we are planning to install a new state-of-the-art Rolm telephone system. We have installed 125 new CRTs to access our more than 700,000 shareholder accounts. We are training scores of new people, and we are acquiring the space we must have. We are in the process of leasing *the entire building* next to the Vanguard Financial Center, already called "Vanguard II." It should be ready for our occupancy during the autumn, and it will bring us together once again.

We will also be working on critical longer-range issues, examining *everything* we do at Vanguard, how we do it, and why we do it, establishing a business planning effort, and seeking quantum improvement in our technology and productivity, without sacrificing quality. Perhaps, most importantly of all, we are looking toward a strengthened spirit of teamwork, dedication, and cooperation, working together as partners and rewarded as such. Indeed, at the end of June, each of you who were here at year-end 1984 will receive your first payment from the Vanguard Partnership Plan, specifically designed so that you will share in the victories we achieved for our clients. (Our new partners who have joined us in 1985 can look forward to their first partnership distributions in 1986.) The plan to make you partners with our officers and our shareholders has been at the top of my personal agenda for five years, and at last our asset growth and our tumbling fund expense ratios have made it possible to implement the plan. I know you will enjoy its growth rewards for many years to come.

In his marvelous book of reflections on his career in public service, entitled *No Easy Victories,* John W. Gardner warned us:

> **Life never was a series of easy victories (nor even a series of hard victories). We can't win every round or arrive at a neat solution to every problem. But driving, creative effort to solve problems is the breath of life, for a civilization or an individual.**

And, I would add, "or an enterprise," especially one with the qualities with which we at Vanguard are endowed.

The Ships of the Line

For at Vanguard, we *have* put together a fine enterprise. We stand for some things that, in my view, characterize few organizations. Consider these attributes:

We are **zealous**—"devoted and diligent." The spirit here is "roll up your sleeves and go to work." Even in the tough times of the last few months, when we have been swamped with investor inquiries and awash in checks, I have sensed an eagerness to help and a willingness to serve, in total, a zealous spirit. I have been, in truth, exhilarated by the experience.

We are **audacious**—"bold, reckless, defying convention." In 1975, Vanguard created a new way of doing business in the mutual fund industry—managing mutual funds solely in the interest of their shareholders. We then assumed the responsibility for shareholder services (1976), then the responsibility for marketing (1977), then for managing our fixed-income investments (1981). We started the first index fund (1975), added new advisers of considerable quality and promise, renegotiated advisory fees time and again, unbundled distribution costs, eliminated all sales charges, cut expense ratios when others were raising fees, and much more. While it would be easy to argue that we made these audacious moves simply to shock our competitors—and surely they did just that—in fact, our unfailing purpose was to better serve our shareholders.

We are **swift**—"capable of moving with great speed"—and we are **sure**—"confident." Our marketing decisions—among the most important decisions in this business—have been made quickly and without hesitation or doubt, almost always with insufficient data and a paucity of evidence. We have made these decisions with a confidence egregiously disproportionate to our knowledge, relying instead on experience, judgment, and intuition. And, while we too often have been timid at it, we have implemented our decisions as if we were totally sure of our direction. This combination of immediate response and enthusiastic determination—of the swift and of the sure—has been one of our most enviable characteristics.

Finally, at our best, we can be **majestic**—"of imposing aspect, grand." Not always, but enough of the time to know we have it in us. We have displayed "a touch of class" to those who own our funds and those who telephone us, in our shareholder reports and in our advertising, in our search for excellence. Without, I hasten to add, any sense of majesty (in the sense of "stately dignity"), we have become one of the proudest names—one of the most majestic names, if you will—in our industry.

Well, I have chosen these words—zealous, audacious, swift and sure, and majestic—not only because I believe them to be apt characterizations but because they too come out of British naval history. Indeed, they are names of British warships counted among Lord Nelson's fleet at the Nile. The HMS *Zealous,* HMS *Audacious,* HMS *Swiftsure,* and HMS *Majestic*—all were in the battle, and indeed it was *Swiftsure* that administered the *coup de grace* that literally blew to smithereens the French flagship *L'Orient,* in an explosion heard 10 miles away. If we can live up to these appellations—no mean challenge—their historical linkage with *vanguard* and *victory* will continue.

The Master of Our Fate?

I can give you no better conclusion to my commentary on the state of the Vanguard at the $10 billion mark than these moving words, describing the person who has suffered severe setbacks on the voyage to victory. They apply to each one of us as human beings, but they can also be read, in a far more mundane way, to speak of Vanguard—our failures, our successes, and, most of all, our determination to prevail. They are the words of William Ernest Henley, in his inspirational poem "Invictus":

> **In the fell clutch of circumstance**
> **I have not winced nor cried aloud.**
> **Under the bludgeonings of chance**
> **My head is bloody, but unbowed.**
>
> **It matters not how strait the gate**
> **How charged with punishments the scroll,**
> **I am the master of my fate:**
> **I am the captain of my soul.**

Captains of our souls we all are, as we sail ahead in the sound ship that I have the honor to command. She is a good ship, ever in turbulent waters, seeking destinations beyond the horizons. So we conclude as we began, on a musical note, with the spirited melodies of Richard Rogers, seeking, as always for Vanguard, *Victory at Sea.*

MAY DAY AND THE
VANGUARD EXPERIMENT

May 18, 1985

*T*EN YEARS AGO, on May 1, 1975—
May Day—The Vanguard Group of Investment Companies com-
menced operations.* It was an appropriate day on which to begin, for
May Day has come to symbolize these two somewhat different but
related ideas:

One, a new beginning, the early vigorous blooming part of life
Two, a revolution, often a sweeping upheaval in ideology or government

Surely Vanguard, a decade ago, was at "a new beginning" in every
sense of the phrase. Our challenge was to build, out of the ashes of a
major corporate conflict, a new way and a better way of running a
mutual fund complex. The Vanguard Experiment was designed to
prove that mutual funds could operate independently and do so in a
manner that would directly benefit their shareholders. Thus, our new
beginning was also, in its modest way, a revolution, both in the ideology of this industry and in its governance structure.

---

*The Vanguard Group, Inc., was incorporated on September 24, 1974, but the
  requisite Securities and Exchange Commission clearance and fund shareholder
  approvals required some seven months to complete.

The First Decade of the Vanguard Experiment

The Vanguard Experiment, it seems fair to say, has been successful beyond our wildest dreams. Consider for a moment some of the customary measures of growth in the context of our first decade:

- Our fund assets were $1.4 billion when we began. Today, assets are $13 billion, a sevenfold increase in just ten years.
- There were eleven Vanguard funds when we began. Today, there are thirty-seven Vanguard funds, including nine that have been formed within the last year alone.
- When we began, we provided solely corporate and accounting services to the funds. Today, we also provide all shareholder services and marketing and distribution services, as well as the investment management services for $5 billion of our assets.
- In 1975, investors were purchasing about $4 million of Vanguard fund shares each month. This year, investor purchases average more than $400 million per month, a 100-fold increase.
- Net cash flow had been negative for forty-eight consecutive months prior to May 1975 and was to continue negative (redemptions greater than sales) for another thirty-two months. In contrast, in the first four months of 1985 alone, we have enjoyed net cash *inflow* of almost $2 billion.
- We had but 28 people on the payroll when we began. Today, Vanguard has 717 full-time crew members.
- Our first budget, for 1975, called for annual Vanguard expenditures of $1.5 million. Our budget for 1985 is $48 million.

Indeed, even the astonishing growth we have enjoyed during our first decade is accelerating as our tenth anniversary becomes history. Only yesterday, Friday, May 17, Vanguard Fund assets crossed the $13 billion mark, compared to $9.9 billion at the start of the year. Our billion-dollar milestones have come quickly, as this record shows:

$10 billion on January 7, 1985
$11 billion on February 4, 1985
$12 billion on March 29, 1985
$13 billion on May 17, 1985

Thus, we have crossed four billion-dollar milestones already this year. Contrast this rate of growth with the length of time required for us to cross and hold our second billion-dollar milestone: *twenty years!* Our assets topped $1 billion in 1959; they did not top $2 billion for once and for all until 1979.

Asset Growth—Not the Only Measure of Success

We point to our asset growth as a convenient reference point from which to measure our success. But I want to underscore that asset growth is only one guide among many, and it is by no means the most important one. The Vanguard Experiment has produced accomplishments far more meaningful than mere asset growth. It has produced excellent returns to our shareholders practically across the board among our funds. It has produced low operating costs for our shareholders, to the point where we are virtually the low-cost producer in the entire mutual fund industry. It has produced a distribution structure under which, in our no-load format, shareholders pay not one single penny of sales charges when they invest with us. And finally, it has produced a high quality of service for our shareholders. While this quality has not been uniformly high—and indeed has suffered rather painfully in the face of enormous transaction volumes during the early months of 1985—surely every person that works for Vanguard knows that service excellence remains a continuing goal, one that we shall most assuredly achieve.

The acceptance of the Vanguard Funds in the marketplace has been sufficiently imposing not only to give us the near crisis in our operations that we faced earlier this year but also to engender a huge influx of new investments into our most popular funds. As a result, we have taken a step virtually unprecedented in the mutual fund industry: We have ceased opening new accounts or accepting additional investments from existing shareholders in three of our most successful equity funds. By limiting the growth and size of Windsor Fund, Explorer Fund, and Vanguard Qualified Dividend Portfolio I, we hope that our portfolio managers can continue to provide the high-quality performance results that they have provided over such a long period of years. While this marketing discipline will certainly slow our growth, I hope it reflects our respect for the integrity of these funds and our willingness to honor the fiduciary duty that we owe to our shareholders.

As we now close down Windsor Fund and Explorer Fund and prepare to open Windsor II and Explorer II, utilizing two new investment advisers, we should recognize that this strategy is possible only under the Vanguard structure. We have the unique ability to provide substitute funds with new investment advisers, to handle additional assets without jeopardizing the existing funds. Thus, in the long run, I have complete confidence that our way of doing business—the Vanguard Experiment—will not only be successful but will indeed give us a well-earned advantage over our competitors in the marketplace. Thus, our action as trustees should not prove contradictory to our business strategy.

There is so much work left to do. And I will take no more time speaking with admiration about the handiwork of the past, no matter how successful it may have been. I think Rudyard Kipling put it well when he presented this warning:

Our England is a garden, and such gardens are not made
By singing 'Oh, how beautiful!' and sitting in the shade.

While that verse can hardly be misunderstood, I am going to take the liberty of putting a sharper point on it by paraphrasing it in Vanguard's context, with this couplet:

Our Vanguard is a warship, but warships lose their might
When crews sing 'O how powerful!' and forget how to fight.

With this thought, I issue a clarion call for your continued discipline and your continued dedication, the discipline and dedication that have propelled us to where we are today. Despite the ambience of this wonderful tenth anniversary celebration, there will never be time at Vanguard to sit back and relax and to enjoy what we have accomplished. Self-adulation should be taken in small doses, for there are no easy victories.

The Rewards of Partnerships

As we work together in the future, we want every person on the Vanguard crew to share in its rewards. I want to remind you all that we have provided the Vanguard Partnership Plan so that each of you will participate in the earnings Vanguard is able to achieve for our shareholders. It is only fair that you share in our earnings, for you helped to create them. We must have your continued help in the months and years ahead. We cannot afford to have you "sit in the shade"; rather, we want you to remember "how to fight" in the never-ending struggle for Vanguard's survival and growth. In return, as we win the competitive battles that lie before us, we want you to share in the rewards—the fruits of victory.

Finally, I want to close with some words from a letter I received from a shareholder just two days ago. You may forget every word that I have said today, but I hope you will remember his words. They are the first words that everyone who joins Vanguard should know and the most important words they should remember about Vanguard. They are, as it were, our alpha and our omega, and I hope that they will be reaffirmed on each May Day anniversary in Vanguard's future. Let me share them with you:

> **All my experiences with you and all your reports on the funds in which we have investments have created a feeling of trust in your integrity and responsibility and good sense. I hope this will never turn out to have been the result of mere window-dressing. . . . If you really are as honest as you have convinced me that you are, don't ever let me down. Integrity seems to be in short supply nowadays. Please stay in the Vanguard of integrity.**

And that principle—*the Vanguard of integrity*—must be the real message of the Vanguard Experiment.

THE IMPOSSIBLE DREAM

December 14, 1985

*F*IRST OF ALL, a warm welcome on this cold day. A welcome to each member of our Vanguard crew, and to your friends and your families, as we gather together for a celebration of the Christmas season, a season of hope and joy, a holiday season to be sure, but let us not forget, also a season of Holy Days as well.

As we gather in this splendid new Vanguard building—the Vanguard Operations Headquarters that stands just a few steps from the Vanguard corporate headquarters here in Chesterbrook—we want to take just a few moments to dedicate this building and to celebrate Vanguard's remarkable growth to the awesome $15 billion milestone. Indeed, in the six weeks since that milestone was crossed on October 31, 1985, our assets have crossed the $16 billion mark, and they total some $16.4 billion at this moment.

When we dedicated our then new corporate headquarters just a bit over two years ago, on September 18, 1983, we had the audacity to call that modest structure "Vanguard Financial Center." (We considered calling it "Vanguard World Headquarters," but that was too audacious even for us!) Today, with the dedication of this second building, it is fair to say that we do have a financial center here. And who is to say that yet another Vanguard building won't arise here one day, giving us, I suppose, "the Vanguard Financial Complex." For better or for worse, that kind of terminology is consistent with the way we are now described in the press: "the giant Vanguard Group." (Could that really be *us?*)

Well, we have surely grown! At our dedication next door, two years ago, our assets were $7 billion; today they are $16 billion. Two years ago we operated twenty-six mutual fund portfolios; today we operate thirty-seven. Monthly purchases of our regular fund shares were running at almost $100 million; today the rate is $400 million. We were then handling 150,000 transactions a month; today we handle 300,000. Two years ago we employed 400 people; today we employ 900. Small wonder that we needed to add a new building to the Vanguard Financial Center!

The Fastest-Growing Company in America's Fastest-Growing Industry

These figures place Vanguard as the fastest-growing major company in the fastest-growing industry in America. Think of that! Our growth has been truly remarkable, indeed astonishing. Most corporations are born, and live, and die without in their entire lifetime ever experiencing the kind of growth Vanguard has enjoyed in the past two years.

Growth is exhilarating, and rewarding, and satisfying. It is, I know, a source of pride to all of us. But it comes only because we have had good people—outstanding individuals both at Vanguard and at our investment advisers—contributing their time and talents to making the Vanguard Funds what they are today, and good people contributing their time and talents to administer our affairs, including helping us through the processing traumas that we have faced as we have struggled to keep pace with our growth. For your efforts, I can offer only my deepest appreciation.

Without our people—without all of you—we would, in truth, be nothing. For a company, if you think about it, is no more than the sum of the individuals who comprise it. As those of you who have heard me philosophize before know, I have a profound respect for what one individual can do. Therefore, in dedicating this building—the third building I have dedicated in my life—I can think of no better dedication than the one I have used twice before. So, I dedicate the Vanguard Operations Headquarters with these same words:

I believe that even one person can make a difference. Thus, I dedicate this building to the individuals in our company—the individuals who got us started fifty-seven years ago, the individuals who work with us today, and the individuals who, God willing, will come forth to assure our future.

Let me give just a few reflections on our $15 billion and $16 billion milestones. This moment in our history is very similar to the events of

73

a year ago, when we crossed $10 billion last January and then crossed $11 billion in just a few more weeks. Remarkably, we added $1 billion of assets before we had time to organize a celebration for the prior milestone. Perhaps having this event happen twice in a single year is the most vivid example of the lightning speed of our growth.

Growth—A Two-Edged Sword

Growth, of course, is a two-edged sword. It reflects our considerable success, to be sure. And it validates the faith we have had in our Vanguard mission. But it places great stress on our organization. And, sooner or later, it obviously means we are no longer a small company.

So our challenge is to manage our growth responsibly and to shape our growth in accord with the values that got us where we are today. We must engage in comprehensive business planning, for example, without letting the plan control the business. We must bring some coordination to our marketing and our development of new products and services, without stifling the intuition and initiative that will always be the best source of innovation. We must have a cogent organization design, without adding needless layers of management and bureaucracy to our structure.

In sum, we must maintain our entrepreneurial spirit. We must continue to be a company in which one person can make a difference and in which people care about one another—and in which, I pray, there is no "we" and "they," whether referring to rank or to department. And surely we must be a company in which every member of the crew is treated fairly. You are entitled to a good place to work, and I hope you agree that this building is a fulfillment of that commitment. You are entitled to a share in the profits from our growth, and when our Vanguard Partnership Plan checks are distributed next June, you will, I am confident, see a considerable increase in your earnings.

It may seem paradoxical to be speaking of the burdens of growth even as we gather to celebrate its blessings. Surely dedicating a building in which 600 people will work means we are growing. And, equally surely, basking in the glory of the $15 billion milestone in the very year in which we passed the $10 billion milestone reflects a rate of growth few companies will ever achieve. Nonetheless, the issue, it seems to me, is no longer how to make Vanguard a *bigger* company but rather how to make Vanguard a *better* company. It will be a challenge to us all, as we focus on higher quality, greater convenience, and enhanced investment performance—all in the name of better service for the investors who have turned over to our responsibility their investment assets. A dream it may be—getting bigger only by being better—even an impossible dream, but a thrilling ideal.

To Dream the Impossible Dream

Writing in *Don Quixote* nearly four centuries ago, Cervantes said that there are "no limits but the sky." I believe that to be true. We must but reach for it, even as we know that our reach will exceed our grasp. A latter-day Don Quixote, in the marvelous musical play *The Man of La Mancha,* put it this way in the "The Impossible Dream":*

To dream the impossible dream,
To fight the unbeatable foe,
To bear with unbearable sorrow,
To run where the brave dare not go.

To right the unrightable wrong,
To love, pure and chaste from afar,
To try when your arms are too weary,
To reach the unreachable star,

This is my quest, to follow that star,
No matter how hopeless, no matter how far,
To fight for the right without question or pause,
To be willing to march into hell for a heavenly cause.

And I know if I'll only be true to this glorious quest,
That my heart will lie peaceful and calm, when I'm laid to my
    rest,

And the world will be better for this,
That one man, scorned and covered with scars,
Still strove with his last ounce of courage,
To reach the unreachable stars.

This, then, is the star that must set our course for the years ahead: the dream of being not just a growing company, not just a successful company, not even just a good company, but an even better company. As we seek that elusive goal, that impossible dream, we will surely be in the vanguard, leading the way both with our crew and for our clients for a long, long time to come.

Part III

A Pause
in the Markets,
Praise
for the Crew,
1986–1990

*T*HE SHARP UPWARD TURN in the financial markets that began in August 1982 (heralded in my speech, "The More Glorious the Triumph") continued for nearly five more years. In April 1987, however, the upsurge ended abruptly. A sharp rise in interest rates caused bond prices to tumble and sent the market areel. Though we were tested by soaring phone volumes and strains on fund liquidity, we weathered the crisis and learned from it. When an overheated stock market got its predictable comeuppance as summer ended, we were ready for it, and came through with flying colors. But the double shock was enough to subdue both bond and stock markets for several years.

Once again, a major factor in our ability to weather these storms so well was our character. In my first speech of this era ("Score," commemorating $20 billion in June 1986, just seven months after we reached $15 billion), I talked of the ominous trends in the fund industry, assuring the crew that we "had not sunk, and will not sink, into this quagmire" of higher management fees, risky funds, and hyped-up performance advertising. I hammered home the message that we were marching to a different drummer. Remaining steadfast to the high principles we had set for ourselves, we would do it *our way.*

By that time, our crew had crossed the 1,000 mark, and it was no longer possible to assemble them at the drop of an asset-milestone hat. So we moved to a cycle of two company gatherings a year—in June for the partnership plan celebration and the distribution of the earnings checks, and in December for a holiday celebration. (As the idea of the *Christmas party* became passé, ever the traditionalist, I persisted in calling it a "Holy Day celebration.") Each occasion gave me the opportunity to mount the pulpit and deliver my sermon (which, for better or worse, is how many crew members came to view it). I continued to

	Total Net Assets[1]	Net Cash Flow[1]	% Change in Assets	Number of Funds	Crew Members	Expense Ratio (%)	% of Fund Assets In:				Annual Return (%)		
							Stock Funds	Balanced Funds	Bond Funds	Money Funds	Stocks	Bonds	Bills
1986	24,961	6,938	51.2	43	1,100	0.46	37	9	38	16	18.7	15.3	6.2
1987	27,059	3,407	8.4	47	1,500	0.40	35	7	28	30	5.3	2.8	5.9
1988	34,206	5,141	26.4	52	1,600	0.40	33	6	26	35	16.6	7.9	6.8
1989	47,576	11,156	39.1	54	1,900	0.35	34	7	23	36	31.7	14.5	8.6
1990	55,817	11,489	17.3	58	2,200	0.35	28	7	25	40	−3.1	9.0	7.9
Cumulative		38,131	27.6								13.2	9.8	7.1

[1] Figures are in $ millions

urge that our growth not be *forced,* driven by opportunism or excess or avarice, but *organic,* the natural result of serving investors effectively.

We had created a company that I wanted "To Preserve, Protect, and Defend," the title of my 1986 year-end remarks. To do so, I told the crew, required not only foresight, but: (1) a *sense of purpose and objective,* (2) *the talent to organize the process for reaching new objectives,* and (3) *people who care—and care deeply—about the institution,* "all who are served by it, all who own it, all who govern it, all who work for it." In that speech, I also suggested that the era of extraordinary growth enjoyed by the fund industry since our inception—an age in which Vanguard's assets had grown from $1.4 billion to $25 billion in just twelve years—was likely dying, to be succeeded by a challenging and exciting new age, but one in which the dimensions of industry growth would be more modest than in the remarkably robust period that had just ended.

The Cruelest Months

The year 1987 didn't wait very long to validate that caution. April was indeed "the cruelest month," as a short-lived threat to the tax-exempt status of municipal bonds led to a stunning tumble in bond prices. Our bond funds suffered major, almost frightening, net liquidations by shareholders, leading to the forced sale of portfolio holdings, often at depressed prices. But the crisis led to the creation of the "Swiss Army" I had suggested in a speech a year earlier—to defend Vanguard, "not by *having* an army, but by *being* an army." As teletransactions and tele-marketing grew in importance, every qualified crew member was trained to handle our soaring telephone volumes whenever they surged.

Gradually, interest rates leveled off, and stability returned to our operations. But only for a few months. The Dow-Jones average had begun the period at 1,500, and continued to rise through the summer of 1987, topping the 2,700 mark as August ended. But after drifting lower in September, the market decline accelerated in early October. Then on "Black Monday," October 19, 1987, the Dow plunged 508 points—a 22.6 percent decline *in a single day*—and touched a low of 1,677, more than 1,000 points below its high just six weeks earlier. It was a stunning day, but despite the chaos, all of our fund prices made the next day's newspapers.

As the news of the decline permeated the investment world, phone volumes soared to unprecedented levels. The Swiss Army responded magnificently to the challenge, and I personally spent almost all day Tuesday on the phones, handling 114 phone calls. I quickly sensed the steadfastness of our investors, and any fear that there would be a panic vanished. Like any taut ship manned by a staunch crew, we weathered the storm. But like April, October was a cruel month, and the shock of the crash subdued stock prices until early 1989. It took two years for the Dow to return to its August 1987 high.

New Bond Funds

The events of 1987 put a temporary damper on industry growth, an overdue reminder that this is a *market-sensitive* business. But we continued to create new funds at a rapid pace, again breaking hitherto untrodden ground. Much of our early emphasis continued to focus on bond funds. I resolved my antipathy to the single-state municipal bond funds (too much concentration of credit risk, I thought) that were rapidly gaining investor acceptance by creating the industry's first series of state-specific *insured* tax-exempt funds, holding *only bonds backed by private guarantors.* (We'd created the first no-load insured *national* municipal bond fund in 1984.)

Two of the long-term funds were accompanied by tax-exempt money market funds for the state, a pattern we would repeat thereafter. It worked well, and by the close of 1990 we'd added two more states, giving us five new tax-exempt bond funds and four new money market funds. (We also added four more taxable bond funds.) But our major innovation of the period took place at the end of 1986, when we formed the first *bond market index fund* available to the investing public. As with the stock market index fund, the success of its bond market counterpart in delivering solid performance to investors—giving them their fair share of bond market returns, no more, no less—was as certain as shooting fish in a barrel. While it took time for our bond index fund to gain acceptance, with $21 billion of assets today it is the second largest bond fund in the world.

New Equity Funds Too

Those fourteen new fixed-income funds dominated our agenda during the 1986–90 period. But we also created an equity income fund, emphasizing dividend-paying stocks. And, again breaking new ground, we formed the industry's first quantitative equity fund, with stocks selected largely by computer programs that evaluate enormous mountains of financial data. The idea was to hold a portfolio that matched the risk characteristics of the Standard & Poor's 500 Index, but would strive to garner a marginal edge in annual return. Vanguard Quantitative Portfolios (whose trademark name was changed to the generic "Vanguard Growth and Income Fund" in 1996) has met that test, albeit by a more modest margin than we had anticipated.

Still innovating, in September 1987 we created our second index fund, and with it an expanded Core Management Group to run our increasingly promising index activities. The new fund was the industry's first Extended Market Index Fund, tracking the Wilshire 4500 Stock Index, which covers the entire market outside of the S&P 500. Used in tandem with the 500 Index Fund, the extended market fund could at last enable investors to conveniently own the *total* stock market at low cost and, we expected, with minimal portfolio turnover. And in 1989 we converted one of Vanguard's actively managed small-cap funds into a small-cap *index* fund, another industry first.

In mid-1990 we also introduced the industry's first *international* index funds. Intimidated by the sky-high valuations in the Japanese market, however, we divided the fund into two discrete series, the European portfolio and the Pacific portfolio, giving investors the opportunity to make their own allocations in markets outside the United States. That has proved to be a wise decision. Since then, the Tokyo market has steadily dropped, and is currently at its lowest level since all the way back in 1985. But the European portfolio has flourished, providing excellent returns relative to its peers. With $5 billion of assets, it is the largest fund in its sector.

Asset Allocation

Learning from the 1987 crash, we also formed Vanguard Asset Allocation Fund. First offered in the autumn of 1988, the fund's managers—Mellon Capital Management, formed by some of the quantitative pioneers of the early 1970s—would gradually modify the fund's target 60/40 stock/bond balance depending on expected future returns in the stock and bond markets. The equity portion of its portfolio is indexed to the Standard & Poor's 500. It has turned in an exceptional performance record, providing returns that approached those of the stock market, but assuming significantly less risk. So, six of our seven equity offerings in this period were index oriented. With the new bond index fund and the other tightly structured, high-quality bond portfolios, nineteen of the twenty-one funds we created in this era sprang directly from the qualities that are at the core of our corporate character.

With our low-cost strategy, our focus on "down-the-middle" funds designed to provide predictably market-like returns would gradually capture the attention of the marketplace and help fuel our growth. These same factors also positioned us to capitalize on another major change taking place in the financial field: the coming of tax-deferred retirement plans. While the acceptance of IRAs and 401(k)s had been low in the early years following their inauguration in 1981, growth was accelerating. IRAs leaped from just 5 percent of our assets when 1985 began to 14 percent when 1990 ended, and the assets of our 401(k) and other pension and institutional accounts accounted for another 24 percent—38 percent of our asset base. Our technology group had prepared us well to deal with the complex administrative details of these plans, and we labored long and hard to provide candid, honest, no-holds-barred educational materials to assure that investors understood both the likely risks and the possible returns. We were ready to stake our claim to market leadership in the retirement plan arena.

From the Highest to the Humblest

As my speeches became coordinated with the distribution of partnership checks to our crew in June, I spoke increasingly of the importance of the hard, detailed, controlled, often mundane work we were called upon to do, all in the name of providing services of the highest quality to our shareholders. As I expressed, over and over again, praise and appreciation for the crew's efforts, I constantly warned of the perils of bureaucracy—*the challenge from within*—and of the need to treat one another, "from the highest to the humblest," with respect, honor, and decency—in short, as human beings.

I also offered the firm's loyalty to the crew in return for their loyalty to the firm, stressing that our management must never forget this message: *Loyalty is a two-way street.* We also began to conduct exhaustive employee surveys (*Crew's Views*, to parallel *Crew's News*, the company newsletter we created in 1986). In my speeches, I candidly reported on the results, sometimes gratifying, sometimes disappointing. We worked to deal with the continued low ratings our crew gave us on compensation levels, even as we reveled in our near-100 percent rating in the crew's understanding and endorsement of Vanguard's mission and character.

Character Above All

Character was never far from my mind when I spoke. In 1987, "Above all, provide value" was a major theme. My year-end talk urged the crew to remain lean and solid, to hold steadfastly to what is right, and to proudly stand for the values that lie at the heart of Vanguard's character. Yes, just "Like a Rock." My first speech in 1988, entitled "Tradition," was intended to reinforce the values of our heritage, and in the autumn talk I gave to our officers when we celebrated our having overcome the negative effects of the Great Crash of 1987, one section was entitled "Character Above All."

During the 1986 through 1990 era, I constantly pressed home the value of our reputation, pointing out how tough it is to build a reputation and how easy it is to destroy one. One highlight came in June 1989 when we marked not only our $40 billion milestone but the fifteenth anniversary of the original "white paper" I wrote to our board in April 1974. In that paper, written amidst our struggle to gain independence for our funds, I had presented our original articles of faith: independence, optimum cost-effectiveness, superior performance, candid communications, efficient shareholder service, and marketing directly to investors, all attributes that I emphasized in my remarks. Six months later in December, pursuing the same theme, I quoted Walt Whitman: "It takes crisis to give courage, and singleness of purpose to reach an objective." Character, once again, was clearly on my mind.

We Lead

As this period drew to a close, my speech to the crew at the 1990 midyear partnership meeting focused on *leadership.* "We Lead" was the ship's motto of the HMS *Vanguard,* and to mark our completion of the first fifteen years of Vanguard's operations, I spoke of our obvious industry leadership in pricing, indexing, quantitative investing, candor, and asset growth, as well as our arguably leading position in service to shareholders. (We had just won first place in the *Financial World* survey for the second year in a row.) But I also emphasized that the operative word for our success was not *lead,* but *we.*

At year-end 1990, my theme was taken from the movie *Field of Dreams:* "If You Build It, They Will Come." That phrase, a wonderfully apt description of the strategy we had followed since our inception, has become almost a Vanguard trademark. In it, I emphasized the importance of our lexicon: Not *employees* but *crew members* would do the "building." Not *products* but *services* and *trusteeship* would be the "it" that we would build. Not *customers* but *clients* were the "they" who would come. (We actually had an informal policy calling for a fine of $1 for using the wrong words!) I closed the talk by driving home the fact that a solid ethical foundation was the only sound basis for any business in which just about all of us on the Vanguard crew would want to spend our careers: *Good ethics is good business.*

The stock market leaped by 32 percent during 1989, only to tumble in 1990 as the Middle East crisis loomed and the winds of war began to blow. Nonetheless, the annual return on stocks, while below the stunning 17.4 percent rate of the previous five years, averaged a generous 13.2 percent. At 9.8 percent and 7.1 percent, respectively, the average returns on bonds and Treasury bills were also lower, but far above historical norms. But the cruel bond and stock market shocks of 1987 had curtailed, albeit briefly, the rate of growth of fund industry assets. Mutual fund assets had grown at a 32 percent annual rate during the previous era. While almost halved, the industry's 17 percent annual growth rate during the current period remained strong.

Vanguard's imposing compound rate of asset growth during this period was far higher—28 percent annually. While that rate too was lower than our 38 percent annual rate from 1980 through 1985, we were hardly discouraged. After all, our assets had increased from $16.5 billion at the outset to $56 billion at the end of the period. The major forces driving our growth included our early pioneering in the bond and money market fund arenas and our remarkable pace of new fund creation—thirty-eight funds at the outset, fifty-eight at the end. Our determination to dominate the fixed-income segment of the industry was reflected in the growth of our bond and money market funds from 48 to fully 65 percent of our asset base. As a result, we grew far faster than our rivals, and our market share jumped by 60 percent during this period. The increase, from 3.3 to 5.2 percent of industry assets, added fully $21 billion to our assets—more than half of our $40 billion increase. While the shifting winds had been strong and gusty, they favored HMS *Vanguard,* and our crew and warship were ready for whatever the remainder of the 1990s held for us.

SCORE

June 4, 1986

*T*ODAY WE CELEBRATE a truly remarkable "score" in Vanguard's history: a score of billions. That is, the twenty billions of dollars of assets that are now under Vanguard's aegis. We reached this mark when assets totaled $20,021,023,000 on April 10, 1986. Now, less than two months later, we have added nearly $1 billion more, and assets at the close of business today totaled $20,906,925,000.

In contrast, it took nearly thirty-one years from our founding in 1928 to July 1959 to reach our first $1 billion of assets. Twenty-three more years elapsed until we crossed $5 billion in August 1982 . . . less than three more years to January 1985 and $10 billion . . . then just ten *months* to October 1985 and $15 billion. Now, *just seven months later,* $20 billion. Clearly, the HMS *Vanguard* is sailing ever more swiftly. A beneficiary of a favoring tide and a strong wind at our stern, to be sure, but it is we who built this warship, and we who sail her, with our own sweat and blood.

As you may know, the derivation of *score* has to do with notches that were made on measuring sticks many centuries ago. The sticks came to have twenty notches, or scores, and a *score* meant "twenty." But this common meaning of *score* then changed over the years—as words are wont to do—to refer most typically to a game or contest, either the earning of a goal or points, or the number of points made by a competitor.

Our $20 billion aggregate score is, of course, the sum of the individual scores turned in by the various Vanguard fund portfolios—now forty-three in number. And here again we are reaching milestone after milestone. Consider these examples:

- Vanguard Fixed Income Securities Fund crossed $3 billion on April 23, 1986. This fund topped $1 billion only a year earlier, in April 1985.
- Vanguard World Fund crossed $500 million in April 1986, with $320 million in the International Growth Portfolio and $180 million in the U.S. Growth Portfolio. When these two portfolios began their independent existence last September, assets were $77 million and $124 million, respectively.
- Windsor II, namesake of our incomparable flagship Windsor Fund, topped $600 million in mid-May, before we even celebrated its first birthday.
- Vanguard STAR Fund, only two months after its first birthday, has $360 million in assets and accounted for one-half of our new IRA accounts this season. Last autumn, *Forbes* magazine called it "the dumbest idea in years."
- The Vanguard municipal bond and money market assets managed by our own Fixed Income Group crossed $7 billion early in May—more than the total of Vanguard assets three years ago. When the transition from external to our own internal portfolio management was made in November 1981, these assets were $1.7 billion.

This brief list of Vanguard funds represents only those with the most striking recent success in the marketplace, funds with twenty-one separate portfolios, eleven of which did not even exist five years ago. It is not only the magnitude of our growth, then, nor even its speed, but its diversity and its pervasiveness that catch the eye.

Tenacity, Determination, and Wellington Fund

Nonetheless, perhaps the most appropriate symbol of Vanguard's success is the milestone that soon lies ahead for a fund that has reflected not only extraordinary growth but tenacity, determination, and clarity of purpose as well. I refer of course to Wellington Fund, the rock on which this organization was built. From its founding by Walter L. Morgan in 1928, Wellington grew to be one of the Big Three of the mutual fund industry. It crossed $1 billion in 1959, and $2 billion in 1965, only to fall on bad times. Beset by a combination of poor performance and an unpopular balanced (stock/bond) strategy, Wellington suffered huge capital outflows for eighteen consecutive years—nearly a score, as it were, of years. Assets dropped to $467 million by the end of July 1982, a decline of more than 75 percent. But we worked to improve performance, to enhance shareholder satisfaction, and to build investor acceptance. And we succeeded. Assets have now more than doubled, to $984 million, and it is only a matter of time until Wellington Fund crosses $1 billion—for the *second* time.

This remarkable recovery should not give us excessive pride, however. In 1959, Wellington was a $1 billion fund among 150 funds in a $16 billion industry; today Wellington is again virtually a $1 billion fund, but among 1,500 funds in a $600 billion industry. It has had a renaissance to be sure, but it also stands as a monument to what Vanguard has had to achieve beyond our founding fund in order to maintain our competitive position. The "only child" of the first thirty years, now, just twenty-seven years later, it has forty-two brothers and sisters. Including a few twins and triplets, they have been arriving at the rate of one every nine months. What a marriage!

As we celebrate yet another aggregate asset milestone, to say nothing of this series of "mini-milestones," we must challenge ourselves to not be overly swayed by abstract numbers. Whether measured in the goals or points we earn, and whether or not we have more of them than our competitors, scores are at best only a superficial measure of what we are about. Even as we bask in the glory of our asset totals, or our investment returns, or our expense ratios, or our profits, or our market share, or our operating standards, I would warn you that scores never—I repeat, *never*—tell the full story of an enterprise. In short, there is something profound in the late sportswriter Grantland Rice's notion,

**When the One Great Scorer comes
To write against your name—
He marks—not that you won or lost—
But how you played the game.**

This is not to say that Vanguard will not be a vigorous competitor. We will. And our competitive position will surely remain secure, provided that all of us, together with our external advisers, meet the high standards that are required of us. But we must not lose sight of our shared fundamental values in this industry's pell-mell rush for asset acquisition and performance prestidigitation. The competition may well be getting out of hand, as we witness two forbidding trends that are almost certain to have unpleasant consequences.

Ominous Trends in the Fund Industry

One, the trend toward increasing mutual fund costs comes at the direct expense of shareholders. Even though aggregate industry advisory fee revenues have grown from the millions to the billions, fee rates are nonetheless being increased. Initial sales loads are being obscured as "contingent deferred sales charges," and many investors will first learn of them when their redemption checks are docked. Other distribution costs have gone underground as "12b-1 fees"—direct add-ons to a fund's annual operating expenses—and they are getting larger and larger. In sum, this industry is engaged in a massive price war. But it is not a typical price war. Ironically, it is a war not to reduce prices but to raise them.

The second disturbing trend is the competition's emphasis on short-term and speculative performance results and their excessive claims about yields. This industry, with the implicit encouragement of the press, is hell-bent on creating new funds—the riskier the better if an equity fund, the higher yield the better if a bond fund. If fifty funds are created, the law of random numbers almost guarantees that at least one will find its way into *Barron's* top performers for the year (or even for the quarter), calling for a photograph of the portfolio management genius whose very randomness has been rewarded. *Money* tells us "the best forty funds to buy now," yet only fifteen of them have completed even five years of history. And mutual fund advertising screams "up an amazing 154.8 percent since December 1984!" and "It's America's number 1 performing stock fund," thus adding hype to performance results in order to grip public attention. Yet these results have already been hyped quite enough by the mere existence of investment returns that have been achieved only in one great bull market, returns that are too often based on high levels of risk, returns sometimes achieved through sharp portfolio manage-ment practices during the early months of a new fund's operation, or, even worse, its incubation.

The practice of playing up performance or yield raises investor expectations to unrealistic levels, often at excessive risk. At the same time, the practice of piling on prices directly reduces investor returns. It is hard to imagine two courses of action more likely to result in col-lision. While not all of our competitors have engaged in these shabby practices, too many have. Vanguard has not sunk, and will not sink, into this quagmire. We will hold to our mission of providing solid and competitive investment returns, along with the highest standards of quality at the lowest reasonable costs.

The Great God Market Share

At this $20 billion celebration, we might as well recognize today that we will pay a price for our discipline. The great god market share is already smirking at us for closing down our three best-selling equity funds and for holding the line on advertising. But I, for one, and I hope every member of our crew, can look him in the eye and laugh. The joy of the "score" we celebrate today is that in a very real sense we have earned our massive point total despite being a one-legged player with one arm tied behind our back. And nothing is more challenging or more fun than that. We have not stood on the "leg" of performance pyramiding, nor have we swung the "arm" of piling cost upon cost, so as to bring more assets into our coffers, thereby increasing profits, the better to have our management company go public in one massive public offering of another hot stock.

No, we have marched to a different drummer. And as we hear the beat of her drum, we cannot help but hear the beat of a popular song that sums up the Vanguard mission. With apologies to Paul Anka and Frank Sinatra, I'll paraphrase it just a bit:

The record shows we took the blows
And did it our way

. . .

We faced it all and we stood tall
And did it our way.

Marching to a Different Drummer

Vanguard will continue to march to a different drummer and to play the game "our way." Our mission precludes a sales-pressured, commission-driven approach to marketing. Our structure precludes ownership, and that is one of our great strengths. I am well aware that the conventional industry structure offers a kind of material and monetary gain that does not exist here. The Vanguard Experiment tests whether it is a necessary condition of the successful enterprise. We have done extraordinarily well without it so far, and I have absolutely no doubt that we can continue to do so. For I agree with the great economist Joseph Schumpeter, who seventy years ago wrote that there were at least three entrepreneurial motives more powerful than money:

1. The dream and the will to found a private kingdom, usually, though not necessarily; also a dynasty
2. The will to conquer: the impulse to fight, to succeed for the sake not of the fruits of success but of success itself
3. The joy of creating, getting things done, or of simply exercising one's energy and ingenuity

The dream of dynasty . . . the will to conquer . . . the joy of creating. That's what it's all about. But I do not mean to suggest that extra financial incentives should not be a major part of Vanguard's program. They must be. Indeed, the idea of incentives to reward all of us for serving our clients faithfully and well is implicit in the structure of our Vanguard Partnership Plan. In substance, we calculate our earnings—based on demonstrated expense efficiencies and tangible success in fund performance—and share them with you. Each crew member's incentive is based on three factors: (a) our earnings per share, (b) the crew member's compensation category, and (c) his or her years of service with Vanguard. Today, we are distributing more than $0.5 million—$518,000—among you. And it is within our power to make this sum grow over the years, perhaps by a substantial amount. Your own partnership payment will also grow as our earnings rise and as your job level and employment longevity increase. This is as it should be, for it is not you who are in Vanguard's debt for our awesome distribution of profits but rather Vanguard that is in your debt for the work that you have done. Please never let us down.

Mathematical Expectations—Animal Spirits?

So with our $20 billion of assets and our half-million dollars in partnership incentives, we have two more "scores" for Vanguard. But we must always remember that numbers are only numbers—quantities on a scoreboard that reports only one measure of an enterprise. I believe that John Maynard Keynes knew this when he pointed out that it was the merest pretense to suggest that enterprise is "mainly actuated by the statements in its own prospectus, however candid and sincere . . . based on an exact calculation of benefits to come." Rather, he urged on us "animal spirits, a spontaneous urge to action rather than inaction," warning that "if the animal spirits are dimmed and the spontaneous optimism falters, leaving us to depend on nothing but a mathematical expectation, enterprise will fade and die."

There is little doubt that we will need our animal spirits in the months and years ahead. The mutual fund industry will have to face the consequences of its exaggerated claims of portfolio performance and its soaring product prices. This industry will also have to face the broader challenges created by ever more volatile securities markets, and ever more volatile investor activity. Let us not forget that, all too recently, we saw "the day they closed down the municipal bond market." Let us anticipate the day—perhaps some "triple witching hour"—when the Dow-Jones average drops not 40 points as it has in the past but 100 points. And let us be prepared, as best we can, for the perhaps massive and precipitous cash flows (exchanges and redemptions) that may be generated even in our own funds as investors act on the emotions that drive markets—optimism and pessimism, disappointment and fear, greed and hope.

The Thesis—A Thirty-Five-Year Perspective

If we understand our work and our business, we can meet these challenges. For this is inherently a simple business of a few fundamentals, and it really has not changed all that much over the decades. As I approach the completion of my thirty-fifth year with this organization one month from today, I am struck—indeed thunderstruck—with how little has changed since I wrote my Princeton senior thesis "The Economic Role of the Investment Company" in 1951. Consider these summary excerpts from its conclusion:

On mission: "The principal function of investment companies is the management of their portfolios. Everything else is incidental."

On confidence: "The only probable causes for a loss of public confidence would be gross mismanagement or the expectation of miracles from management."

On service: "The investment company must continue to serve shareholders as it has in the past, with management operating in the most efficient, honest, and economic way possible."

On costs: "Future growth can be maximized by concentration on a reduction of sales loads and management fees."

And in conclusion: "The optimum role of the investment company is to contribute to the growth of the economy, and to enable individual as well as institutional investors to share in this growth."

Obviously, these excerpts are equally valid today. But if we can heed these warnings and adhere to these time-tested principles, we at Vanguard will be proud of how we played the game. And, who knows, over time we may well win it too. But keep in mind that our scores—yesterday's, today's, and tomorrow's—are just for fun, and just for keeping track. More important are our energy, our ingenuity, our will to conquer, our animal spirits. With them, we shall live and flourish as long as we have an insightful and wise vision of the future and the enduring faith to remain steadfast to the high purpose we have set for ourselves.

VANGUARD: TO PRESERVE, PROTECT, AND DEFEND

December 12, 1986

*O*UR CELEBRATION this evening is without precedent in Vanguard's annals. Given the rapid growth of our organization and the difficulty of convening our crew on short notice, we are taking this opportunity when we are all together to celebrate the Christmas and Holy Day seasons to also celebrate our $25 billion milestone—but not *after* crossing it, as is our tradition, but some days or even weeks or months *before* it is reached.

At the close of business today, the assets of The Vanguard Group of Investment Companies were at $24.9 billion. With our net cash inflow from investors running at the astonishing rate of more than $500 million per month, it is difficult to see that even a significant stock market shock could long keep us from our tantalizingly close milestone, particularly given the fact that our equity funds—where the main market risk lies— make up only slightly above one-third of our asset base. So, I hope that, by anticipating it, I have not hexed the achievement of the $25 billion mark. Indeed, if we don't soon soar past that mark, a colossal storm that you will not soon forget lies immediately over the horizon.

So congratulations and deep appreciation in advance to each one of you who has helped us reach this goal. We have come a long way since Vanguard was established in the autumn of 1974. Consider the growth in our assets:

- Then assets were $1.45 billion. Today they approach $25 billion.
- Then our group comprised eleven fund portfolios. Today there are forty-three.

- Then we had not a single fund with assets over $1 billion (Wellington Fund had dropped below $1 billion, on its way to $500 million). Today we have seven portfolios with more than $1 billion, and it is only a matter of a few months until there are ten.

Consider the growth in our cash flow. When we abandoned, in 1977, the broker-dealer network that had supported us (to a greater or lesser extent) for nearly fifty years, investor purchases of our funds were running at the rate of $5 million per month. Today, after nearly a decade with our no-load, no-retail-salesperson strategy, investor purchases are running at the rate of $5 million per *hour* (at least if we assume a seven-hour day, a limit that not so many of us are able to stay within).

Over the twelve years of our history, our assets have grown at a rate of +23 percent per year. At that remarkable rate, our assets would be $58 billion in 1990 and $460 billion in the year 2000. Happily, however, a 23 percent growth rate is unsustainable. But even at a 10 percent rate, Vanguard's assets would be $37 billion four years from now and $95 billion at the turn of the century. And if rates of anything like this magnitude are sustained—as you will hear later on, there may well be some major obstacles in sustaining them—we will all have our work cut out for us to preserve, protect, and defend the institution for which we are together responsible.

For some years now, one of my principal concerns has been that growth not be allowed to deprive us of the character that got us here in the first place. In my $20 billion speech last June, I described them as "our energy, our ingenuity, our will to conquer, our animal spirits." We risk losing these values if we seek growth at any price. Is bigger better? Does growth make us a stronger company? A more efficient company? A more profitable company? A company that is more personal, or more hospitable, or more fun? Grow we must, and grow we will, for, as John Cardinal Newman said, "Growth is the only evidence of life." But it must be not growth forced by opportunism or excess or avarice, but growth that is the natural result of serving investors effectively.

The Switzerland of an Industry at War

The philosophy that the best growth is organic rather than forced enables Vanguard today to maintain a sound balance in a burgeoning industry that seems to have lost it. The participants in the mutual fund industry—established firms that have been around for a half century, as well as new firms that are bereft of history and tradition—are at once engaged in a price war, a product war, and a performance war:

- The price war is a paradoxical battle to increase, beyond any reasonable level, the prices investors pay to own mutual funds, so that fund managers can undertake massive marketing expenditures for sales commissions and advertising.
- The product war is a fight to introduce new mutual funds, perhaps 700 or more in 1986 alone, often speculative and always untested.
- The performance war is a contest to see which funds can add the most hype to their records—by reaching to the very extremities of prudence and beyond for the largest equity returns and the highest bond yields.

Each war is fought for the same territory—the investor's financial assets. Each war reinforces the sins of the others, in one massive triple-pincer attack aimed at speedy victory—the acquisition of these billions of assets at any price, at a time when markets are heady and prosperity rife, and when too many investors are unconcerned about risk and unaware of cost.

Perhaps it goes without saying that, in this war, Vanguard is marching to a different drummer: We are not raising prices but lowering them; introducing not speculative funds but funds that are conservative and relatively predictable; committing not a veritable fortune to tout yesterday's so-called miracles but a modest advertising program that speaks common sense. It takes the courage of one's convictions to hold to this utterly contrarian approach, but courage we have, and conviction we hold.

Indeed, I can't resist comparing Vanguard's strategy in the financial war being waged today with the strategy that a small mountain-ringed nation in central Europe has followed since the year 1515. Switzerland's strategy has been to let the great powers of Europe fight their own wars and to let them pay the terrible price involved. Prussia, Germany, Austria, Hungary, England, Serbia, Russia, France, Spain, Italy: these nations, many of which have come and gone, have fought the same wars, for the same territories, over and over again. But for nearly

95

500 years, Switzerland has maintained its neutrality by being prepared to protect its fortress nation not by *having* an army, it is said, but by *being* an army.

This strategy has kept Switzerland peaceful and prosperous, with its own distinctive culture, values, and ethics. It has been the envy of a Europe that has been savaged by war for centuries, and, not incidentally in view of my analogy with Vanguard, it has been the place to which concerned investors seeking a safe harbor for their capital turn at the first sign of crisis. And we at Vanguard, like the Swiss, shall also maintain our values, hold ourselves to higher standards, and let our competitors, old and new, engage in the utterly self-defeating price-product-performance wars which they have declared. We can stand aloof from these wars, provided that we are ever willing to preserve our standards, protect our own enterprise, and defend our independence.

Caring for an Institution

So it behooves us, above all, to believe in this institution we know as Vanguard. To do so, despite the Switzerland analogy, we need to maintain the characteristic American virtues: optimism, candor, high expectations, hard work, and achievement. These are the qualities cited by Howard M. Johnson, chairman of the Massachusetts Institute of Technology, in a speech he gave back in 1972. While he was speaking of the challenges facing private foundations, he might just as well have been anticipating the standards underlying the creation, just two short years later, of a business institution that would be known as The Vanguard Group of Investment Companies:

> There is always a point in time when the longer view could have been taken and a difficult crisis ahead foreseen and dealt with while a rational approach was still possible. How do we avoid extremes? What do we do when short-range competition may preclude a longer view? How can sustainable growth be achieved? Only with foresight—the central ethic of leadership— for so many bad decisions are made when there are no longer good choices.
>
> If foresight is needed to protect an institution, what are the requirements necessary to make it work? Clearly the first requirement is the sense of purpose and objective. Little can be gained without knowing where one wants to go. Second is the

96

talent to analyze, organize, and manage the process for reaching new objectives. Second-rate talent will not suffice to meet
first-rate objectives. Finally, and let me surprise you by emphasizing this third need, we need people who care about the institution. In an increasingly impersonal world, I have come to
believe that a deep sense of caring for the institution is prereq-
uisite for its success.

The institution must be the object of intense human care and
cultivation: Even when it errs and stumbles, it must be cared for,
and the burden must be borne by all who work for it, all who
own it, all who are served by it, all who govern it.

Caring, we know, is an exacting and demanding business. It
requires not only interest and compassion and concern; it
demands self-sacrifice, wisdom and tough-mindedness, and discipline. Every responsible person must care, and care deeply,
about the institutions that touch his life.

Over the years since Dean Johnson spoke those profound words, we
have worked together at this young and vibrant and confident and
dedicated organization to strive for these lofty goals. That they will
never be fully realized here at Vanguard—nor indeed anywhere here
on earth—is not the point. Rather, if we truly care about our organization, our partners, our associates, our clients, indeed our society as a
whole, then their set of goals will be our guiding star.

As we have grown—by doing our work, in our way—we have
become one of the largest financial institutions in the United States.
This simple fact, which we too often take for granted, places upon Vanguard the burden of sharing the responsibility for the future of our
financial system, and thus for our society as a whole. Among all the
thousands of asset management institutions in this nation, The Vanguard Group of Investment Companies ranked ninety-seventh just five
years ago, fortieth when 1986 began, and as we approach the $25 bil-
lion milestone with 1986 drawing to a close, we may now well rank as
high as thirtieth. That we here together tonight—with all of our weaknesses and imperfections—share this responsibility is both exhilarating
and more than a little frightening.

Our securities markets, to be sure, are at record levels today. Financial assets—stocks and bonds—are the preferred place for investors to
have their investments. But there are serious signs of stress in our U.S.
financial system, not the least of which are the excesses in the invest-

ment company industry today that are so similar to those that presaged the Great Crash that began in 1929. At the same time, the world financial markets are interactive and interdependent. What we have at once is the leveraging of America at a time of prosperity, the inability of the third world to meet its debt service, exotic new multinational financial instruments—unregulated and of unknown magnitude. The present exuberance in the securities markets that manifests itself all across the globe is indeed a strange bedfellow to these perils.

Vanguard cannot solve these problems itself, though perhaps we ultimately can play a role in their resolution. But what we *can* do is no less than live up to our continually heightened responsibility for our clients' growing billions of assets by having the discipline not to "jump on the bandwagon" of speculation and excess that is all too rampant in the world financial system and in the U.S. mutual fund industry today.

"We Are the Movers and the Shakers . . ."

In short, we must do all we can to preserve, protect, and defend our organization and our values, to say nothing of preserving, protecting, and defending the investments our clients have entrusted to us. There are today perhaps 1.5 million investors—down-to-earth, honest-to-God human beings with real needs and aspirations—who believe that we offer them sound investment programs, with clearly delineated risks, at fair prices. *We must never let them down.* At this time in history, it is a lonely job requiring us to dream our own dreams, not only about the past age in which our assets exploded from $1.4 billion to $25 billion but about the challenging and exciting new age that may well lie before us. The late poet Arthur O'Shaughnessy said it well:

> **We are the music-makers,**
> **And we are the dreamers of dreams,**
> **Wandering by lonely sea-breakers,**
> **And sitting by desolate streams;**
> **We are the movers and shakers**
> **Of the world for ever, it seems.**
> **We are the dreamers of challenge**
> **To make of each age what it's worth;**
> **For each age is a dream that is dying,**
> **Or one that is coming to birth.**°

°I hope that the poet would forgive me for tinkering with the fourth couplet.

It matters not whether the halcyon era of the mutual fund industry that began in 1979 is ending in 1986. If it is—if it is—a new age will inevitably come to birth. In either case, Vanguard is ours—all of ours—to preserve, protect, and defend.

A NEW ERA

Monday, June 8, 1987

Welcome to the second annual Vanguard Partnership Plan party. This evening I want to talk seriously with you about a new era for Vanguard. The era of prodigious, ever-accelerating growth—all that most of you here tonight have ever witnessed at Vanguard—is now behind us. Times have changed: We face the challenges of a new era in which growth will be slower and our standards must be higher. These challenges will be met and surmounted only if we shape this enterprise—its people no less than its philosophy—to meet the stringent demands that lie ahead.

At our $25 billion party last December, I predicted that a challenging and exciting new age may well lie before us, emphasizing that if the halcyon age of the mutual fund industry that began in 1979 was ending as 1987 began, Vanguard could meet the challenge. In this context, I urged you to accept the notion,

Each age is a dream that is dying
Or one that is coming to birth.

Seven years ago, an age of rapid growth came to birth at Vanguard. Readers of the Holy Bible will not be surprised that this new age began after a discouraging seven-year era of attrition, seven years of want that were to be followed, as it turned out, by seven years of plenty—seven years of famine, then seven years of feast. We can mark the year as 1980, when our assets finally topped the $2.6 billion level at which we had peaked in 1972—eight years of zero growth. And we can, a bit arbitrarily, mark the specific day in 1980 as September 17, when we reached the $3 billion asset milestone. Since then, we have been one of the fastest-growing companies in one of the fastest-growing industries in America. And we have celebrated this growth every step of the way.

We enjoyed celebrations at $4 billion in 1981, at $5 billion and $6 billion in 1982, at $7 billion in 1983, at $8 billion and $9 billion in 1984, and $10 billion in February 1985. With our growth accelerating beyond our ability to celebrate at every $1 billion, we shifted to a $5 billion cycle, celebrating $15 billion in 1985, $20 billion in June 1986, and $25 billion in December 1986. At the close of business today, Vanguard assets will total $29.4 billion.

But I believe that our pace of growth—an annual asset growth rate of nearly 40 percent over the past seven years—is now clearly slowing, and we must now look ahead to focus more on making this a better company, and less on making it a bigger company. Beginning tonight—right now—we must accept the challenge of working together to make this not just another financial services company but a company that is the pride of its clients and the envy of its competitors.

Five-Year Annual Returns: Stocks 27 Percent, Bonds 21 Percent

Let us spend a moment on the background of the era of dazzling growth that we have enjoyed. The primary source of our growth, and make no mistake about it, was our environment—the financial markets in which we work. There is simply no historical parallel to the incredible pair of bull markets we have enjoyed during most of that era. In the past five years, the annual rate of return on common stocks has averaged +27 percent—by far the best single five-year period of the past six decades, over which the average return has been just +10 percent per year.

Even more striking, the rate of return on long-term U.S. Treasury bonds has averaged 21 percent in the past five years, by a huge margin one of the two best five-year periods in the past six decades, over which the average return has been only a puny +4 percent per year. Clearly, if one gives any credence whatsoever to the lessons of history—and I do—the rates of return on stocks and bonds achieved over the past five years are simply unsustainable on a long-run basis.

What is more, these high returns have been achieved when bank deposits—the financial mainstay of the U.S. household—have provided ever-lower returns. For example, the yield on a six-month certificate of deposit reached an all-time high of 13 percent early in 1982; today it yields 6 percent. Small wonder that millions upon millions of investors have shifted their assets from short-term investments with fixed values (savings accounts) to long-term investments with variable values (stocks and bonds). Bluntly stated, however, the compelling advantages of long-term investing come hand-in-hand with significant risks to principal.

The prime beneficiary of this convergence of circumstances—high returns on long-term investments, rapidly diminishing returns on short-term investments—has of course been the mutual fund industry. A decade ago, our industry accounted for just $1 billion of the $160 billion of annual discretionary household savings flow, or less than 1 percent of the total. But by 1986, mutual funds accounted for $209 billion of $298 billion of new savings, or 70 percent of the total. There is, as far as I know, *no precedent in the financial history of America* for any significant category of financial institution to enjoy anything even remotely resembling such a 100-fold increase in market penetration. Truly, "we never had it so good."

Mutual Funds—An Idea Whose Time Has Come

Victor Hugo said that "an invasion of armies can be resisted, but not an idea whose time has come." Given the circumstances I have described earlier, the mutual fund industry was nothing less than "an idea whose time had come," evidenced by its 30 percent growth rate since 1980. With our astonishing near-40 percent growth rate, Vanguard was not only a participant in this growth but one of the major institutions leading the way.

Part of our leadership can, I believe, be attributed to our fundamental strategic principle: *Above all, provide value.* Part can be attributed to our clarity of focus: *Mutual funds are our only business.* Part has been the result of our innovation: *Create new investment companies when—but only when—they meet a sound and durable investor need.* Part is the result of our good fortune: *Investment performance that surpasses most of our peers, most of the time.* And part, it almost need not be said, is the direct result of the dedication of our people: *The Vanguard crew.*

With all of our success, we may have allowed pardonable pride in our achievements to develop into hubris—that is, excessive pride bordering on arrogance. We were well aware that investing in long-term bonds (U.S. Treasury bonds, GNMAs, corporate bonds, municipal bonds) involved interest rate risk—the risk of fluctuating market values. But, in retrospect, I think that we were not adequately aware that—by virtue of the very advantages we offered, such as higher yields, lower expenses, no sales commissions, and the absence of transaction charges—Vanguard had attracted the assets of many clients who were at the highest levels of intelligence, education, wealth, decisiveness, financial sophistication, and willingness to shift their assets from one type of investment to another, in the entire mutual fund industry.

April Was the Cruelest Month

The hard evidence came abruptly as April began. Interest rates surged upward, and we entered what was one of the most volatile bond markets in memory. The yield on the benchmark thirty-year U.S. Treasury bond rose from 7.5 to 8.7 percent in a matter of weeks—with its price declining from 100 to 88, or 12 percent. In this baneful environment, a truly massive cash flow out of our long-term bond funds and into our money market funds began—first as a rill, then as a rivulet, then as a river, finally as a flood. During the subsequent two months, cash redemptions and net exchanges out of our bond funds exceeded $2 billion—more than 20 percent of their assets—as investors moved to protect themselves against the sharp upward thrust in interest rates.

Alas, in retrospect, we now know we should have heeded T.S. Eliot's warning:

**April is the cruelest month . . . stirring
Dull roots with spring rain.**

Well, April *was* the cruelest month. And if interest rates were the spring rain, they surely stirred at least some of our roots—those many Vanguard shareholders concerned above all with short-term preservation of their principal. That some 80 percent of this cash outflow ($1.6 billion) represented exchanges within The Vanguard Group, and thus did not diminish our asset base, is no small consolation. But, while our assets remained at about $29 billion, we nonetheless experienced two major sets of problems. First, our communications and processing systems were strained to near the breaking point by the transaction overload. Our telephone volumes leaped almost overnight from 8,000 calls per day to 16,000 during mid-April, as investors deluged us with exchanges from our long-term fixed-income and municipal bond portfolios to our money market funds. All of this activity, of course, came right at the time of the usual surge in IRA activity. Only a truly heroic effort by our client services staff enabled us to escape catastrophe in our telephone service.

The second stress point appeared in the securities markets. Mutual funds poured huge amounts of fixed-income securities into the marketplace for sale, in order to raise cash to meet the redemptions and exchanges. Particularly in the municipal bond market, liquidity left a great deal to be desired, as dealers began to sharply reduce their bids—the prices they would pay for blocks of bonds. With each drop in prices, more investors moved out of bond funds, requiring more bond sales, reducing prices still further. We were witnessing the paradigm of the vicious circle, and Vanguard was a major participant in it. Only another truly heroic effort, in this case by our portfolio managers and fund accounting staff, enabled us to raise the requisite cash in a devastated marketplace.

We must not ignore the lessons of the cruelest month. To state the obvious, we cannot again come so close to the edge of our ability to respond to the transaction requirements of our investors. We must, and we shall, provide greater answering capacity, better technology, and ample standby staff reserves for the utterly inevitable contingencies that will always be part of this volatile, market-driven business.

The No-Load Fund Investor and Financial Flexibility

We also must recognize—to an extent that might have seemed unbelievable as April began—that investors in no-load mutual funds demand far more financial flexibility than direct holders of securities, and indeed more than owners of broker-sold mutual funds. Recent evidence suggests that transaction activity (redemptions plus exchanges out of regular mutual funds, as a percentage of their total assets) is substantially higher among no-load funds. Shareholder activity in no-load funds currently runs at an astonishing annual rate of about 70 percent, while such turnover in funds charging sales commissions runs at about 20 percent—less than one-third as large. At 40 percent, Vanguard's transaction activity has been way below that of the typical no-load fund, but it is still a very large number, the implications of which are not yet entirely clear.

We have always known that our typical Vanguard client is better educated and wealthier than the typical fund investor. We now know that, in addition, he or she is more ready, willing, and able to move his or her assets among our funds. In short, our prototypical client is a financially astute investor who knows what he or she wants, when he or she wants it, and how to get it.

As the mutual fund research service *Strategic Insight* recently pointed out, "The way people go about making financial decisions is a key distinguishing characteristic among mutual fund customers. . . . People who seek the help of brokers and financial planners . . . are *decision-dependent.* . . . [T]hose who feel comfortable enough on their own to select, switch, or sell mutual funds are *independent decision makers.*" Decision makers, says *Strategic Insight,* spend significant time studying matters relating to money management; they desire detailed, thorough, and diverse sources of information; they seek stimulation, excitement, and challenge; and they are "highly responsive to opportunities and risks in the constantly changing investment environment." To me, that sounds like a great many Vanguard clients.

Facing Tough Issues

Vanguard's obvious attraction to well-informed, sophisticated, and independent decision makers carries implications far beyond our transaction processing capability. It touches on enormous issues, including how we manage the assets entrusted to us. (For example, should we maintain large cash reserves in our funds?) It touches on our asset-size ambitions. (For example, are smaller portfolios more or less liquid than larger ones?) It touches on the assessment of transaction costs. (Should we redeem in kind? Should we impose redemption fees?) And it touches on our marketing strategy vis-à-vis our competitors. (To what extent should we limit exchange frequency?) How do we attract the investors we want? Should we in fact *prefer* that certain types of investors put their money somewhere else, at Fidelity, or at Dreyfus, or at T. Rowe Price? These are real-life issues, complex and far-reaching, with no simple answers. One of our challenges, clearly, is learning how to deal with them effectively and realistically. It will be no small task.

For me, then, the cumulative weight of evidence points to the end of an era of overwhelming and pervasive growth. To begin with, a 40 percent growth rate simply cannot sustain itself. The fluctuating stock and bond markets that establish an inevitably volatile environment for mutual funds will not continue to provide returns of +20 to +30 percent each year. Indeed, we have just witnessed the powerful market forces unleashed by a modest—if astonishingly abrupt—shift in interest rates. And surely one day, probably sooner rather than later, a stock market plunge will unleash similar forces. Finally, Vanguard faces these challenges with a new awareness that our client base is exceptionally active in terms of money mobility, and exceptionally demanding in terms of service.

The cumulative impact of these factors lends credence to the likelihood that Vanguard is entering a challenging new era of more limited growth that will require us to focus our strategies and policies on a relatively small number of critical issues. Let me be crystal clear that I regard such a change as an unmixed blessing. Change means excitement. Change means renewal. And change must mean progress. But if we are sailing into an era of change in turbulent waters and with an uncharted course, we must sail with the best sailing orders and the best crew we can find. Let me speak first about the orders; second, about the crew.

Above All, Provide Value

To state what may be obvious, the standing orders will not change from the five basic elements of our leadership that I earlier described. Let us call them the "orders" contained in *Vanguard's Manual for Officers and Crew:*

1. Above all, provide value, keeping operating costs paid by investors at the lowest levels in this industry and offering fund shares to investors without loads or hidden sales charges.
2. Hold to our course, concentrating our primary focus on the industry we know best, mutual funds.
3. Innovate soundly and sensibly, making intelligent bets on the future while never ignoring the lessons of history.
4. Generate rewards for our clients, consistent with the risks they expect, and generally surpass competitive norms.
5. Maintain a crew of dedicated people, who have signed on to Vanguard's mission.

These sailing orders are by no means easy to carry out. Temptations abound to do the easy thing, to take the shortcut. But we must maintain our principles, to the best of our ability, if we are to survive and prosper in the new era that almost surely lies ahead.

Meeting High Standards of Service Excellence

And there is of course one more order that is worthy of special emphasis, today more than ever: Meet high standards of service excellence for our clients. Clearly, we have done so in the past, as witnessed by the gratifying responses to our shareholder surveys (84 percent say our service is "excellent" or "very good"; only 0.5 percent say "poor"). But we can and must do better. Even at today's high service levels, I receive far too many letters calling attention to a variety of serious problem areas: difficulty in reaching us by telephone, delayed confirmations and dividend checks, inaccurate account registrations, failure to correct errors and, heaven forfend, failure to return promised phone calls. (One frustrated client recently asked me why we are open 168 hours a week for marketing information but available only 40 hours for client service.) While I also receive letters praising many of you for your helpfulness, expertise, and courtesy, on balance the "Bogle barometer"—my spot indicator of Vanguard service, based on shareholder letters sent directly to me—is registering stormy weather, a fact that I am sure will surprise few of you who interface directly with our clients.

Nonetheless, we have come a long way in bringing our overall service quality to today's high level. But having come so far, we must now raise our sights in the new era that lies before us. For the expectations of the American consumer for service quality are rising every day, as more and more organizations, through their service excellence, respond to the challenge. Vanguard must act to meet these expectations, not merely react to them.

There are at least a few corporations that we must emulate. In our business, Fidelity is the king (or at least according to what the Vanguard shareholders who also own Fidelity funds tell me). Personally, I have never called American Express, at any hour of the day, without hearing a pleasant voice and receiving an immediate response. And, so it is said, Federal Express employees are trained *not* to pick up the telephone until the first ring *ends*—think of that! (Apparently callers are surprised if they hear a voice without a ring.) We must dedicate ourselves to meeting, and then surpassing, the lofty standards set by these determined service providers. So, from today forward, using all of the resources at our command, we must take the requisite actions to move down the long, long road toward service leadership.

Crew's Views—*And We Are Listening*

Of course, such leadership will not be achieved without the support of our entire crew. And we do not deserve your support unless we do everything in our power to make Vanguard a good place for you to work. Our recent *Crew's Views* employee survey indicates how much we have to do to accomplish that objective. In some areas, such as corporate image and job security, our ratings are high, both on an absolute basis and relative to other financial services firms. In others, notably compensation and job training, our ratings are low—again, both on an absolute and relative basis. As you know from the recent special edition of *Crew's News* that reported on the survey, we have major action programs in place to deal with many of these issues, and we shall proceed to make further changes based on what we have learned.

If I discouraged easily, I would have been gone from this institution by early in 1979, after witnessing seven consecutive years of capital outflow from 1972 through early 1978 (seven years of famine!). But I must confess to being initially discouraged by the overall thrust of our survey—that on balance our plusses and minuses average out, with the net result that we are "just another" financial services firm—no better, no worse. However, you should know that I do not remain discouraged for very long. It took me perhaps as little as twenty to thirty seconds to realize that the survey was a blessing (albeit in heavy disguise) that gave us the opportunity to make Vanguard a better organization—and indeed an organization better postured for the new era that lies before us.

To do what we must do—to carry out our five commands (value, concentration, innovation, performance, and dedication) as we provide service excellence for our clients—will indeed require a good crew and a good ship. One of you commented in our *Crew's Views* that "the chairman always makes our company sound like a storybook company whenever he makes a speech. If he only knew. . . ." Well, I do confess to being an idealist, but I am enough of a realist to know that Vanguard could not be confused with heaven. Heaven, after all, is not supposed to exist here on earth. But this self-evident fact does not mean that we should not all work together to make this ship the best that it can be. It is, I emphasize, a shared responsibility of crew and officers alike. In this context, I reiterate a thought I expressed to you last December: *If we are to succeed, every responsible member of the Vanguard crew must have a deep sense of caring about this institution.*

The Vanguard Partnership Plan that has generated the incentive rewards we will be receiving in a few moments is one of our major efforts to assure that your management indeed cares. *You who have shared in the burdens of sailing this ship must also share in its blessings.* "Every employee a partner" is an article of faith at Vanguard. While our survey produced no great outpouring of appreciation for the partnership plan (and elicited but three comments, all negative), I have no intention of becoming discouraged by that reaction either. Thus, we shall modify the plan so as to make it more responsive to the needs of you for whom it was designed. At the same time, in the new era we anticipate, I warn you that earnings will not be easy to come by. And we—every one of us—shall have to work hard and cooperatively even to maintain Vanguard's earnings that are the basis of the partnership plan, to say nothing of increasing them at the near 50 percent growth rate of the past four years.

Speaking in Hard Words

Ralph Waldo Emerson urged us to "speak what you think today in hard words." I have tried to meet that challenge this evening. In these utterly unpredictable times, it is also fair to heed Emerson's next words: "and tomorrow speak what you think in hard words again, though it contradicts everything you said today. A foolish consistency is the hobgoblin of little minds." While it may be a bit grandiose for me to characterize what lies before this organization as a "new era," there is no doubt that we have before us turbulent weather, a hard sail, and an exciting voyage. If we who are officers and crew *work together* to make sure that the HMS *Vanguard* is a sound ship, and *care together* that she is a good ship, we can—with perseverance and enthusiasm—succeed in our mission, no matter what surprises fate holds in store for us.

LIKE A ROCK

December 6, 1987

As we celebrate tonight, 1987 is drawing to a close. Simply put, it has been one of the most remarkable, most difficult, most cataclysmic, years in the modern financial history of the United States. A year with two bear markets in bonds. A year with a single day—Black Monday, October 19, 1987, the day of a great crash in the stock market—when the Dow-Jones Industrial Average declined 508 points, wiping out in a single day nearly one-fourth of the market value of all U.S. equity securities. A year in which the investment of capital in stock and bond mutual funds plunged from a decidedly positive net inflow of $20 billion in January to a decisively negative net outflow of $13 billion in October. In short, a year about which you will one day tell your children and grandchildren, "I was there."

I am proud to state that Vanguard performed "like a rock" during this historic year. Our ship not only weathered the storm but emerged from it stronger, taller, and more battle ready than when the storm first appeared on the horizon. My sense of pride in every one of you, working together for the greater good, caring about our clients, caring about one another, and caring about this institution, is, in truth, beyond the power of mere words to convey. So, all I can say, from the bottom of my heart, is "thank you. I am proud of you."

There are lots of measures of the Vanguard performance that give me special pleasure. Let me give you just a few examples:

- Our fund net assets were $25 billion when the year began. Despite the deluge, they are $27 billion today.
- Our net cash inflow for the year will total some $3.5 billion. This figure, to be sure, obscures an extraordinary volatility, with inflow

of $1.1 billion in January and outflow of $0.4 billion in October. (The October loss, however, represented just 1.5 percent of assets; in November, our cash flow turned positive once again.)

- Our 1987 operating expense ratio—a critical measure of the value we deliver to our shareholders—will improve by at least 10 percent from a 1986 ratio that was in turn the best in Vanguard's history. We remain the industry's low-cost provider of services, and by a larger margin than ever before.
- Our 1987 investment results were very competitive. All five of our money market funds outpaced industry norms. Among our bond funds, thirteen of fifteen provided strong returns relative to other comparable funds. Among our twenty-three equity-oriented funds, all but five met or exceeded our performance standards vis-à-vis competitors with similar objectives.
- Our fund accounting group provided closing prices with better than 99 percent accuracy. In stark contrast to the omnipresent z (no price available) provided by most competitors in the next day's financial pages, Vanguard's Black Monday prices were there for shareholders to see.
- Our administrative groups will handle a record total of some 4.5 million purchase, redemption, and exchange transactions in 1987, at high levels of accuracy and timeliness.
- Our client services and investor information telephone groups will handle more than 3.5 billion phone calls from shareholders. Our service levels reflected solid performance despite incredible volatility—45,000 calls in our lowest week, 117,000 in our highest.

To be sure, in each of these areas there was the inevitable "room for improvement." There always is. But there is no doubt that we would be the envy of our competitors. As measured not against the theoretical *ideal* world of perfection but against the practical *real* world of performance, we met each test—met it "like a rock."

Prepared: In Philosophy, Strategy, Operations, and Organization

What underlies our remarkable accomplishments in such a tempest-tossed environment? The key factor is that we at Vanguard were ready for it. We were prepared—prepared for it philosophically, prepared for it strategically, prepared for it operationally, and prepared for it organizationally. Let me spend a few moments on each.

First, *philosophy.* "The philosophy that the best growth is organic rather than forced enables Vanguard today to maintain a sound balance in a burgeoning industry that seems to have lost it." When I said these words in my talk to you at our Christmas party a year ago, I had no idea of what lay ahead; but we were surely wise to have maintained our discipline—"the discipline not to jump on the bandwagon of speculation and excess that is all too rampant in the world financial system and in the U.S. mutual fund industry today." In short, in December 1986, it seemed clear that the halcyon age of the mutual fund industry was coming to an end. If we agree with Lavoisier that "fortune favors the prepared mind," Vanguard was ready for the new era—"the age that is coming to birth" in the poem I read to you last year—in which we now find ourselves.

Second, *strategy.* A year ago, I described our strategy as a "Switzerland strategy," under which, like that mountain fortress nation in central Europe, we would "maintain our values, hold ourselves to higher standards, and let our competitors, old and new, engage in the utterly self-defeating wars that they have declared." Vanguard fought in none of these wars—"not the price war, to increase costs to shareholders so as to fund a massive marketing effort; not the product war, to introduce new, untested, and speculative funds; not the performance war, to reach to the very extremities of prudence and beyond for the largest equity returns and the highest bond yields." So our disciplined strategy of having a balanced array of relatively predictable and conservative mutual funds—some offering safety, some offering income, some offering growth potential, all seeking to provide value—obviously proved a major asset in 1987.

Third, *operations.* In my admittedly subjective judgment, Vanguard provided the highest level of service of any major fund group during 1987, in large measure by reason of our excellent performance during October's stock market crash. In an independent industrywide survey taken in June, only Fidelity rated higher (and by just a hair). But Fidelity "crashed" in October, reportedly turning away 150,000 phone calls on October 19 alone. By contrast, thanks to good operating management, extensive training, and responsive telephone technology—and to our having learned a priceless lesson, as we should have, from our frightening experience in the April deluge of phone calls—we were prepared for the volumes engendered during the October crash. Our cross training of the investor information staff enabled us to send squad after squad of Swiss Army "shock troops" to handle wave after wave of client service calls.

The spirit demonstrated by our organization—working together, with a common goal—was one of the most rewarding experiences of my entire business career. It is no secret that a client who cannot reach us in times of peril can become a client in panic. Not only was there no sign of panic among Vanguard shareholders but their generally calm— if concerned—reaction to the October crisis stood in stark contrast to the hyperreactions of the press, the investment community, and even some major financial institutions that should have known better.

And fourth, *organization*. We could not have sailed successfully through the storms and shoals of 1987 without a fine organization—a crew of dedicated people who cared about our voyage. For too long, I fear, we had sought your loyalty to Vanguard without adequately considering Vanguard's loyalty to you. The year began with a survey of employee opinions about this company, and you told us some things that were not pleasing to hear but that nonetheless had the ring of truth. We carefully evaluated your comments, we spelled out a program of response to your concerns, and we took appropriate action— in training and supervision, in facilities, in compensation and benefits. I believe that one of the principal reasons that we weathered October's shocks so well is that we had taken affirmative action—prompt, tangible, and enthusiastic—to work together to make Vanguard a better ship for its crew.

Serving Honest-to-God Human Beings

Now, of course, 1987 is virtually history. (Amen!) Where do we stand as 1988 begins? I believe that we are the rock of this industry. We are as strong as any competitor, and far stronger than most. While we have suffered some redemptions, most of them, more likely than not, have come from investors with an opportunistic orientation that belies what Vanguard is all about. Remaining is our truly awesome shareholder base of perhaps 1.8 million investors whom I described a year ago as "down-to-earth, honest-to-God human beings with real needs and aspirations, who believe that we offer them sound investment programs, with clearly delineated risks, at fair prices." I emphasized— indeed I underscored—that *we must never let them down*. Well, during the chaotic year now drawing to a close, we did not let them down. We provided them with high-quality service, at reasonable cost, and with investment results that, if hardly likely to be described as spectacular, were fully consistent with each Vanguard fund's specified objective and risk profile.

And let us not lose sight of the fact that, despite the October crash, nearly all of our shareholders continue to prosper. Tough as it was, the crash did little more than absorb the gains achieved in the first eight months of the year, and the investments of our equity fund sharehold-ers through November were largely intact. Similarly, the high interest rates on bonds were generally sufficient to offset the combined April and September price declines, and, on a total return basis, the invest-ments of our bond fund shareholders were also largely intact. So, those hundreds of thousands of investors who joined Vanguard before, or even during, the great twin bull markets in stocks and bonds that began in mid-1982 have by and large enjoyed strongly positive returns and substantial enhancements to their financial assets. And, of course, the returns for our money market fund shareholders just keep rolling along, in good and bad times alike.

This huge base of 1.8 million investors, whom we have served well, represents the rock foundation on which Vanguard enters the new era. As long as we continue to serve them well, they will surely add to their investments here—most importantly those 600,000 who already invest regularly through retirement plan accounts [IRA, 401(k), 403(b)]. To give you an idea of the confidence we have maintained despite the resounding market tremors that intervened, in the last month alone our shareholders made 120,000 additional purchases of Vanguard fund shares, almost exactly equal to a year ago. That stability in the face of adversity is hardly a sign that investors are disenchanted with the val-ues we offer.

We also begin 1988 with a massive and imposing asset base that has a remarkably healthy balance—a balance that will give us both ample participation in good securities markets, and ample protection in bad. Specifically, our $27 billion of assets today comprises:

- $8 billion in money market funds
- $8 billion in bond and income funds
- $11 billion in equity funds

Come what may—higher or lower stock prices, higher or lower inter-est rates, for that matter, hell or high water—we are well positioned for the year ahead.

Finally, we begin 1988 financially strong and profitable. During the year now ending, Vanguard reached new high levels of earnings. While the stresses and strains we have faced engendered a marked slowing of the pace of our growth, it is safe to say that the earnings that you share through the Vanguard Partnership Plan will increase once again to record levels, as they have each year since the plan began. And literally hundreds of you—those who have crossed the one-year, two-year, and five-year (and even, for a few, ten-year) service thresholds—will receive these higher earnings on something like twice as many shares as last year. I dare say, after this challenging year, you made this money the old-fashioned way: "You earned it."

Like a Rock

Yes, Vanguard, like a rock, is ready for whatever 1988 throws at us. As we move toward the start of a new year, with prospects that are at once exhilarating and frightening, let me conclude by striking two broad themes for your consideration. The first theme is competition. We work in a marvelously competitive industry. To the regret of many investors, however, competition has worked perversely in recent years, producing a discreditable picture of rising prices, debased products, and disillusioning performance—the *destructive* competition to which I alluded a year ago. During the coming year, I hope we can work together to help restore *productive* competition in the mutual fund field, with a focus on providing value to investors, as befits the long tradition of this industry. In *The Lessons of History,* Will and Ariel Durant remind us that *"life is competition. . . . Competition is not only the life of trade, it is the trade of life. . . . Competing groups have the qualities of competing individuals: acquisitiveness, pugnacity, partisanship, pride."* Let us all recognize these qualities in ourselves, and enjoy the competition, even as we strive to make it productive for our investors.

The second theme is laughter. In spite of my optimistic and even brazen remarks this evening, I do not know—nor does anyone know—what lies before us. (Indeed, it wouldn't be very interesting if we did!) So, as 1988 soon begins, be prepared for surprises—even unpleasant ones. And be prepared for challenges—even Herculean ones. It is said that Scaramouche "was born with the gift of laughter and the sense that the world was mad," and I expect that in 1988 we may need both of those qualities more than ever. Indeed, they are part of our heritage.

The commander of the HMS *Vanguard,* Admiral Horatio Nelson, wrote: "I could not sail these perilous seas in safety, if I did not keep a sense of humor." Two hundred years later, our seas are no less perilous; and I urge each of you to maintain good spirits, a caring attitude, and a sense of humor as we work together to maintain Vanguard as the rock of this industry. Ever the idealist, I believe that we will succeed.

When he sang these lyrics of "Like a Rock," Bob Seger was not describing Vanguard. But he might have been: "We were lean and solid everywhere . . . We held firmly to what we felt was right . . . We stood arrow straight unencumbered by the weight of all these hustlers and their schemes, . . . We stood proud—we stood tall, high above it all. Like a rock."

Thank you and good night.

TRADITION

June 13, 1988

I HAVE CHOSEN "tradition" as the theme for my comments this evening, for I want to remind each of you of the traditions—the vision, the philosophy, the core values, together composing, if you will, the corporate character of Vanguard—that are central to making this enterprise what it is today. It is in a sense paradoxical to consider these *old* traditions at a rite of celebration for a *new* tradition—for this is but the third partnership plan party at which we present to each of you as a member of our crew your share of the substantial and growing earnings we are generating for the shareholders of the Vanguard funds.

But it is especially timely to discuss tradition in the year 1988. For this year will mark the sixtieth anniversary of the first Vanguard fund—Wellington Fund, founded on December 28, 1928. Enduring through six decades of war and peace, prosperity and depression, and political change, Wellington's traditional conservative investment principles, which continue to dominate what The Vanguard Group is all about today, are every bit as valid now as when the fund was founded all those years ago.

The year 1988 also marks a remarkable milestone for a remarkable gentleman, without whom we would *all* be somewhere else—one can only imagine where we might be—this evening. In just six weeks, on July 23, Walter L. Morgan, founder of Wellington Fund, will reach his ninetieth birthday. It is Walter Morgan, a pioneer and surely the dean of the mutual fund industry, who set the sound investment principles, the spirit of fair dealing, the organizational continuity, and the integrity without which we never could have come so far.

It is hard to imagine that in the early days of the Industrial & Power Securities Co. (as Wellington Fund was known until 1933), he was able to do so much completely on his own—from filing the original Delaware charter, to bringing in the fund's initial capital from a handful of investors, to keeping the books of the company in his own hand. To this day, I look with awe at that initial journal and recognize the familiar hand that wrote "capital stock subscriptions receivable" for 100 shares, and 1,000 shares, and 60 shares, until the initial $100,000 was raised and the fund began operations.

And so the fund was started—just before the Great Crash of October 1929. (Its parallels with the Great Crash of October 1987 were almost uncanny.) Its conservative balanced program, with a large bond and cash reserve position, helped to moderate the sharp decline that common stocks—Wellington's included—were to experience through 1933. The result was an enviable record of relative performance that made raising additional capital easier—although surely not easy—in the years ahead. This original journal—but 146 handwritten pages—carried Wellington Fund through 1938, when assets reached the then-enviable total of $4 million. (The first real milestone was reached when assets topped $1 million late in 1935. I do not know whether or not that was when the tradition of having milestone celebrations began, but if it was, the number of participants at the party would have been very small!)

I could not begin to do justice to all of Walter Morgan's fine qualities—intelligence, grace, integrity, ambition, generosity, competitive spirit, breadth of vision, range of interests—the list is too long. But I would like to tell you about one quality that made an enormous difference in the life of one man: his interest in young people, his confidence in their abilities, his willingness to cede to them substantial responsibility if he thought they could handle it ("pile it on them" might be more accurate). When he, a loyal Princetonian, took on a shy, crewcut, boyish-looking, insecure, energetic, serious, and terribly ambitious young man who had himself worked his way through Princeton and who had, in the year 1951, just graduated, he gave me my first break. I guess it is fair to say that his decision to hire me made a difference, for the better I hope, in the future development of the Wellington organization, and the creation and founding of Vanguard.

Remember Who Gave You Your First Break?

A wonderful public service ad, sponsored by United Technologies, appeared several times in the *Wall Street Journal* during the late 1970s and early 1980s. It was entitled "Do You Remember Who Gave You Your First Break?" Here is part of what it said:

> **Someone saw something in you once. That's partly why you are what you are today. It could have been a thoughtful parent, a perceptive teacher, a demanding drill sergeant, an appreciative employer. . . . Whoever it was who had the kindness and foresight—two beautiful qualities—to bet on your future. In the next 24 hours, take ten minutes to write a grateful note to the person who helped you. . . . Matter of fact, take another ten minutes to give somebody else a break. . . .**

Well, I did take those recommended ten minutes to write that grateful note to Walter Morgan. And I hope that I am not exaggerating when I say that his initial kindness to me and his future trust in me helped to begin—in a time almost infinitely surpassing a second ten minutes—what I fervently hope has now become a Vanguard tradition: the idea that people should be given a break, should be encouraged, and should be respected. That is the central basis for our philosophy that "even one person can make a difference," embodied in the Vanguard Awards for Excellence that will be presented later this evening.

Out of this long and mutually rewarding and supportive relationship between my mentor and me has come a tradition of executive continuity, first at Wellington, then carried over to Vanguard when we began to administer the affairs of the funds in 1975. Remarkable as it may seem, we share the privilege and honor of having been the only two persons to have served as chairman of the board of Wellington Fund over what will soon be six full decades. And I expect that, when it comes to its conclusion, the twentieth century will have witnessed just three Wellington board chairmen in all. Out of this extended record of continuity—it may well be unique in the annals of American business—has come our focus on core values rather than peripheral adventuring, our focus on a long-term vision rather than short-term opportunism.

I should note that our fund directors have played a constructive and supportive role in our tradition of continuity. Over a period of sixty years, just forty-five directors have served on a board averaging ten members. From the first—Walter Morgan—to the newest—John Brennan—they have been a valuable asset. Speaking particularly of our "independent directors"—those who are not officers of Vanguard—they have been a dedicated crew, ready, willing and able to make the tough decisions that are often required in a rapidly changing and competitive world.

Creative Insight—With Discipline

How radically the world of Wellington Fund and The Vanguard Group has changed would be difficult to overstate. Let me give you a few examples: During the first thirty years of our sixty-year history, our sole mutual fund was Wellington Fund. The number, as it were, doubled when Windsor Fund began in 1958. During the next fifteen years, through 1973, we added the modest total of seven more funds to our "product line." But during the past fifteen years, we have added forty-one new funds—sixteen in the past three years alone. To say that this pace of development has placed great strains on our organization, and in particular on the training and knowledgeability we expect of our crew, would be something of an understatement. But investors are becoming more specialized in their focus, more particularized in their demands and expectations. We have been "in the vanguard" of the industry in terms of creative foresight in forming new funds that would find prompt public acceptance, even as we have been disciplined in providing only such funds as would meet sensible, durable, long-term investment standards.

To give a dramatic picture of how much this radical change has impacted Vanguard, all we need do is look at our line of mutual funds fifteen years ago, just before Vanguard was founded. As 1973 began, we had *no* bond funds and *no* money market funds. Indeed, the money market fund had not even been conceived. Yet today, the assets of our sixteen bond funds total $8 billion, and our seven money funds total $10 billion. Together they compose fully 60 percent of our asset base—a graphic reminder of how much Vanguard's creativity has contributed to our success (and, heaven knows, how much similar creativity has contributed to the success of our competitors).

Typical of the mutual fund industry, our growth has traditionally been more spasmodic than sustained. We experienced little growth—

even on a very small asset base—in the years 1936 through 1943, again in the years 1964 through 1966, and once again in the years 1971 through 1978, which included a 45 percent asset drop in 1973 and 1974. Clearly, our asset growth has again slowed over the past year. At $31 billion today, Vanguard fund assets are just a hair above the $30 billion total reached when we held our second partnership party one year ago, albeit only a hair below their record high of $31.5 billion reached last August.

Growth Levels Off

Most of you here this evening have experienced the impact of this leveling off in our growth. In the aftermath of the Great Crash in the stock market and the two "minicrashes" in the bond market that preceded it, the mutual fund industry has suffered a major decline in investor purchases of shares, and an even larger drop in net cash inflow. Specifically, during the first four months of 1988, regular fund purchase volume has fallen 68 percent below the same period in 1987, from $92 billion to $29 billion. Net cash flow has plummeted from an *inflow* of $56 billion to an *outflow* of $1 billion. These dramatic changes—and Vanguard's declines have been roughly comparable—bear silent witness to the fact that the mutual fund business, which has traditionally been extremely market sensitive, remains so today. Beyond doubt, it will remain so in the future.

Of course, the money market fund has provided "an anchor to windward" that has been of inestimable value both to Vanguard and the industry during this massive slowdown in regular fund cash flows. (Our money market and short-term fund assets have risen from $5 billion to $10 billion since March 31, 1987.) Nonetheless, transaction activity for Vanguard—happily, with respect to redemptions and exchanges, less happily with respect to new accounts and investor telephone inquiries— has slowed perceptibly. So, while we continue to grow in assets, and continue to generate positive net cash flow (estimated at a solid $2.4 billion for the first half of the year), the pace of our new hiring has dwindled to a trickle. I can tell you, however, that, in the tradition of caring that we have developed at Vanguard, we expect no layoffs, and we will do everything in our power to avoid them.

Now let me take a few moments to discuss some of the long-standing traditions that have become part of the fabric of this enterprise. I'll mention just three of those that I regard as most important: the tradition of balanced investing; the tradition of focusing on the long-term investor; and the tradition of fair dealing with our clients.

Three Traditions: Balance, Long-Term Focus, and Fair Dealing

BALANCED INVESTING   For our first thirty years, balanced investing in bonds and equities alike was our sole stock in trade. It was a significant distinction; indeed, I am told that in the old days, representatives of the balanced fund sector of this industry would often snub those of the stock fund sector at industry meetings. (Or was it the other way around?) While this rivalry has long since vanished, however, we have still hewed to the tradition of balance. As recently as in our 1987 annual reports, we reminded the shareholders of all of our funds that one of the basic rules of investing is "Be balanced. . . . A portfolio of stocks, bonds, and cash reserves is a sensible way to hedge against the future's uncertainties." The only difference, really, is that today's balance by Vanguard investors, rather than being ready-made in a single balanced fund, is mostly custom-made, with each client's deciding on a variety of stock and bond funds that meet his or her own precise risk-reward profile.

LONG-TERM INVESTING   Both our fund line and our marketing strategy have traditionally focused on investors whom we expect to remain with us over an extended period of years. We have tried to avoid short-term fads and fashions, emphasizing conservative funds with predictable investment characteristics rather than high-turnover funds with narrow or speculative objectives that are unlikely to endure. (Industry-sector funds—steel, autos, and so on—for example, were in vogue in the 1940s, then disappeared from view, only to be reincarnated in the frothy markets of the mid-1980s, and now are waning in the postcrash era.) The net result has been that, with remarkable consistency throughout our history, our redemption ratios (and now our redemption/exchange ratios) have been about one-half of those of our competitors.

As you know, we have had to maintain some discipline in this process: Our decision earlier this year to place stringent limitations on exchanges (the most stringent, I believe, in the entire industry) was taken with full awareness that we risked the loss of significant assets from market-timers. But while we have lost some assets, the reaction from shareholders has by and large been positive, as exemplified by those words from a shareholder who wrote me a few weeks ago: "I congratulate and thank you for this policy. . . . I feel it fairer if I do not have to pay for the constant switchers and trampers. . . . It is a policy with integrity."

FAIR DEALING WITH CLIENTS   We have written so much about Vanguard's remarkable expense ratio advantage that it hardly bears repetition here today. But you should know that this tradition extends way back in time. In the early 1950s, Wellington Fund was one of the first mutual funds to provide a sliding scale of fees that declined as assets rose, thus sharing the manager's economies of scale with the clients. And in a memorandum to Walter Morgan in 1959, I proudly noted that "Wellington Fund's rank in the mutual fund industry in keeping expenses low has improved from twelfth to seventh among 151 funds." I should add that the Vanguard earnings in which we all share today are importantly based on the truly incredible strides we have made in reducing our costs, even as our competitors are increasing theirs.

Last year, we operated at an expense ratio of 0.40 percent; the average major competitor charged more than *twice* as much (0.82 percent); the average of all mutual funds was more than *three times* as much (1.25 percent). We are now, by a large margin, the low-cost provider of services in the mutual fund industry; clearly our tradition of fair dealing continues. Thanks to the U.S. Securities and Exchange Commission, moreover, a complete and honest statement of fund expenses is, as of May 1, required in the prospectus of every mutual fund. This mandatory full disclosure of costs will serve to bring Vanguard's remarkable advantages into clear public focus.

When to Celebrate, What to Cast Aside

Now I recognize that tradition is not an unmixed blessing. It can substitute inertia for action; it can encrust and stultify; however vital in the past, it can cast a pall over the future. T.S. Eliot put it well when he said, "Tradition is not enough; it must be perpetually criticized and brought up to date." And we have indeed been able to cast aside some of our traditions when the time came to do so. One example is the great strength of our earlier traditional focus on one product that carried us from our modest beginnings in 1928 to industry leadership in the 1940s and early 1950s. However, almost without warning, that asset turned into a liability, and we had to turn our single-fund focus to the offering of a wide spectrum of funds, beginning with Windsor Fund in 1958. If we dragged our feet in making this transition, we quickly made up for lost ground and were soon in the vanguard of leadership as the multifund complex became the basic structure of our industry.

An even more dramatic example of our abandonment of tradition was our sudden shift from a broker-dealer, sales-charge, seller-driven marketing strategy to a no-salesman, no-load, investor-driven strategy in 1977. It would be hard for me to convey to you the trauma of that change. The stock brokerage firms had put on our books essentially every dollar of our then $2 billion asset base. The Vanguard funds had been, in a real sense, the very paradigm of the dealer-distributed mutual funds. Our large national team of wholesale representatives had been working effectively with the brokers for decades, and rare was the industry gathering at which our executives were not prominent participants and major speakers. Feelings about this 180-degree turn in distribution strategy—pro and con—ran high. One of our directors who opposed this radical departure from the past said simply, "It will be the holocaust." Well, it was not. The better judgment was made by our counsel, Raymond Klapinsky, when his first words on learning of the proposal were: "It would be the smartest thing we could ever do." It was. And thus a new tradition was born.

Of course, our greatest break with tradition occurred when we rejected the long-standing industry practice of having the mutual fund complex controlled by an external "management company." The creation of Vanguard in 1974 meant that, uniquely in industry annals, mutual fund shareholders would thereafter be represented by their own directors, officers, and staff, rather than the directors and officers and staff of a company that was in business to make a handsome profit from conducting the fund's affairs. With the Vanguard Experiment, the funds would be operated with the sole focus on shareholder value.

From this decision flowed nearly all of what we at Vanguard, building largely on the three sound traditions I have earlier described, have created. We have enjoyed the independence, operated with the integrity, thrived on the idealism that together are, I hope, bringing us ever closer to what was recently described by management guru Tom Peters (*The Search for Excellence*): "The fleet-footed organization of the future [is] . . . a glowing, healthy, breathing corporate center . . . where the glow comes from management's availability, informality, energy, hustle, and the clarity and excitement of the competitive vision, philosophy or core values." (In a word, *tradition*.) Add to this concept several others—"not written rule, but rule by example, rule by role model, rule by spirited behavior, rule by fun and by the vigorous pursuit of a worthwhile competitive idea"—and you can recognize Vanguard's exciting aspirations.

Loyalty Is a Two-Way Street

One of our competitive visions, of course, is to be not only the low-cost provider but also the high-quality provider of financial services. The achievement of our quality goals will, I think, depend far less on formal measurement standards and controls than on how each of you employed in this enterprise conduct your daily work. We must have the front-line members of our crew, in Mr. Peters' words, "controlled not by a supervisor, middle management, or a procedure manual, but by the clarity and excitement of the vision . . . an extraordinary level of training, the obvious respect they are given, and the self-discipline that must accompany exceptional grants of autonomy."

And so the movement from adversarial relations to partnership relations is becoming, in his view, one of the biggest shifts being made by American companies. The shift is away from the tradition of control from the impersonal, out-of-touch, walled-in corporate hub, in which managers are "cops," and employees are expected to be orderly to a fault. Were Tom Peters here this evening, witnessing this very tangible experience in "partnership relations" and the sharing of partnership profits, I know that he would applaud what he was seeing, even as he was astonished (since he appears to have a large ego) that we have been moving in this direction for years, without the benefit of his not inconsiderable wisdom and counsel. *It is really incredible that it has taken most American companies so long to realize that it is simply not right to ask those who do the daily work to be loyal to the corporation without making the same commitment, with the same fervor, that the corporation will be loyal to them in return.* And that concept of two-way loyalty—of mutual caring, if you will—must itself become a Vanguard tradition.

Let me conclude with a brief summation: From the inception of Wellington Fund in 1928, through founder Walter Morgan's ninetieth birthday in 1988, tradition—the force exerted by the past upon the present—has played a major role in the success of this enterprise. So it will through the rest of the twentieth century and beyond. Nonetheless, true to Ecclesiastes' teachings, we have recognized that "there is a time to keep and a time to cast away . . . a time to plant and a time to pluck up that which is planted . . . a time to cast away stones and a time to gather stones together." With the vital traditions of our heritage, we are building a good enterprise; when we have departed from past traditions, we have usually done so with wisdom and insight; and we are establishing new traditions that should ever renew and ever fulfill Vanguard's spirit and promise.

REJOICE!

THE FIRST ANNIVERSARY OF THE GREAT CRASH

October 19, 1988

Rejoice in your sufferings in the knowledge that suffering produces endurance, endurance produces character, character produces hope, and hope does not disappoint us.

—The Letter of Paul to the Romans (5:3)

EXACTLY ONE YEAR AGO, virtually every person in every financial institution in America experienced a day of suffering. There was little reason to rejoice on October 19, 1987, forever to be known as "Black Monday," when stock markets all over the world were driven to the edge of chaos in the Great Crash. It was a decline utterly unprecedented in the annals of the securities markets—in speed (one day), in magnitude (off 22.6 percent), and in volume (600 million shares). And yet, just as in Saint Paul's words, that suffering—at least here at Vanguard—did lead to endurance, did strengthen our character, did produce hope. Now, a year later, we can affirm, and affirm triumphantly, that hope did not disappoint us.

Fortunately, Vanguard was singularly well prepared for that day of unpleasantness. We were *mentally* prepared, having discussed for a year or more the coming end of "the era of dazzling growth" during which the securities markets had achieved the highest returns in their recorded history. Every crew member knew we were moving into a new, more difficult era. We could not be sure precisely when the new era would begin. However, viewing trends from a biblical perspective brought us remarkably close to pinpointing *the exact date* of the market's crisis.

The Prophecy of Joseph

Vanguard had survived seven years of privation, enduring consistent cash outflows, month after month, in the years 1973 through 1980. And we then were to enjoy seven years of plenty in the years 1980 through 1987, prospering as the markets soared, and as our business strategy succeeded beyond our wildest dreams. A bit arbitrarily, as I admitted in June 1987, we marked that turn from famine to feast as occurring on September 17, 1980, the date we reached our $3 billion asset milestone. The seven subsequent years, then, would have ended on September 17, 1987, just one month before the Great Crash. The Old Testament's Joseph, in his amazing coat of many colors, seems to have touched on an enduring principle when he made his seven-year prophesy to the Pharaoh (Gen 41:25).

We were also *mentally* prepared, having previously developed a massive program of extensive staff training and cross-training, enhanced telecommunications, and more efficient ways of processing high transaction volumes. As a result of the April bond market collapse, six months before October's stock market debacle, we recognized how quickly we could experience truly massive changes in telephone and transaction volumes and how ill prepared we were to deal with them. In short, we learned from our April suffering, and we took the appropriate actions to meet new threats down the road. So we were ready for the challenges we were to face. Providentially, we had also taken major forward steps in our employee relations program to gain the loyalty and confidence of our crew—and it hardly hurt our morale that a broad range of compensation increases for our staff had been implemented just six weeks before the crash.

Now recall with me what happened on Monday, October 19, 1987. The stock market opened weak, down 50 points on the Dow-Jones Industrial Average, following a 110-point loss the previous Friday. It got progressively weaker during the day, and it was down 300 points by 3:00 P.M. Finally, it closed in chaos, off 508 points at the bell. Soaring phone volume throughout the ensuing week brought us 114,000 phone calls—many urgent (and, in retrospect, unwise) requests to exchange holdings in our equity funds into our money market funds, and many more pleas for guidance—a near-immediate 100 percent increase over normal volume levels. The assets of the Vanguard funds dropped by $2.1 billion—*in one day*—to $26.9 billion. It was a historic day, one about which, as I mentioned to you last December, you will one day tell your children and grandchildren, "I was there." We suffered, yes; but we also endured.

Vanguard's Strength: Our Spirit, Not Our Size

And I believe that our endurance on that day of near catastrophe—despite the pervasive doubt, disappointment, and disenchantment all around us—had a major impact on Vanguard's character. We proved to our clients—and, far more importantly, to ourselves—that Vanguard could take the hardest imaginable punishment that the financial markets could hurl at us, and remain steadfast, proud, resilient, even cheerful. There is no question in my mind that, on that dark day a year ago, we were the best-performing company in this beleaguered industry. Working together, the Vanguard crew proved that, in the crucible of history, we had the strength to endure an extraordinary—perhaps once in a generation—event without a hint of panic or desolation. Indeed, I believe that our endurance during those difficult days confirms that which we all know: *The strength of Vanguard is not its size but its spirit.*

In the twelve-month aftermath of Black Monday, which we commemorate—perhaps with mixed emotions—this evening, some remarkable things have happened. The prophets of doom were, as is so often the case, plain wrong. Black Monday was not the harbinger of world financial collapse nor the precursor of a great economic depression. Rather, it was the classic bursting of the balloon of grossly inflated stock prices. Only in the context of what came before Black Monday, and what was to come afterward, can its significance be fairly assessed. So let us not forget (as so many have) that from the beginning of 1987 through the August 25 high, the stock market had risen by +42 percent, giving us in eight months a return more characteristic of four years. Next, the −33 percent drop through October 19, in which $1 trillion of equity market value was erased. And then, right up to today, the unexpected rebound of +28 percent. On balance, the investor who stayed the course from 1987 through 1988 has enjoyed a return of +21 percent, just about what stocks are supposed to provide over a two-year period, based on historical norms.

I am pleased to report that the rebound in Vanguard's total assets since the crash has been the strongest of any major fund group in the mutual fund industry. Our assets are now fully $6 billion above the distress levels of a year ago, and they total $33.2 billion—the highest level in Vanguard's history. The 22 percent gain in our asset base is nearly *three times* the 7 percent gain reflected in mutual fund industry assets. So we have clearly demonstrated more than mere endurance; we have demonstrated solid growth, and we have demonstrated remarkable progress vis-à-vis our competitors, in this terribly competitive world.

Character Above All

I do not believe it is hyperbole to say that success in the competitive arena depends, in the final analysis, on character. As an organization, Vanguard has just such character, and I pray that each one of you will join me in assuring that we shall never lose it. If our suffering on Black Monday helped to produce our endurance through its aftermath, and that endurance helped to strengthen both our individual and our corporate character, and that character in turn produced our hope—not the pessimism, the fear, the self-doubt of so many others—for the year that was to follow, then hope most assuredly did not disappoint us. For we have enjoyed a marvelous year, a year bright with accomplishment, a year shining with success, a year that will ever remind us that, together, we can move mountains.

Of course, we remain with Joseph's ominous seven-year cycle. Did *another* seven-year period of privation begin on October 19, 1987? Well, as our figures so clearly affirm, it certainly was not manifested in the first of those seven years. But, if the positive signals sent in that first year turn out to be ephemeral and prove to be wrong—and indeed they could, make no mistake about it—Vanguard is once again prepared. With $13 billion of our assets invested in stocks, $9 billion in bonds, and $11 billion in money market instruments, the exposure of our $33 billion asset base to another sharp stock market decline, and even to another depression, is well within tolerable limits. I reiterate, however, that size—even when measured in the tens of billions—is not the most important part of our strength. No matter what may come, no matter what tomorrow may hold, it will be our spirit that will prevail—our willingness to work effectively, positively, productively, cheerfully, and together. In short, our character will shape our future, and our hope will never disappoint us.

So, let us all rejoice!

THREE ANNIVERSARIES . . .
AND ONE TO COME!

December 17, 1988

*I*N A FEW SHORT WEEKS, The
Vanguard Group of Investment Companies will complete what will be
beyond any doubt, the finest year in our history. We—all of us
together—are gathered here this evening to bask in the delight of
accomplishments of a truly remarkable year, one that is a signal credit
to every member of our crew. I thank you, enthusiastically and sin-
cerely, for your own contributions to our success, and to our team
effort.

It is fitting that 1988 be a *record year* for us. For it is a year in which
we celebrate anniversary milestones for not one, but three, of our Vanguard funds:

- Wellington Fund will, on December 28, celebrate the sixtieth
  anniversary of its founding in 1928 by industry pioneer Walter L.
  Morgan. While there are some 2,653 U.S. mutual funds in existence today, only two others, as far as I know, have ever before
  reached that milestone.
- Windsor Fund, on October 23, celebrated the thirtieth anniversary of its founding. As the second fund in what was to become
  known as "The Vanguard Group," Windsor increased our product
  line by 100 percent. In a real sense, it was our first step toward
  the fifty-five portfolio complex we have today. This anniversary,
  combined with Wellington's, means that we have now experienced the same number of years—thirty—as a "multifund" complex and as a "single-fund" firm.

- W.L. Morgan Growth Fund, named of course for Wellington Fund's founder, will celebrate, on December 27, the twentieth anniversary of its founding in 1968. Our use of the "Morgan" name was challenged by two major financial firms—Morgan, Stanley & Co. and The Morgan Guaranty Trust Company—but, as 1968 drew to a close, we prevailed. Interestingly, in recent years both firms have entered the mutual fund field.

So, even in this brief thumbnail history of our anniversary funds, I hope that I have given you some sense of our background and tradition, beginning with our balanced fund, adding a growth and income stock fund, then adding a capital appreciation fund. This triumvirate truly represents the foundation of what we call "Vanguard" today.

The Finest Year in Our History?

Let me spend just a moment to make my case that 1988 is the finest year in our history. It rests on four pretty solid pillars: our asset base, our competitive growth, our investment returns, and our operating performance.

First, Vanguard assets are today at an all-time high of $34.1 billion. What is more, these assets are almost ideally balanced among the three principal classes of financial assets—very close to one-third equity funds, one-third bond funds, and one-third money market funds. Come what may, we are ready for it.

Second, when the full story of 1988 is told, we will rank number 1 among our major competitors in terms of asset growth. Vanguard's assets have grown by 26 percent during the year now ending—nearly four times the +7 percent increase we expect for the industry. For a firm like Vanguard, hardly hell-bent on mindless growth no matter what the cost, this accomplishment approaches the incredible.

Third, the investment returns earned by our funds for their shareholders were, without doubt, the best in our history. If a few other years have witnessed higher *absolute* returns, none have rivaled our *relative* returns for 1988. Fully thirty of the fifty portfolios for which we use "peer groups" for comparative purposes have outpaced their returns by (as they say) "statistically significant" margins. Only two of our fifty were rated subpar, with the remaining eighteen meeting competitive norms. (What, you may ask, does "statistically significant" mean? Well, for one example—admittedly the best one I have tonight—when Windsor Fund provides a return of 30 percent for its shareholders in 1988 and its peer group returns +12 percent, we are talking about "statistical significance" at the world-class level.) So, heartiest congratulations to our advisers—our external managers and the people in our internal fixed-income and core management groups—for a series of sensational achievements.

Fourth, we enjoyed, in my considered judgment, our "best-ever" operating performance. The retail services and institutional services groups—our major interface with our clients—did an outstanding job. But equally impressive were some other key groups that too many of us take for granted—financial accounting, fund financial services, private label, systems and data processing, retail and institutional marketing, legal, and business planning. Coming out of the ashes of the Great Crash, of course, the mutual fund business—traditionally market sensitive—experienced much lower volumes that were at once both a bane and a blessing. At Vanguard, for example, investor purchases of our regular funds will be down by 45 percent to 2.4 million. This slowdown, if not unexpected, gave us the opportunity to consolidate our organization. What is more, it was a nice plus to see exchanges drop by 50 percent to 330,000, and phone calls subside by 30 percent to 2.6 million. (In contrast, Fidelity receives some 50 million calls annually; my envy for that high-volume strategy remains subdued.)

Since the pluses in our year well outweighed the minuses, 1988 will almost certainly be the best year in our history in terms of Vanguard's earnings. So we expect that the earnings per unit for our Vanguard Partnership Plan—when we all share in its distribution next June— will also reach a record high. I am compelled to add a note of conservatism, however; given our increased financial commitments—to compensation and benefits, to staffing and training, to data processing, and to systems development that will be required to keep us competitive during the decade of the 1990s—our earnings growth rate will be significantly below the very high rates achieved in recent years. But "lower growth" is a far cry from "no growth," and the Vanguard Partnership Plan continues in its goal of having this entire enterprise focus on profitability, enhance it, and share in the rewards.

The Crew's Views *Improve*

As the crew of a very redoubtable HMS *Vanguard,* we go into 1989 with great strength. For as 1988 comes to a close, we have a solid reaffirmation that this great warship is sailing the true and proper course. Your ship's officers have just received the results of our *Crew's Views* opinion survey—and it offers refreshing evidence of progress in the major problem areas you identified in the first of such surveys back in 1986.

In order of your concern level, the four most significant areas for improvement you identified were pay, job training, management, and communications. In each of these four areas, your evaluation of Vanguard has risen significantly, and in some cases even massively, since the previous survey. What is more, your overall evaluation of Vanguard is now, almost uniformly and across the board, at a more favorable level than the evaluations of other financial services organizations by their own employees.

We know, of course that we can—and must—continue to achieve progress in these areas. Having said that, I would note that steady progress is the order of the day, and I would not expect to see a repeat of the quantum jumps we implemented in 1987. Your views on your compensation as a totality—including pay, and benefits, and the Vanguard Partnership Plan—are far more positive today, as is your evaluation of our top management and our training and development programs. I know that we have much room for improvement. But I ask you to recognize that we cannot solve all of the world's problems at Vanguard, that there is, sadly, a small minority of people who will never be satisfied, and, to state the obvious, that Vanguard will never be paradise. Nothing on this earth ever is. But to make Vanguard a better place for you to work—with enjoyment, with advancement, with confidence, with enthusiasm—better every day, in every way, remains our enduring goal.

I must add that I was delighted with the unvarnished enthusiasm you displayed in two special areas of the survey:

- First, 87 percent of you believe that *Crew's Views* is a good way to tell top management what you think.
- Second, 92 percent of you rate *Crew's News* as an effective source of information.

These are important statements, for we *must* have your candid opinions, and you in turn must be fully informed about Vanguard if we are to continue our extraordinary success in serving investors. In this context, I was particularly impressed with your response to two questions we asked under the caption, "Company Image." Fully 95 percent of you believe you understand "the values and objectives of this organization."

And 91 percent of you believe that Vanguard is "highly regarded by the general public." In both cases, in a response certainly as gratifying as it was astonishing, 0 percent disagreed. (The remainder were not sure.)

Our Coming Fifteenth Anniversary

At the outset, I mentioned the three milestone anniversaries—of Wellington Fund, of Windsor Fund, and of W.L. Morgan Growth Fund—we celebrate in 1988. But in the title of my talk, I also promised to address not only "anniversaries past and present" but "anniversaries yet to come." For in the autumn of 1989, The Vanguard Group will celebrate the fifteenth anniversary of its creation—on September 24, 1974—a brand-new name in the mutual fund firmament. As you know, the Vanguard Experiment represented an attempt to determine whether or not a mutual fund group could survive, serve, and prosper by operating independently, solely in the interests of its shareholders. That our assets have grown twenty-five-fold during this fifteen-year period—from $1.3 billion to $34.1 billion—suggests that the results of that experiment are no longer in doubt.

Far more important than mere asset growth, however, is the growing reputation of our name, the growing force of our values. Simply put, it would be *impossible* to buy—at any price—the kind of public recognition that we enjoy today, most recently exemplified by the Vanguard profile in *USA Today*. Enjoy with me the headlines: "Funds offer strong, safe, asset growth. . . . Vanguard draws investors. . . . While the industry has floundered, . . . Vanguard sales have been healthy. . . . For investors, Vanguard method pays." That article and numerous other articles with a similar focus, if more terse and less expansive, reflect what we have been able to accomplish—not just one or two of us, but *all* of us, working together.

So let us savor the spirit of Vanguard, and the spirit of the season, for just a moment. And then, as is our custom, when the business day begins next Monday, let us return to the challenge of the day-to-day life in an imperfect organization, the challenge of serving investors faithfully, the challenge of volatile and uncertain securities markets, the challenge of competing—and winning—in a marketplace that is demanding of our best, and unforgiving of anything less.

Thank you, and God bless you all.

AT THE PINNACLE

June 7, 1989

I AM PLEASED to welcome each one of you—members all of the Vanguard crew—to our fourth annual partnership plan party. It is here and now that we express our appreciation for your contribution to our success, and honor our obligation to share with you the fruits of that success, distributing partnership checks that reflect the bountiful financial benefits that we have earned for the 2 million clients who have entrusted their assets to our care. The earnings we achieved for our clients again reached record-high levels in 1988, and so did the earnings we share with you at this symbolic meeting.

All of you share in the solid increase in our calculated earnings per unit. And many of you will receive those earnings on a larger number of units than a year ago based on lengthened service at Vanguard, or perhaps a higher compensation grade—a manifestation of the increasing responsibility you have assumed. So, it is a day both exciting and enriching.

$40 Billion

It is also, in a remarkable number of ways, a day to celebrate milestones. Just four weeks ago, on May 12, 1989, Vanguard assets crossed the $40 billion mark. That asset increase of $6 billion, in a year not yet half over, enabled us to surpass the fund asset totals of yet three more of the largest mutual fund companies, moving us from fifth- to second-largest among all of the independent mutual fund organizations. What is more, if our $40 billion of assets hardly threatens the $80 billion total of our largest competitor (Fidelity), it is some $2 billion ahead of the third-ranking firm (Dreyfus), $24 billion ahead of the fourth (T. Rowe Price), and $30 billion ahead of the fifth (Scudder) of the Big Five direct marketing mutual fund organizations. (Just for the record, the *next* five competitors in order of asset size have *combined* assets of $20 billion, or one-half of our total.)

We began the decade of the 1980s with just $2.4 billion of assets. Our climb to $40 billion reflects an incredible growth rate of 35 percent per year. During this decade, while total assets of the mutual fund industry rose by ninefold, Vanguard assets rose by seventeenfold, nearly twice as much, and we have become a dominant factor in the financial services field.

Putting Vanguard "On the Map"

In short, in the past decade we have, together, put Vanguard "on the map." Not bad for an organization in which not a single one of our mutual funds even carried the "Vanguard" name when the decade began. (Until April 1980, our only use of the name was in our operating company, The Vanguard Group, Inc.) Indeed, if "Vanguard" has not yet become a household name for all investors, it is surely precisely that for independent, intelligent, self-motivated individual investors, and it is the benchmark against which other fund organizations are measured by corporate investors.

But far more important—at least to a dyed-in-the-wool idealist like me—is that "Vanguard" is not just a name that is well known but it is one that is well respected and favorably regarded by our clients, by the press, and by the public. (The fact that our name is a curse word in the halls of our competitors is an added plus.) We have done something far more important than merely building a name; we have built a reputation—a reputation, in the ideal, for investment performance, for investor service, for investment value, and for business integrity. And this reputation will be far more important in determining our success during the nineties than all of the dry statistics—however imposing— that have defined our success during the eighties.

The End of a Fabulous Decade

A second milestone, of course, marks the end of the decade of the 1980s, now rushing in upon us. It has been a wonderful decade for financial assets. The return on equities will average some 17 percent a year, second best among our six decades of history. The return on bonds will average some 12 percent a year, which makes this the best decade in history—indeed, it is more than double the returns of the next best decades (the 1930s and the 1970s). In short, despite the devastating 33 percent drop in the stock market in August through October 1987, and the two bond market bludgeonings of that same year, it has been a fabulous decade for investors who stayed the course.

And organizations like ours also benefited enormously from two other events: one, the emergence of the money market fund as a major factor in America's savings, and two, the positive tax environment that gave us, among other benefits, the individual retirement account and the 401(k) corporate thrift plan. With our combined money market and thrift and retirement plan assets now at $22 billion, you can see that developments that we neither invented nor controlled helped us generate more than one-half of our awesome asset base. Never underestimate the role of good fortune in our success!

Competitive Strategy—The Secret

To be sure, our competitors also had the benefit of this salubrious environment for investing in mutual funds. So it is worth spending a moment on the strategy that gave the extra momentum to our growth. *Strategy*, as defined by the *Oxford English Dictionary*, Second Edition, is "a plan for successful action . . . in circumstances of competition." And, as I hope you are well aware, our strategy has differed from those followed by our major competitors in at least four material respects:

1. To provide the highest quality of investor services, *at the lowest possible cost*
2. To provide excellent investment performance, *across the board*, in stock funds, bond funds, and money market funds alike
3. To innovate, *without opportunism*, with funds whose purposes are sound and whose returns will track benchmark standards
4. To distribute our funds on a pure no-load basis, *quietly, candidly, and without stridency or hyperbole*, giving the investor the *essential information*—on risk, on return, and on cost—required to make an intelligent decision

I continue to be amazed—even flabbergasted—that not one of our competitors seems to incorporate even a single one of these elements in its entirety. They seek quality service, but they seem to ignore cost; they seek good performance in their equity and bond funds, but they are apparently unconcerned with their money market funds, where high price is the functional equivalent of low performance. Sometimes it seems to me that the stark simplicity of our strategy is what confuses our adversaries, who have yet to realize this basic fact: *Vanguard's secret is that there is no secret.*

The Role of Market Share

Strategy, then, comes down to the actions and reactions of business organizations in an environment of vigorous—indeed, almost unfettered—competition. Its success can be measured straightforwardly, by the standard we call *market share,* the relative participation of competitors in a free marketplace. By this standard, we have done unbelievably well during the 1980s, when Vanguard's market share of the assets of all direct marketing mutual funds has increased by 86 percent—from 9.4 percent in 1980 to 17.5 percent today. Put another way, whereas one of every eleven of such fund shareholders owned Vanguard funds a decade ago, today we attract one in every six.

I am aware that these market share percentages may seem small, but in fact they have engendered a truly enormous addition to our asset base. If our market share had remained at the initial 9.4 percent level, today we would be managing $20 billion of assets. At a 17.5 percent share, however, our assets are $40 billion. Thus, fully *one-half* of our asset base—and no mean portion of the increase in our partnership earnings—has been earned through the success of our strategy vis-à-vis the strategies of our competitors.

You should know that the abiding interest in share of market that I have had through my entire business career—all thirty-eight years of it right here—is based on its logic as a *measurement of strategic success.* I would emphasize that it is far less important to me as an *objective.* After all, it would be easy to build share by offering funds that pander to the fads and fashions of the moment, by magnifying each idiotic whim of the securities markets (that is, puffing stock funds only in times of market exuberance), or by spending astronomical amounts of fund shareholders' money in advertising that is too often grossly misleading and lacking in the most primitive elements of candor. Our two largest competitors are using precisely such a "Joe Isuzu" strategy today to hawk their "new" money market funds. But I hope it will not surprise you to learn that Vanguard has no intention of using such tactics—even if the consequence is a short-term loss in our market share. In the long term, we will continue to build share by staying the sensible four-point strategic course, outlined earlier, that is the foundation of everything we do at Vanguard.

Vanguard's Original Articles of Faith

I've talked about our $40 billion milestone and about the milestone that the decade of the 1980s represents. There is one other milestone that I would like to discuss with you this evening: It took place fifteen years ago, in April 1974, when we completed the white paper (five volumes of text and tables) that the fund board of directors was to accept as the basis for the formation and incorporation of Vanguard in September of that year.

Vanguard, as many of you know, is a company that might easily never have existed. If you will forgive me a personal note, it was born of a corporate conflict between some other senior officers of Wellington Management Company and me. It was shaped by one of the really exciting battles of my life—a fight for my own career and reputation. And it was decided, time and again, by frighteningly hairbreadth votes at each moment of decision by the board.

And yet, as I reviewed that aging white paper a short time ago, I could not help being impressed with the durability of our founding principles. At the very outset, the Vanguard Experiment called for "corporate, business, and economic independence for the group, . . . an environment and incentives that will enable it to attract and retain qualified people . . . and a structure consistent with the future environment, including 'consumerism' and new standards of business ethics."

In this document, we also set forth our articles of faith, the central elements of our long-range strategy:

Consistently superior performance . . . optimum cost-effective arrangements for fund administration and investment advisory service . . . effective communications with shareholders . . . efficient shareholder account maintenance . . . appeal to the broad savings market . . . marketing of new products to assure respon-

siveness to the changing environment . . . a new no-load distribution channel . . . and direct marketing to employee savings plans and personal retirement plans.

These principles and strategies, set down in writing fifteen long years ago—and I have quoted them verbatim—remain intact today. They form the articles of faith that were the foundation for our not inconsiderable success during the decade of the 1980s, culminating in the achievement of our $40 billion milestone just four weeks ago. Indeed, I think it is fair to say that, as we meet today, we are at the very pinnacle of our success.

Reaching the Pinnacle

I am sure it is obvious to you that I take great pride in reaching that pinnacle, and I hope you share that pride. But even as we take pride in what we have accomplished together so far, we must beware of the proverbial biblical injunction that "pride goeth before destruction, and a haughty spirit before a fall." All human history is replete with examples of this warning. The ancient Greek historian Herodotus told us in 425 B.C. that "it is the gods' custom to bring low all things of surpassing greatness." Edward Gibbon, writing *The History of the Decline and Fall of the Roman Empire* in 1780, noted that "the vicissitudes of fortune spare neither man nor the proudest of his works, and bury empires and cities in a common grave."

And so, in view of these consummately sensible warnings, what should Vanguard do to avoid having the grim lessons of history repeat in the coming decade of the 1990s? I believe there are two fundamentals: One, we must continue to do what we do best, independently and resolutely, ignoring the cacophony of our competitors. And two, we must all recognize that the greatest challenges of the coming decade are more likely to come not from without Vanguard but from within it.

Strategies for the 1990s, and the Challenge from Within

Continuing to do what we do best—to stay the course we have set for ourselves—will take discipline and courage. I have every confidence in the durability of our basic strategies, even as I can see some changes in emphasis during the coming decade. For example:

- Focus on our mutual fund activities but have an open mind about complementary activities.
- Enhance our low-cost-provider status but spend what we must—wisely—to remain competitive.
- Maintain the investment advisory relationships—external and internal—that have yielded such good performance but better articulate our performance standards.
- Increase our focus on our existing index, quantitative, and short-term ("safe") funds, even at the expense of having fewer new funds.
- Maintain our pure no-load status but be ever more aware of the value of having no outside organizations—nobody—between our clients and us.
- Maintain our retail marketing effort and image but emphasize the effectiveness of candor (as in our *Plain Talk* brochures) as a marketing strategy.
- Unequivocally, be the best in service. Clients expect perfection, so, through more effective systems and technology and an ever more dedicated organization, we shall strive to give it to them.

In short, if we maintain our strategy—and strengthen it as we go—the same factors that brought us competitive success in the past decade should continue to do so in the decade that lies before us.

But a second ingredient will also be required: We must meet the challenge from within Vanguard. This organization has succeeded not only because of *what* we are but because of *who* we are. And the challenge from within—to keep our crew motivated, stimulated, compensated, excited, caring about this institution, "onboard" if you will, with the conviction that Vanguard's mission is worthwhile—is ours to solve. We must work toward greater job satisfaction, more innovation at all levels, more enlightened management; work, in short, toward the greater good, cooperatively and with respect for one another, from the humblest to the highest among us. Writing in *Julius Caesar,* Shakespeare noted that "the fault, dear Brutus, lies not in our stars but in ourselves," a reminder to each one of us that if we fail to shape our future success, we will have only ourselves to blame.

$1.1 Trillion? . . . The Tyranny of Compounding

There is little doubt in my mind that simply being aware of the challenge from within will help us to surmount it. But it will be no easy task, for I am confident that we look ahead to an era of continued growth in our organization and in our assets, with all of the extra challenge that implies. During the 1980s, we have grown, as I have noted, at a 35 percent annual rate. We will not continue at this pace to be sure, but, just for fun, an extension of that growth rate would take us to $1.1 *trillion* of assets as the twenty-first century begins. More realistically, however, even if we were to grow at 20 percent during the coming decade, our assets would be $343 billion in the year 2000; at "only" 10 percent, $121 billion. This is "the tyranny of compounding," and it clearly produces a lot of money. But whatever our growth may be, *managing* it—even as we strive to retain the values, the character, the integrity that got us, in barely fifteen years, to where we are today—is no mean challenge.

Mindful of Edward Gibbon's warning that "all that is human must retrograde if it does not advance," we must continue to grow. But our growth should not be forced, not be growth for growth's sake, nor should our growth exceed our capacity to manage, nor should it be based on opportunism or excess. Rather, our growth should be organic, natural growth, sensible growth based on our confidence in staying out of step when everyone else is marching to the wrong tune, disciplined growth that flows from the inherent value of what we have to offer.

A Time for Reflection

So, at the very pinnacle of our success, it is a time for sober reflection by each of us who labors here at Vanguard, who labors in "the little company that almost didn't exist." (We might begin by reflecting on what we might otherwise be doing this very evening, and, perhaps more tantalizingly, just where our $40 billion of assets would otherwise be!) We must realize that we have increased our challenge because of the lofty standards we set for ourselves—and met by ourselves—over the past fifteen years during which we put Vanguard on the map. And we must realize that our record, the envy of our competitors, has made us their target, and they have now begun the battle to knock us off our pinnacle. (I do love a good fight, and just the thought of it gets my heart beating a little bit faster!) When the smoke clears, however, I have no doubt that we will have honored our Vanguard tradition: winning—and winning with class.

Finally, we must realize that, in this wonderful business, wild winds and turbulent tides will ever beset us. But we will continue to win—with class—if all of us in this crew but navigate our ship with judgment and purpose, remembering, as Gibbon also reminded us, that "the winds and the waves are always on the side of the ablest navigators."

Thank you for your attention, and thank you for being Vanguard.

THE INDIVIDUAL AND THE
INSTITUTION

December 10, 1989

*P*REPARING FOR THIS TALK, I
opened one of my reference books, and a yellowed newspaper clipping
tumbled out. It was a *New York Times* editorial, written at the end of
1979 and looking ahead to the decade of the 1980s. Quoting Walt
Whitman, it said, "It takes struggles in life to make strength, it takes
principles to make fortitude, it takes crisis to give courage, and singleness of purpose to reach an objective." The editorial concluded that
our generation's task for the eighties was "not only to understand what
needs to be done but to accomplish it."

Those words could easily have been a prophecy for Vanguard.
When 1980 began, we were limited in our resources (assets of $2.4 bil-
lion), stagnant at best (just $1 million of cumulative cash inflow since
our inception in 1974), and very small (131 crew members). We had a
stock market crash just behind us and—although we did not know it at
the time—a bond market crash just ahead. We had a new way of doing
business—the Vanguard Experiment, under which, for the first time,
mutual funds would operate independently and on an at-cost basis—
with no way of knowing whether or not it would work.

What is more, we were facing revolutionary changes in the mutual
fund industry. Money market funds were to become its largest component, with bond funds not far behind. Equity-oriented funds—our traditional bread and butter—were to become within the decade the
smallest component of our industry. And, believe it or not, this business was then run with archaic telephone systems and limited reliance

on computers—in both cases pallid forerunners of what we have today. The larger fund families had perhaps a dozen funds. We were, in short, a midget industry, unsophisticated but well intentioned, and hardly poised for what lay ahead.

And what lay ahead, of course, can probably be fairly described as the most remarkable explosion of growth and progress in American financial history. (That may sound hyperbolic, but I don't think it is.) Armed with new funds that would appeal not merely to our traditional *investors* but to *savers,* and entering a decade that was to be the most favorable in all history for financial assets, the mutual fund industry's asset base grew tenfold—from just short of $100 billion at the outset of the decade of the 1980s to nearly $1 trillion at its conclusion.

The Rise to Industry Leadership

In this environment, as you well know, Vanguard became an industry leader, in both total assets and in rate of growth, and *the leader* in both cost efficiency and service quality. Let me support these remarkable claims of leadership with a few facts and figures:

- As to total assets, our $47 billion marks Vanguard as the second-largest independent firm in this industry (and, among regular funds, the largest no-load firm). A decade ago, we ranked number 8, so we have leap-frogged the asset totals of six of our seven largest competitors.
- As to growth, our assets rose nineteenfold during the decade, nearly double the tenfold growth of the industry. We grew, then, at a compound *annual* rate of +35 percent, an astonishing accomplishment.
- As to cost-effectiveness, our operating expense ratio in 1989 will be about 0.36 percent. Incredibly, our *lowest* cost competitor incurs expenses more than 110 percent higher. (Total annual expenses—excluding sales charges—for the *average* mutual fund run in the range of 1.4 percent, or nearly 300 percent above ours.)
- As to service, our surveys tell us that 82 percent of our clients rate us as "excellent" or "very good." Less than 0.5 percent rate us as "poor." With respect to our *toughest* competitor, only 5 percent of our joint shareholders rate its service as better than Vanguard's.

Institutional Character—Individual Quality

Two of the elements cited by Walt Whitman relate to our institutional character, and both have been crucial to our success. They are, first, "that it takes principles to make fortitude," and second, "that it takes singleness of purpose to reach an objective." These attributes are those of Vanguard as an institution. We have stuck to our high principles, striving to be, as one shareholder described it a few years ago, "in the Vanguard of integrity." And our purpose has remained singular—to put the interests of our clients first and paramount, no matter what the issue. In an industry that too often tries to be all things to all people, our steadfast course may well be unique.

But the other two of Whitman's four elements are individual qualities—strength and courage. "The struggles in life that make strength" and "the crisis that gives courage" are surely attributes not of institutions but of human beings. And, despite these easier days—when we sail on calm seas, with wind and tide at our back—those of you who were part of our voyage during even the latter part of the 1980s well know through direct experience the struggles we've had and the crises we've faced—in volatile financial markets, in surging telephone volumes, in processing overload, in competitive conditions where we've fought with one hand tied behind our back. All I can say is that we have overcome these handicaps and emerged at the top. You, ladies and gentlemen of our crew, have a great deal to be proud of. You have been a source of pride to Vanguard. And I am proud of you in a magnitude that you could hardly imagine.

The Challenges Ahead

But enough of the past decade. The *next* decade is almost upon us, and there is no use—and indeed, in this busy enterprise, no time—for resting on our laurels, however well deserved. So let's look ahead at some of the challenges we face:

- *Volatile financial markets:* In a generally uncertain world, it is a near certainty that the nineties will *not* be a reprise of the eighties in terms of the abundant returns on financial assets. It would be foolhardy to anticipate and plan for another "Golden Decade," so we should bank on more modest investment returns for our shareholders, with the hope that the overall environment will remain a positive one.

- *Heated competition in the marketplace:* Our competitors don't like being beaten (especially by Vanguard!), and they are going all out to recoup the huge market share that we have captured from them. Apparently, they'll stop at nothing in their efforts, even waiving their management fees—temporarily, of course—to attract dollars into their new money market funds. More profoundly, however, Vanguard's very existence has established price competition—long overdue—in this industry, and if our competitors are dragged, kicking and screaming, into giving their customers a fair shake, well, that is not without redeeming social value, even if it slows our growth.

- *Even more heated competition for investment performance:* I simply do not believe that our competitors can make major inroads on our remarkable cost advantage, and thus the consistent past superiority of our money market funds should remain intact. With our competent professional management and our cost advantage, our bond funds should also at least match, and more likely exceed, the competition. Thus, our challenge lies principally in the equity arena. Here, we are coming off a lackluster year in 1989—albeit at the end of an excellent decade in total—but we must be prepared to work with our present equity advisers for performance excellence, and to retain new advisers as necessary. Our recent manager selections (especially for Windsor II, Equity Income, Asset Allocation, and World-US) have been distinctly positive, and we are both emboldened and determined to make the tough decisions that may be required in the years ahead.

- *Service enhancement:* We have made remarkable strides to attain our leadership role in quality of service. Other major financial firms will not only try to match us but will try to surpass us. The huge investments we are about to make in the development of a new, state-of-the-art, shareholder services system should help to keep us in the lead.

Our challenges, of course, are not limited to the boundaries of the financial services industry but rather, go far beyond. For example:

- *The state of the nation:* It is no secret that America is being challenged from within. Our willingness to pile on astonishing layers of debt is but one indicator; others would include the disgusting erosion of ethical values on Wall Street, in Washington, D.C., and elsewhere; the growing gap between poverty and plenty; and the near-failure of our educational system in meeting the needs of those who need it most. As a nation, we must take major steps to resolve these problems.

- *Finally, the challenge of the wide, wide world:* In the increasingly interdependent global economy, no longer is the United States the master of its own fate. But the incredibly swift erosion of Russian imperialism, and the remarkable move toward market, rather than controlled, economies—even within the Soviet Union itself—gives the hope of a rebirth of freedom. We can only hope and pray that those stirring pictures we saw of cheering Germans atop the Berlin Wall represent a durable reality, and with it a marked lessening of the threat of global war.

Well, I hope the preceding litany of challenges for the 1990s—some of which are far beyond our control, some within our province to solve—gives you enough to think about tonight. But whatever obstacles lie before us, our opportunities are limitless if we all work together. So I now want to return to my theme "The Individual and the Institution" and to talk with you about working together, and specifically the *relationship* between the *individual*—each of you in our crew—and the *institution* itself—the good ship *Vanguard.* I want to reemphasize—and underscore—the theme of caring. For only with a mutual sense of caring can we make this the kind of enterprise that will meet its lofty standards, goals, and values.

Exactly three years ago, in this same theater, at our then $25 billion milestone, I quoted the words of Dean Howard M. Johnson, chairman of the Massachusetts Institute of Technology, and I would like you to recall them with me. Speaking of the requirements necessary to make an institution work, he said:

> **We need people who care about the institution. In an increasingly impersonal world, I have come to believe that a deep sense of caring for the institution is requisite for its success.**
>
> **The institution must be the object of intense human care and cultivation: even when it errs and stumbles, it must be cared for, and the burden must be borne by all who work for it, all who own it, all who are served by it, all who govern it.**

> **Caring, we know, is an exacting and demanding business. It requires not only interest and compassion and concern; it demands self-sacrifice, wisdom and tough-mindedness, and discipline. Every responsible person must care, and care deeply, about the institutions that touch his or her life.**

I emphasized that this philosophy of caring—caring about our partners, our associates, our clients, indeed our society as a whole—must be our guiding star if we are to preserve, protect, and defend Vanguard.

Caring Is a Mutual Affair

As I reflected on that theme for my remarks this evening, however, it occurred to me that having a crew that cared about Vanguard was only half of the message that I intended to deliver. So let me deliver the other half now: *Caring is a mutual affair.* Surely, if we are to meet our goals, not only must the individual care about this institution but this institution must care about the individual. What does such caring mean? Well, at least these five things: respect, opportunity, environment, communications, and compensation:

- *Respect for each of you, from the highest to the humblest among us:* Each one of you deserves to be—and will be—treated with courtesy, candor, friendliness, *and respect for the honorable work you perform.* And if you are not, I'm half inclined to make this rule: "If you denigrate the work of any member of the crew, you must try it for half a day yourself." (A lot of your officers—including me—could not meet that challenge, so it is a rule unlikely to be violated.)
- *Providing each of you with an opportunity for career growth, participation, and innovation:* Developing career paths at Vanguard—an enterprise in which so many are asked to do jobs that are sometimes routine and mundane but that are always essential—has been a challenge. We must meet that challenge. But it is a simple fact that we need your enthusiastic participation in your job—whatever it may be—if we are to make Vanguard work effectively because the people on the firing line know a lot more about problems and solutions than the rest of us will ever know.
- *Maintaining an attractive, efficient environment in which you do your work:* We've done fairly well here, I think, but it gets

tougher as the original Vanguard campus (one building) has become four buildings, and is now six. We are engaging at this moment in the development of a "master plan" for our facilities in the 1990s, and I can assure you that our standards will be maintained and enhanced. Certainly, when I looked at our new space-age Technical Operations and Distribution Center on Saturday (their moving day), I was more convinced than ever that we can meet this test.

- *Keeping you informed with a meaningful communications program:* The well-received *Crew's News* is but a part of it. Heaven knows, these speeches I prepare and deliver are my way of informing you about our organization, our objectives, and our values. Regular staff meetings, business planning sessions, and the like are also part of it. To be sure, effective communications is a challenge that is never truly achieved, but recognizing its importance is a good place to begin. Communication is not a one-way street—management to staff. Rather, we expect our crew members to communicate with management through such channels as our periodic surveys (*Crew's Views*), our open-door policy, and even the weekly luncheons I enjoy with small groups of crew members. These informal luncheons have enabled me to chat comfortably with some 275 of you so far, with lots more to come.

- *Paying you fair compensation:* One of the most difficult challenges of a competitive business enterprise—with limited resources but unlimited needs—is to pay people fairly. We are acutely aware of this challenge, and we seek to provide this combination: (1) realistic and competitive salaries; (2) exceptional fringe benefits, to provide you with generous insurance protection and savings via our retirement and thrift plans; and (3) an equity incentive in our earnings, through the Vanguard Partnership Plan, in which you share in the rewards we generate for our shareholders. *I know of no other company in America in which every employee—without putting up one cent of capital—shares in its earnings.* Just for the record, each of you, on the average, receives an additional $490 of these fringe and partnership benefits for every $1,000 of your salary. This is hardly an insubstantial add-on, and we remain committed to an ongoing standard of fairness.

151

Let's Not Allow Process to Triumph over Judgment

Putting all these aspects of mutual caring together, it occurs to me that the greatest challenge of all is to maintain our "small-company" values as we become an ever larger company—that is, to maintain personal relationships in an environment that could easily become impersonal and to work together as human beings with hopes and aspirations and responsibilities that must be always respected. In my few dark moments, my greatest fear for Vanguard is that it becomes a giant, impersonal, boring bureaucracy where nobody cares about anything or anybody. It is incumbent on our entire management team to fight to our dying day to hold back the great tide of process—of paper and policies and regulations and procedures—that could overwhelm all that we have tried to achieve.

I am not foolish enough to think we can operate this demanding, disciplined service business by relying solely on everyone's goodwill and good intentions. We must operate in an efficient, businesslike manner. But I ask you to be aware that every time we replace common sense and sensitive judgment with formal policies and set procedures, a small part of the battle is lost. If we look exactly like a giant mutual life insurance company—my nightmare—we will be just that, and both our personal enjoyment and our competitive success may well be lost. So for heaven's sake, let's all work to make Vanguard a firm in which judgment has at least a fighting chance to triumph over process.

As I mentioned at our partnership party last summer, if we continue to grow at a rate of +35 percent during the 1990s, our assets will be just short of $1 trillion at the start of the year 2000. That is hardly in the cards, but even at +20 percent, assets would reach $300 billion; at "only" 10 percent, $122 billion. So, thanks to growth that begets growth—I called it "the tyranny of compounding"—we will almost certainly become a larger organization with each passing year. If we *all* work together to manage it with compassion, integrity, judgment, and respect for the human beings who earn their livelihoods here, and with a sense of mutual caring—a two-way street that runs both from the individual to the institution *and* from the institution to the individual—we can indeed preserve, protect, and defend what we have built.

Three weeks from now, when we enter the 1990s, we will do so as a sound enterprise, strong and lean, with success that has begotten more success, and with a strong name and a respected reputation. As in the

1980s, using Whitman's metaphor, we will again face struggles and crises, and we will again deal with them with singleness of purpose and sound principles. Taking the liberty of speaking for "the Institution," I close by saluting "the Individual"—each one of you—for your efforts, and I ask you to join me tonight in looking forward to the new decade, with curiosity, with excitement, and with confidence.

WE LEAD

June 23, 1990

A LITTLE OVER A MONTH AGO, on April 30, 1990, Vanguard completed its fifteenth year of operations. As it has turned out, that fifteenth year was a landmark year for us, a year in which our hopes of 1975 turned into realizations, our goals became realities, and our strategies begat success in the marketplace to a degree that was, in candor, unimaginable at our inception fifteen years ago.

In sum, Vanguard has emerged as the leader of the mutual fund industry. And this is only as it should be, given not only our history but our heritage. For each warship in the Royal Navy has a special badge—a distinctive mark that identifies its crew. For the HMS *Vanguard,* the badge depicts in gold a pugnacious lion holding a spear, topped with a crown of sails, with *Vanguard* printed atop a field of cerulean blue.

In addition to their crests, many of the warships also have had their own mottos. The HMS *Vanguard* had a motto, and it sets a singularly appropriate theme for my anniversary message. The motto echoes the naval battles of yore but also foreshadows this modern era of competitive business battles. It is: "We lead."

We Lead

We lead. Of course, we have always believed that we were the leader of the industry—and in a sense, we have been. But what is different about our fifteenth year is that, really for the first time, our "leadership" now has "followership" throughout this industry. Indeed, I think that it is fair to say that seldom in the annals of business history has a single company dominated the direction of an entire industry the way that Vanguard has dominated the affairs of the mutual fund industry during 1989 and 1990.

If you think that this claim is an exaggeration, consider these facts: (1) We lead in pricing strategy; (2) we lead in index fund development; (3) we lead in quantitative investment techniques; (4) we lead in providing complete and candid disclosure to investors; and (5) we lead in service to shareholders. And, as a result of this leadership in the key areas that are driving this industry today, despite furious challenges by our major competitors, (6) we lead in asset growth. In all, it is an imposing record of leadership, in which each member of our crew has made a contribution, and in which each one of you can take special pride. Let me briefly summarize each of these six points.

1. Leadership in Pricing

Our pricing leadership is now legendary. Vanguard, indeed, has brought long-overdue price competition to the mutual fund industry. Our unit expenses have been described as "lowest cost," "microscopic," and even "stingy," as we have lowered our expense ratio by 40 percent since 1980 (0.58 of assets to 0.35 percent) while our principal competitors, astonishingly, have *raised* theirs by the same 40 percent (0.62 to 0.86 percent). In a decade, then, our margin of advantage has risen from 4 basis points to 51, an increase of 1,175 percent!

By early 1989, the magnitude of our low-cost advantage could no longer be ignored—and Fidelity and Dreyfus responded. Stung by our success, our two largest competitors were forced to start low-cost money market funds. Low cost, that is, achieved only by waiving all fund expenses "for a period of time," after which their expenses will revert to levels—if lower than those of their high-cost sister funds— well above ours. Together, they have spent tens of millions to bring in billions, while Vanguard (in *Business Week*'s words) "has remained prosperously above the fray."

If the remarkable increase in our share of the market during the 1980s has been slowed by this illusory price competition—founded on gimmickry and half-truths—it still continues to rise. Nonetheless, emboldened by their pale imitations of Vanguard's low-cost strategy, the Fidelity Spartan Fund product line has now been expanded to nine bond and money market funds, and the Dreyfus Premier and General product lines now encompass twenty-two funds. Surely more price competition—and, I hope, more *durable* price competition—is on the way. While it will, obviously I think, erode our massive competitive advantage, it will not eliminate it. And since the investing public is the beneficiary of the competition, that can only be a wonderful step forward for our industry.

2. *Leadership in Indexing*

Our leadership—indeed, our virtual monopoly—of mutual fund market indexing has also stung our two giant rivals. They have figured out—in 1990—what we figured out in 1975, when Vanguard Index Trust began: that the colossal advantages of matching securities market indexes—complete diversification, low portfolio turnover, no advisory fees—make index funds formidable competitors for conventional actively managed funds. (In fact, during the past five years, the unmanaged Standard & Poor's 500 Composite Stock Price Index outpaced 74 percent—three of every four—actively managed equity mutual funds.)

Finally copying us, Dreyfus and Fidelity have started their own index funds and are waiving expenses "for a period of time," as they spend millions on disingenuous advertising. (Do you sense a pattern emerging here?) But so far at least, they have enjoyed no noticeable success in the marketplace. And even if they are successful, they will be where we were way back in 1976—with a single Standard & Poor's 500 Index portfolio—just at the time that we have expanded our index concept to encompass six portfolios, including two for smaller stocks, two for international stocks, and one for the bond market. So our followers still have a lot of catching up to do.

3. *Leadership in Quantitative Investing*

Our leadership in quantitative investing—essentially, using the power of the computer to strive to enhance the results of a selected market index—is also being followed. Here, we began with Vanguard Quantitative Portfolios in 1986, the first quantitative fund. While quantitative investment techniques are rife outside the mutual fund industry, they are just beginning to emerge within the industry. (As in the case of market indexing, it takes time for mutual funds to get the word.) Perhaps no more dramatic example of this emergence exists than the fact that the legendary John Templeton—that fundamental analyst of securities all over the world, and one of the great money managers of this generation—recently acquired one of the major quantitative research organizations for his own firm.

We have, as you know, now taken our second step along this road by adding two quantitative managers for Morgan Growth Fund, and we have promulgated the standard by which we will measure our success: the performance (and hence the portfolios) of other growth funds. Our cost advantage—critical to our quest for superiority—means that even if we only tie, we win. You can expect more utilization of these new techniques by Vanguard funds, even as more fund organizations most assuredly will follow us, forced to enter the fray by the pressure of competition.

4. Leadership in Full and Candid Disclosure

We lead, too, in disclosure to fund shareholders. Morningstar's *Mutual Fund Values* recently began rating the quality of mutual fund shareholder reports and awarded Vanguard the *only* A rating among the independent fund complexes (Fidelity got a C+ and Dreyfus a C−). Our competitors may well have to follow our lead in disclosure because regulations will require them to. Earlier this year, the staff of the Securities and Exchange Commission proposed a requirement that each fund provide a "Management Discussion and Analysis" to its shareholders, including comparative data on fund performance. If this requirement is adopted by the commission, our competitors will be dragged—kicking and screaming—into making the kind of factual, complete, and candid disclosure that we have made to shareholders throughout our entire history.

And full disclosure may come even if the Commission fails to act. Because I believe that the investing public will demand it. And, if the marketplace demands full disclosure, our rivals will simply have to provide it in order to remain competitive. In short, if disclosure is good business, good businesses—and our competitors are that—will provide it. So once again, they will be bending every effort to emulate Vanguard's lead.

5. Leadership in Service

As I am sure you all know, we lead in shareholder services too. "The Vanguard Group is tops with mutual fund investors" was the simple declarative opening statement in *USA Today*, reporting on the *Finan-*

cial World survey of 10,000 mutual fund investors. We had been a hair's breadth from the top of the list in the previous two years, but it is always a special treat to be rated number 1 by an independent survey. Special thanks to each one of you who contributed to our victory.

To be sure, I personally receive each week some twenty letters from shareholders citing an array of problems that attest to the fact that we have not yet reached perfection. But perfection must be our goal. To remain ahead of our competitors will require the best people, the best processing, the best systems that are available. One year from now, we hope to have our marvelous new shareholder system working for us— and for our clients—and it will take us to a new level of service excellence. It must, because—let's not deceive ourselves—our competitors are also driving for service superiority. In this area, indeed, there will be no easy victories.

6. *Leadership in Asset Growth*

Because we now lead in these critical areas of pricing, indexing, quantitative investing, shareholder reporting, and client services, we also lead the industry in asset growth. With a 39 percent increase in assets, Vanguard was the fastest-growing firm in this industry in 1989— almost *inconceivable* for a firm of our size, now the second-largest independent firm in the mutual fund industry. And, despite the "pricing challenge" of Fidelity and Dreyfus, we continue to be the fastest growing among the direct marketing firms. Indeed, during the period from the close of 1988 through the first quarter of 1990, our asset increase (+48 percent) was tops among the Big Five of direct marketing: Dreyfus (+41 percent), Fidelity (+35 percent), Scudder (+26 percent), and T. Rowe Price (+17 percent) were all satisfyingly behind.

Having said that, I hope that I have made it clear that, while we lead the industry in growth today, our pace may slow in the years ahead. To state the obvious, as our competitors observe our success and mimic— at least to some degree—our strategy, Vanguard's leadership will be harder to come by. Put another way, as we march to our own drummer—seeking long-term investors, following conservative fund policies with clear objectives, and eschewing massive advertising campaigns built on half-truths and hyperbole—building our "share of market" against these wily competitors will be more difficult. Nonetheless, we shall ignore any short-term aberrations in our competitive position, realizing that Vanguard will be in this business for a long, long, long time.

Looking Back to Our Founding

We did not, of course, establish overnight, or even in the past few years, the leadership that I have just described. Rather, we have been working on it since Vanguard began operations fifteen years ago—the anniversary we are now celebrating—a period that surely reflects our willingness to take the long view and to hold our principles intact. That steadfastness, perhaps paradoxically, not only failed to dampen our growth but actually accelerated it.

There are only eight crew members who have witnessed, firsthand, how far we have come. The vast majority of you will have to witness our growth through our key operating statistics, and I ask that you not only consider them but share my pride in the remarkable growth we have achieved during the past fifteen years:

- *Fund assets* . . . up from $1.4 billion to $53 billion. Incredible!
- *Number of fund portfolios* . . . up from twelve to fifty-seven. Five times over!
- *Cash flow* . . . from −$52 million *outflow* to $11 billion inflow. Unbelievable!
- *Operating budget* . . . up from $1.5 million to $174 million. Expensive!
- *The crew* . . . up from 28 members to 1,978 members. A huge crowd!

These numbers speak for themselves. In a word, they say "WOW!" as they portray the explosion that took us from being a tiny cottage enterprise in 1975 to the corporate enterprise we are in 1990.

Looking Ahead to More Competition

Continuing the growth rate reflected in these numbers is simply not in the cards—partly because of the law of diminishing returns, and partly because of more heated competition. This competition will occur in two principal arenas: (1) performance, investment return; and (2) price.

As to performance, you may have noted that I failed to say that "we lead" in the returns that we are providing to shareholders, for we cannot claim to be the across-the-board champion in *every* mutual fund category. (And even aggregating fund returns to see who is number 1 is a daunting and imperfect task.) But, if not *on* the top, we are assuredly *at* the top in every major industry segment.

In the money market sector, only a jaundiced few would argue that we are not the leader. In the fixed-income sector, we are surely *among* the leaders. And in the equity sector—while it depends on the time periods selected and the weight given to each fund's asset size—we are not far behind. Indeed, independent ranking services—*Business Week, U.S. News and World Report, Mutual Fund Forecaster, Consumer Reports,* and *Changing Times*—took up the challenge of assessing performance leadership, and Vanguard consistently emerged—often among 100 firms or more—in the top 5 percent. So there is substance to my enthusiasm for our past standing, even as there is confidence in my expectations for the future.

The other principal manifestation of the battle ahead will, I believe, be price competition. And, while there is no doubt whatsoever in my mind that Vanguard will continue to be *the* low-cost provider by a wide margin, our pricing superiority may not expand very much from the competitive margins I mentioned at the outset. As investors become aware of the impact of fund expenses on their investment returns—especially on the more modest investment returns that we expect in the 1990s as compared to the returns that we enjoyed in the Golden Decade of the 1980s—costs will become increasingly crucial.

Let me expand my earlier expense comparison in two ways: (1) considering *total* costs, including not only expense ratios but sales commissions for funds which levy them; and (2) expanding the field to include virtually the entire industry, not merely our major competitors. The results are astonishing. Our advantage is: (1) enormous versus the highest-cost providers; (2) huge versus the average-cost providers; and (3) large even against the lowest-cost providers of services in this industry.

Consider these figures: The typical cost for an investor in an average fund is 1.7 percent of assets per year; for the highest-cost 10 percent of all funds, it is 2.1 percent; and for the lowest-cost 10 percent of all funds, it is 0.7 percent. But for Vanguard, the all-in cost was just 35/100 of 1 percent last year. In short, even measured against the *lowest-cost* funds, Vanguard provides investors with savings of 50 percent!

Considering these differences, it does not require a Nostradamus—or even one of his latter-day successors in prophesy, say, Jean Dixon—to confidently predict that the rock on which Vanguard is founded—having our funds run solely in our clients' interest, on an at-cost basis—will be just as firm a foundation tomorrow as it is today.

We

I have focused on the word *lead* to this point. But let that not obscure the fact that *lead* means nothing unless prefaced by *we*. *We* are those here tonight, and those who came before us, and those who will follow us. *We* includes, heaven knows, not only those who have the highest order of responsibility for the future of this corporate enterprise but also those members of management who direct our day-to-day operations, and surely those with equally important but perhaps more routine jobs, those who have the responsibility for satisfying each client and for assuring that every task under the sun that we perform is carried out effectively.

In the more competitive world that is coming—I hope that I've persuaded you of that—*we* will determine Vanguard's success. *We* will have to increase our efficiency by performing every task more effectively. *We* will have to be better leaders, better data processors, better accountants, better marketers, better investment advisers. And *we* will have to provide an even better level of service. These are easy goals to reach, if—and only if—*we* work together, with respect for one another, with cooperation, with intelligence, and, perhaps most of all, with energy, good humor, and enthusiasm. Together, *we* can reach our goals.

Your contribution is being recognized tonight by the distribution of your share of the earnings from the Vanguard Partnership Plan in 1989. This plan should say two simple but important things to each of you: First, that the officers and directors appreciate your contribution, and second, that when we earn so much for our clients, it is only fair that you who help to create the earnings should share in them. We are alone in this industry with such a plan—*every crew member an owner*—but I fear that this final area in which we lead is unlikely to be copied by our competitors. So much the better for us!

A Warning

Despite the past success that we have achieved together, let us never forget the favorable role that time and chance—the good times in which Vanguard has sailed, and the favoring winds of chance that we have enjoyed—have played in our race for leadership. Ecclesiastes had it right when he warned:

I returned, and saw under the sun that the race is not to the swift, nor the battle to the strong, neither yet bread to the wise, nor yet riches to men of understanding, nor yet favor to men of skill; but time and chance happen to them all (Eccl 9:11).

Thank you again—each one of you—for helping us to make the most of time and chance, the time and chance that has favored us on our exciting voyage, in a race about which tonight it can be unequivocally stated: "We lead."

IF YOU BUILD IT, THEY WILL COME

December 14, 1990

ONE OF THE MOST memorable and poignant motion pictures of recent years was *Field of Dreams.* It is a story about a determined (one might even say "driven") idealist who is told—we're never quite sure by whom—that if he builds a baseball diamond in his cornfield, his deceased father and his Chicago White Sox teammates will come and play there. Until the hero acts, the mysterious voice just repeats, over and over, "If you build it, they will come."

"If you build it, they will come." That, it seems to me, is an appropriate theme for our annual Christmas celebration this evening. For in some respects, the story of *Field of Dreams* is the story of Vanguard. It is almost as if someone had come to us in the dead of night and uttered those same words: If you build it, they will come.

Let's begin by deciding who "you" is—and what "it" is—and who "they" are.

- **You,** in the collective sense, means all of us who are Vanguard employees—those who have come before, those who are here tonight, and those who will take our places in years yet to come. As employees of this fine enterprise, we have together done the hard work required to make Vanguard into the highly regarded firm that employs us today.
- **It** would certainly be our product line. We presently offer some fifty-eight fund products, many of them the best in their fields. These products have been designed with care and discipline,

with a clear definition of risk, and with specific investment objectives, which, much more often than not, have been achieved over time.

- **They,** finally, are our customers, the investors who buy our products. And if we meet their financial needs, these customers will not only buy more, but they will endorse these products to their relatives and friends, who will become our customers as well.

Three Little Words

As those of you who have been paying careful attention may have noticed, however, the three key words that I have just used—*employees, products, customers*—are the *wrong* words. Indeed, I have demanded that they be excised from our Vanguard lexicon. Why?

- We do not have *employees*—people who work here with the understanding that if they do exactly as they are told they will be paid a fixed wage in return. Rather, at least in the ideal, we have *crew members,* working together in partnership, from the highest job to the humblest, sharing in the earnings we generate for our owners, and doing our best to assure that the HMS *Vanguard,* as our crew's proud symbol, sails purposefully and on course through calm and rough waters alike.

- We do not have *products*—something manufactured for consumers, aggressively advertised, impulsively purchased, and finally used up (by eating or drinking or spreading or spraying, or *something*). Rather we have *investment companies,* but I don't object if you call them *mutual funds,* or *programs,* or *services,* or *trusts* in which the "fiduciary duty of trusteeship" are our watchwords.

- We do not have *customers*—those whose never-ending cycle is purchase and consume, purchase and consume, purchase and consume, and whose loyalty is based more on transitory special sales, or glamorous packaging, or the fads and fashions of the day than on valuable and durable service. Rather, we have *clients,* intelligent investors who have chosen to enter into what we expect will be a long-term professional relationship with us.

Amazingly, the three little words that we eschew sum up as well as anything else—maybe even *better* than anything else—what this enterprise that we call "Vanguard" is all about. For we are, in a very real sense, an enterprise without employees, an enterprise without products, an enterprise without customers. Think about that!

Management guru Peter Drucker, and indeed the executives of most of our nation's corporations, would be appalled. They would say that a firm without employees, products, and customers simply could not exist. But we exist—we are! And we transcend mere existence—which would really be quite boring—by our diligence, our discipline, our ideals, and our competitive spirits. We not only exist, but we thrive! And we have built one of the most successful financial enterprises of the age.

It is true. **We** have built something quite out of the ordinary, something of which we all can be enormously proud. Our success is attested to by an almost unimaginable asset total of $55 billion. We have grown at an astonishing pace of 28 percent annually during our fifteen-year history. Few companies have ever achieved that rate of growth—four times the 7 percent average pace of American business—over an extended period. And we have built our enterprise—**it**—and earned that growth by providing productive investment performance and high-quality investor service that have received almost unremitting praise from independent analysts and financial journalists throughout the year that will shortly end.

And **they** have come. Our clients have beaten a path to our door as, Emerson-like, we have built a better mousetrap. Today, we have approximately 3 million shareholder accounts, including all of the participants in our corporate pension plans. We establish as many as 3,000 new accounts on a normal business day. So long as *we* measure up to our responsibilities, there is no reason why *they*—new clients, or existing clients adding to their current investments, or investing in a second or third or fourth Vanguard fund (or more!)—will not continue to tramp that path in the years ahead until it becomes hardened like a rock.

Building on a Firm Foundation

When we build, to state the obvious, we must build on a firm foundation. In our case, it is our unique Vanguard corporate structure. We are, of course, the only mutual fund management company that is owned by the shareholders of its mutual funds, rather than by an external corporation with its own set of stockholders. Thus, our profits—and, measured in the hundreds of millions, they are not inconsiderable—revert to our fund investors, not to outside investors in publicly held or closely held corporations. Thus, we are in essence the only mutual mutual fund complex!

This structure is, I think, what provides Vanguard with the opportunity to conduct its affairs on a high ethical plane. Since we are owned by our clients, it is not very difficult to operate our funds in their interest, to strive to keep their costs within reasonable bounds, to write shareholder reports with candor (no matter how painful!), and to provide first-class service. I have heard it said that to be successful, a business should treat its customers as if they owned the company. Much of our success flows from the self-evident fact that our clients do *own* Vanguard.

I am well aware that we live in an era in which ethics seem to have taken a back seat to greed. Scarcely a day goes by without some new evidence of wrongdoing, or at least of skating too close to the edge of proper behavior. And it is really quite pervasive. Consider:

- *On Wall Street, disgusting financial crimes:* Michael Milken, who got away with massive fraud but did get caught for a few of his crimes, has been given a jail sentence that, at long last, will make white-collar crime less attractive. Ivan Boesky and Martin Segal, one the giver, the other the recipient, of a suitcase containing $250,000 in cash, a payoff for inside information (now there's a class act!) have been convicted. And many others too.
- *In Washington, grave ethical lapses:* Witness "the Keating Five," five U.S. senators in a hearing before their peers (paradoxically including that pillar of probity, Jesse Helms) who were found to have exerted undue influence on the savings and loan regulators. It is a sorry sight.
- *In the world of entertainment, fakery:* It is funny as a cute trick but tragic as a sign of the times that two singers—I think they are called the "Milli Vanillis"—won a Grammy music award, only to be forced to surrender it when it became known that they were lip-synching the voices of others.
- *And on Madison Avenue, fraud:* A company known for its probity has stooped to faking an advertisement that shows a truck crushing a line of cars in which only the Volvo remains unscathed—thanks to a few strategically positioned steel beams! This ethical violation stung me particularly since Volvo—with its emphasis on value, durability, sensibility, and safety—always seemed to me sort of the Vanguard of the auto world.

Measured against these grotesque standards, there are tens of thousands of firms that look pretty good, and we would surely be among them. If we are not angels—and we are not—we do run an ethical enterprise. And perhaps paradoxically, that has been one of the keys to our business success. Let me give you two instances in which our ethical values proved to be good business during 1990.

The Value of Candor

One of our most important values is candor—tell the whole truth and nothing but the truth, with no strings attached, and let the chips fall where they may. Sometimes it feels pretty good: A year ago, in our annual reports, we told our clients not to expect in the 1990s a repeat of the Golden Decade of the 1980s, during which the returns on financial assets were the highest in history. And as soon as 1990 began, we had sharp declines in the stock and bond markets, followed during the summer by even sharper declines as the Persian Gulf crisis brought the world to the brink—of war. Shareholders who followed our advice—"hold a mix of stocks, bonds, and cash reserves that meets your own goals and risk tolerance, and then stay the course"—easily weathered the storm, perhaps bloodied but nonetheless unbowed.

Sometimes it hurts: Early in 1989, we warned Windsor Fund shareholders to beware of a possible bad year for the fund, noting that "no investment account—whoever its manager, whatever its objective—outperforms the stock market consistently, year after year." This warning was borne out not only in 1989 but again in 1990, when the fund's stunning decline caused me to begin my letter in the just-published annual report with these words: "This is my twenty-first chairman's letter to you; . . . by all odds it is the most difficult one I have ever had to write." You just don't find these kinds of words or thoughts in the pallid reports of our competitors. But easy or hard, right or wrong, this candor is a simple manifestation of our respect for the intelligence of our clients.

The Value of Organic Growth

A second value in which ethical behavior is proving to be good business is our relaxed attitude toward growth. While we are an extremely competitive group of people—we love to win and we hate to lose—we compete on our own terms. We spend modestly on advertising. As an investor, why would you want your money used to bring in more investors? In our advertising, we describe all three fundamentals of investing—return, risk, and cost—while most other fund promotions focus on—indeed, hype—the first and ignore the second and third. And we simply do not advertise our funds when they are hot and easy to sell. We do like to take business away from our competitors by building our market share, and this we have done consistently, year after year. But never forget Vanguard's two principles of market share: (1) It is a measure, not an objective, and (2) It must be earned, not bought.

By this standard, we are doing very well indeed. In spite of the furious attack—aimed directly at Vanguard—by Dreyfus and Fidelity, our market share has remained intact. Temporary fee waivers on their new so-called prime money market funds have left their combined share of market roughly unchanged, so they are sneaking the costs back into place, and doing so bit by bit, in the hope that their shareholders won't notice. Their expense ratios are now about the same as ours, and they will apparently move up 50 to 150 percent above ours during the coming year. They are now repeating this scam with their U.S. Treasury money market funds, and I expect that the outcome shall be about the same. In any event, during the past two years they have each spent perhaps $50 million (of their shareholders' money!) on advertising and increased their money fund assets by $11 billion each; we have spent about $4 million, and our money fund assets are up $9 billion. That is, we have spent about 8 percent as much on advertising but have garnered 80 percent of the asset increase. It should go without saying that this ratio is good—clear evidence that what we built, we built well . . . and they came.

These two behemoth competitors also had the temerity to challenge our almost proprietary leadership in the field of indexing—matching the market—where we now have seven funds, each performing *exactly* in accordance with our expectations. Here, despite their customary fee-waiver gimmickry, their combined asset total remains below $100 million, compared to our $3 billion index fund asset base—earned, not bought, over the past fifteen years. Discussing index funds, Morningstar's *Mutual Fund Values* said: "Dreyfus may be better at self-congratulation, but in our book, Vanguard is the true people's hero. . . . If Dreyfus and Fidelity think it's going to be easy to supplant Vanguard as the country's best purveyor of index funds, they're fooling themselves." (Perhaps you can see why *Mutual Fund Values* is rapidly becoming my favorite publication!)

Mutual Funds: Just Another Business?

Together, these values of candor and a relaxed attitude toward growth have been the major reasons for the success that we have achieved. Having said that, I want to be clear that I am not impugning the business practices of our rivals. They are doing what too many consumer products businesses have been doing since time immemorial: operating as close to the edge of proper conduct as they think they can get away with. What I am doing is disputing their implicit philosophy that providing advisory services to mutual funds is "just another business."

Surely they want to serve their fund investors, just as we do. But they also want to serve their private owners, who control their funds and in essence set their own fees. I believe, however, that "no man can serve two masters." Matthew, at 6:24, said that 2,000 years ago; it remains good advice today. So, we have formally recommended to the Securities and Exchange Commission that the forthcoming Investment Company Amendments Act include an express statutory standard of fiduciary duty for fund directors and investment advisers.

In a real sense, then, the lines are drawn. On the one hand, there are the aggressive marketers of mutual funds, spending lavishly on marketing and promotion to bring in even larger amounts of assets to manage, and thus to earn even larger profits for themselves. That, indeed, is the American way of business. On the other hand, Vanguard stands alone—not much concerned about growth in the short run, confident that it will do well in the long run. We like it that way! It is, for us, a luxury to act on the principle that the best growth is organic and not forced, and comes naturally from within. I am in fact elated to have Vanguard as the test case of whether the different drummer of trusteeship can succeed in a world of industry and commerce.

I hasten to add—as if you do not know it!—that we are not an enterprise unflawed. Working at Vanguard, no matter how enlightened our organizational principles, is not heaven on earth. Investing at Vanguard, no matter how cost competitive our funds, is, regrettably, not an assurance of consistently high investment achievement. Future growth for our enterprise, no matter how extraordinary our past growth, and no matter how assured its continuation may seem today, must be earned and reearned, again and again, by continuing to provide the kind of client services, investment performance, and disciplined innovation that have become, and must remain, our standards.

Challenges for the Coming Year

As we enter 1991, then, we must strive to overcome each of these challenges. Our new *Crew's Views* survey will give us yet another opportunity to make this a better place to work. The development of our new quality management program will help us to work more effectively together. Our new VAST shareholder accounting system will enable us to maintain our reputation for first-class client services.

In 1991 and beyond, however, we will pay the price for our subpar equity fund performance in the past year—and that is as it should be. When our Windsor Fund flagship disappoints, it does so not only for most of us personally but for all of us professionally. However, we can take great comfort from the fact that the $40 billion of our asset base that comprises money market, bond, and stock index funds continues to provide both expert management and competitive returns. Our leadership in these areas—based importantly on our low cost—will surely again be challenged in the marketplace by our competitors, if only on the basis of legerdemain.

So the coming year will surely again be one of challenges. We know of the risks in our nation's financial system, and the exposure of money market funds to them. Neither is the stock market, despite the consolidation during 1990, without high risk. Even excepting these two big risks, however, our remarkable rate of past growth will almost surely slow during the coming year. In short, even though we are among the most successful firms in what seems to be the *only* successful sector of the financial services industry (just consider banks, thrifts, and insurance companies!), we must run a tight ship and be ever prepared for stormy weather.

Good Ethics Is Good Business

Let me conclude by referring to my original theme. What we—all of us together—have built rests on a solid ethical foundation. For me, no other foundation is worthwhile, or even acceptable. Our candor in presenting the facts and our discipline in seeking growth have not only failed to inhibit our success but have actually fostered it. *Good ethics is good business.* The proof of that thesis rests on the self-evident fact that, every day and in ever-increasing amounts, existing clients are adding to their investments and to the number of Vanguard funds that they select, and new clients are joining us in droves. So the record is clear that *we* have built *it* and that *they* have come. And the challenge for this enterprise in the years ahead—this enterprise with neither employees, nor products, nor customers—is simply this:

If we build it *ever stronger*, they will *continue* to come.

That quotation doesn't have quite the rhythm and ring to it, nor the sonorous tone, that we heard in *Field of Dreams*. Neither does it have the sentimental evocations of baseball and forgotten heroes, of corn-fields and Iowa. Nonetheless, it is a worthy vision—a dream—for us all, working together as a crew to assure that The Vanguard Group of Investment Companies is the best that it can be in serving our clients.

Part IV

Pressing On Regardless, 1991–1995

W HEN THE ERA 1991 through 1995 began, even a 100-day war in a Middle East desert couldn't slow a stock market recovery from the dog days following the 1987 crash. While the Iraqi invasion of Kuwait in the autumn of 1990 had knocked the Dow-Jones average down from 3,000 in July to 2,365 in October, the onset of war and its speedy resolution in February 1991 marked the beginning of a vibrant chapter in stock market history.

Breaking out of the doldrums of the late 1980s, stocks provided a fabulous 30 percent return in 1991 and then leveled off for three years, only to explode in 1995. That year's near-38 percent gain carried the Dow to 5,200, more than double its late 1990 level. As interest rates tumbled, bonds, too, were little short of sensational. In 1980, bonds provided a 16 percent return, then, like stocks, leveled off for three years, only to explode again in 1995 with a remarkable 18.5 percent gain. With our powerful line-up of stock, bond and balanced funds, few fund firms were as well postured as Vanguard for this double bull market.

Bond Funds, Balanced Funds, and Index Funds

Once again, an important factor in our growth was the formation of new funds. Another twenty-nine Vanguard funds came to birth during the years 1991 through 1995, bringing our offerings to eighty-two funds. Our goal was to play to the strengths of our character—conservative objectives, long-term policies, indexing, structured portfolios, and low costs. We filled substantially all of the gaps in our bond fund

	Total Net Assets[1]	Net Cash Flow[1]	% Change in Assets	Number of Funds	Crew Members	Expense Ratio (%)	% of Fund Assets in:				Annual Return (%)		
							Stock Funds	Balanced Funds	Bond Funds	Money Funds	Stocks	Bonds	Bills
1991	77,143	15,123	38.2	58	2,600	0.32	30	8	32	30	30.5	16.0	5.7
1992	98,102	18,806	27.2	68	3,100	0.31	32	9	35	24	7.6	7.4	3.6
1993	127,164	22,477	29.6	69	3,500	0.30	34	10	36	20	10.1	9.7	3.1
1994	131,934	10,676	3.7	79	3,550	0.30	36	11	30	23	1.3	−2.9	4.2
1995	180,136	24,857	36.5	82	3,900	0.31	4π1	11	28	20	37.6	18.5	5.7
Cumulative		91,939	26.4								16.6	9.5	4.5

[1] Figures are in $ millions

line, adding an intermediate-term and a short-term U.S. Treasury bond fund in 1991, and then two other intermediate-term funds—for corporate bonds in 1993 and for California tax-exempt bonds in 1994. Early in that year, building on the success of our Total Bond Market Index Fund, we also created the industry's first (and still only) bond index fund *triad* consisting of a long, intermediate, and short-term portfolio. This move was another vote of confidence in the inevitability that indexing not only works, but works especially well in the bond fund arena, where the dispersion of returns among similar funds is small, and low costs detract only minimally from the more modest returns expected of bonds.

On the balanced-fund front, we entered the period with just four funds and emerged with eleven. My indoctrination in the value of balanced investing during all those earlier years at Wellington Fund had left its mark, and in 1992 we created the industry's first balanced *index* fund, followed in 1994 by a series of four LifeStrategy Funds. These funds were basically combinations of underlying Vanguard stock index funds and bond index funds, with equity allocations ranging from 20 percent (LifeStrategy Income) to 80 percent (LifeStrategy Growth).

On the equity fund front, we created three more index funds, beginning in 1992 with the world's first Total Stock Market Index Fund, as well as the first Growth Index and Value Index funds, based on indexes that divided the stocks of the Standard & Poor's 500 into those two distinctive investment styles. All told, our commitment to the principles of indexing couldn't have been more deliberate nor more obvious: Twenty-five of our twenty-nine new funds followed indexlike strategies.

I include in this group another major Vanguard innovation: *the fund industry's first series of tax-managed funds.* While most managed funds are rendered abjectly *tax inefficient* by their extraordinary portfolio turnover (then about 80 percent per year), our standard index funds had been remarkably *tax efficient.* But we wanted to create a series in which tax efficiency would take precedence over index matching. We sought this goal both by pursuing tax-sensitive, index-based investment strategies so as to minimize *portfolio* turnover and by imposing substantial penalties on shares redeemed during the early years so as to minimize *shareholder* turnover. Why it had taken until 1994 for us to respond to the obvious need for tax-efficient investing remains a mystery. Why we could be so late and yet still be first is an even greater mystery. But our tax-managed funds—Growth and Income, Capital Appreciation, and Balanced—have been a signal success.

When Marketing Pressure Overwhelms Good Judgment

Confession being good for the soul, I must admit to making another mistake. Not having learned what I should have from the experience of the sector funds we formed eleven years earlier, in 1995 we inaugurated a new series of Horizon funds, designed for investors with long-term time horizons who were willing to take extra risks. Two funds were worldwide in focus (Global Equity and Global Asset Allocation). Another (Capital Opportunity) pursued highly aggressive equity strategies, ill-implemented by its first external adviser, but then successfully replaced by Primecap Management. The fourth fund (now Strategic Equity) followed a computer-oriented quantitative strategy, and it has generated acceptable returns. With the exception of the Primecap-managed fund, however, marketplace acceptance was modest. While investing more aggressively in narrow market segments may make sense, there seemed few truly long-term investors in evidence. The Global Asset Allocation Fund no longer exists; the "Horizon" name has vanished. The lesson, I suppose: While no one hits a home run in every appearance in the batter's box, you'll have a better batting average if you don't swing at marketing pitches.

Our 1992 introduction of the Admiral series—four funds investing in U.S. Treasury obligations, differentiated by carrying long, intermediate, short, or money market maturities—however, was indeed a home run. Its echoes continue to reverberate throughout Vanguard and will ultimately reverberate throughout the industry. The genesis of the Admiral concept was the obvious insight that, since the costs of handling a shareholder account are relatively fixed, larger investors generate substantial economies of scale. The sooner we could deliver these economies to our investors, the better. For it would only be a matter of time, I thought, until our competition would have to offer lower-priced funds to their larger investors, a market-segmentation strategy under which they could at least pay lip service to Vanguard's cost advantage.

The Admiral Treasury Funds, with $50,000 investment minimums and minuscule expense ratios, were designed to attract and retain substantial investors. They were also our way of firing a shot across the enemy's bow—letting our rivals know that they'd better get ready for even tougher price competition. Indexlike in character, these funds delivered exactly what they promised: a fair share of each Treasury bond sector's return. In 1994, in order to make lower costs available to investors with higher share balances in other Vanguard funds, we applied to the U.S. Securities and Exchange Commission for approval to offer shares in several series, differentiated solely by their expense ratios. Six years later, in 2000, the concept became fully embedded at Vanguard. We now offer an Admiral class of shares in fifty-two of our Vanguard funds, providing our substantial and long-term shareholders with even lower expense ratios. Already, nearly $60 billion of Vanguard assets—one-fourth of the $225 billion of assets held in regular accounts by individuals at Vanguard—carry the Admiral imprimatur.

Creative Destruction

My speeches during this period continued to focus on *character.* The first talk, in June 1991, explored the theme "Creative Destruction," pointing out how the fund industry had been the beneficiary of a sea change in the way American families invest, becoming a creative destroyer, as it were, of the thrift and life insurance industries. Similarly, Vanguard itself was becoming a creative destroyer of some of the most venerable firms in the fund industry itself. In this speech, and in many of its successors, I also focused on the inner workings of our organization—crew member attitudes, compensation, benefits, communications, service. And I often spoke of world events that would affect our lives, such as the dismemberment of the Soviet Union in 1991, comparing its impact to the call to arms for America at Pearl Harbor fifty years earlier, and even with Lord Nelson's destroying Napoleon's dream of imperial conquest at the Nile two centuries before.

In my 1992 speech, "Press On Regardless," I emphasized to our crew members the importance of riding out the inevitable triumphs and disasters in the financial markets and in world affairs, and of subordinating our own personal concerns to the greater good. I also stressed our need to constantly reexamine our own business strategies. To remind them both of our success and our fragility, I recounted the myth of Icarus, who flew so close to the sun that his waxen wings melted. Renouncing complacency, I reported that some of our policies—*but none of our principles*—would promptly be changed. Killing a series of what many senior crew members considered "sacred cows" at Vanguard, I said we must spend the resources necessary to lead the industry in technology; we must provide financial advisory services to investors; and we must engage directly in active (if quantitatively oriented) investment management. With assets then at $86 billion, I repeated my warning at our $8 billion milestone eight years earlier, stressing the danger to any company doing as well as we were: *to think we can do no wrong.*

I also began to speak even more bluntly to the crew. The theme of my year-end 1992 speech ("A Willing Foe and Sea Room") was all about *battle.* Our proposal to finance a new office campus (our crew then numbered 3,000, on its way to 5,000 in 1996 and to 11,000 in 2001) was, astonishingly, protested to the Securities and Exchange Commission by Vanguard rival Fidelity. As the fight warmed, I regaled the crew with excerpts from a letter written to Fidelity by a shareholder of funds offered by both firms. The shareholder had sent me a copy of the letter, which was scathing in its criticism of our rival. Perhaps I shouldn't have used the firm's name in my talk, but I had a chip on my shoulder and was in a feisty mood. Fidelity soon wisely withdrew its protest, but I wasn't about to stop battling. The last quote in my speech read: "Life is a kind of campaign. People have no idea what strength comes to one's soul and spirit through a good fight."

A *Fighting Spirit*

Surely a fighting spirit—not just my own but Vanguard's—is an element of character, and my next speech, in June 1993, was entitled simply "Character." I explained who we were and what we stood for, buttressing my own obviously subjective opinion about Vanguard's character with the objective opinion of Dr. Michael E. Porter of Harvard Business School, perhaps America's preeminent expert on corporate strategy. A few weeks earlier, to a packed house at the general membership meeting of the Investment Company Institute, he had described us as the *only* firm in the industry that had differentiated itself from the pack with a "genuine, unique, sustainable competitive advantage," built directly on the character we had established. Our rivals in the audience were not amused. But he was right.

I was confident that our fighting spirit was indomitable and that our competitive advantage was both unique and sustainable. And I was emboldened by our burgeoning asset base and our plummeting expense ratio—from 0.51 percent in 1985, it had fallen nearly 40 percent, to 0.32 percent in 1991. We at last had the resources to invest heavily in the investor services we would depend upon for our future growth. The lion's share of our spending was on technology, as we developed an acronym-laden series of new computer systems—for individual share-holders (VAST), for 401(k) plans (VISTA), and for fund accounting (COMPASS). And in the biggest commitment of all, we built and occu-pied a handsome but efficient new campus in Malvern, just a few miles down Route 202 from the Chesterbrook offices we vacated.

Other commitments were also substantial. We became an early advocate of using technology to enhance our shareholder services, developing and then regularly enhancing our website, assuring that "Vanguard.com" would be in the, well, vanguard of the Internet. We opened our first off-site operation center in Phoenix in 1994, and a year later made our first foray across international waters when we decided to launch Vanguard/Australia in Melbourne. In the same year, we started our Personal Financial Services group, offering for the first time advisory and asset management services, at a modest fee. And we also began the Vanguard Variable Annuity program, ultimately offer-ing thirteen Vanguard funds in annuity wrappers. In the variable annu-ity arena, most products were substantially overpriced, and it was easy to recognize our huge opportunity to serve investors by providing a low-cost alternative. As in the case of our brokerage operation eight years earlier, I insisted that we not fritter away our shareholders' resources on marketing. Rather we would grow organically, relying on press coverage and word-of-mouth rather than costly advertising.

When we moved to our new campus late in 1993, my dedication speech struck the same patriotic theme I had used when I dedicated both the new Wellington building in 1973 and Vanguard's first build-ing of its own in 1983. Like our new campus, both were close to Valley Forge National Park, and we continued to use our Valley Forge postal address. Just as America went through her first challenge at Valley Forge in the winter of 1777–1778, I reiterated in my talk, our land and our institutions were once again being challenged, and it was up to our own institution to respond. All of us on the crew must do our best each day to make ourselves, our company, and our nation just a little bit bet-ter. As I ended my remarks, the bell atop the tower on our new cam-pus tolled "America the Beautiful."

Let the Wisdom of the Past Illuminate Our Future

In my final speech of this period, at the partnership meeting in June 1995, I took the opportunity to remind our crew of our now firmly established character. These were the ten elements I singled out: (1) Our nautical heritage—Vanguard, victory, valor, discipline, and gallantry. (2) Our mutual respect: "Even one person can make a difference." (3) Our approach to business: "If you build it, they will come." (4) Our celebrations: the milestones that mark our progress. (5) Our motto: "Press on, regardless." (6) Our spirit: entrepreneurship, creativity, and a "can-do" attitude. (7) Our risk: to forget where we came from. (8) Our tradition: to preserve it, but to perpetually criticize it and bring it up to date. (9) Our constant reminder: While we are in command of our own ship, we are in the presence of a power mightier than our own. (10) Our duty: Care for the institution!

Throughout this five-year era, the favoring winds of the financial markets had given powerful impetus to our voyage. Stock returns averaged 16.6 percent per year, only a bit short of the fabulous 17.4 percent annual return recorded in 1980 through 1985. Bond annual returns, at 9.5 percent, were also nearly as good as in the previous period. Only Treasury bill returns of 4.5 percent were significantly lower than in our earlier years. This salubrious environment helped us to a 26 percent annual growth rate that was only a percentage point below that of the previous five years. By the end of 1995, our assets had reached $180 billion. Our market share continued to grow, rising another 23 percent, from 5.2 percent in 1990 to an all time high of 6.4 percent at the year-end 1995. And in 1993 we passed the Merrill Lynch funds to become the second-largest mutual fund complex in the world.

Changing market conditions changed our asset mix dramatically. Stock funds rose from 28 percent of our assets as 1991 began to 41 percent of our assets as 1995 ended, and balanced funds nearly doubled, from 7 to 11 percent. Bond funds virtually held their own (25 versus 28 percent), and money market funds, with a dominant 40 percent share of our assets in 1990, fell to just 20 percent. At the close of the period, half of the assets we managed were equities, half fixed-income. Come what might, that balance was a perfect place to be.

But it was no time to rest on our laurels. In the final words of my final speech of this era, I told our crew that the best way to prepare for the rapidly approaching twenty-first century would be to rely not on the outer support of plans, programs, and policies, but upon the inner strengths of character: *resiliency and resourcefulness, discipline and cooperation, endurance and courage, and, perhaps above all, faith and hope.* We had developed those strengths. It was up to us to keep them.

CREATIVE DESTRUCTION

June 17, 1991

"CAPITALISM IS by nature a form of economic change that not only never is but never can be stationary." These profound words of Professor Joseph Schumpeter—a voice in the wilderness up to his death in 1950 but now recognized as a seminal economic thinker—encapsulate my theme at this 1991 celebration of the Vanguard Partnership Plan. Despite the fact that it is often painful and always disquieting, change is what drives our nation's system of capitalism. Change is essential to our progress. And progress, in turn, using Schumpeter's expression, depends upon the process of "creative destruction."

There are few better examples of creative destruction than the financial services sector of our economy. Here, I would argue, the mutual fund industry has been the single most important agent of change. As the purveyor of better investment programs and better services, at better prices, our industry has prospered, while the process of creative destruction has driven other once-dominant financial institutions to falter, and sometimes to fail.

Hard statistical facts provide powerful support for this thesis. On the losing side, the most obvious manifestations are thrift institutions and life insurance companies, and the biggest beneficiaries are surely mutual funds. Forty years ago, a young man writing his senior thesis at Princeton University—yes, he had a crewcut even then!—noted that mutual fund assets of $2.5 billion "looked small in comparison" with $54 billion in life insurance reserves, $74 billion in savings deposits, and $50 billion in U.S. savings bonds. In short, mutual funds represented only about 1.5 percent of the $180 billion total of these basic savings programs.

Today, forty years later, the combined savings assets held by these competitive institutions total $3.6 trillion—a 20-fold increase. However, mutual fund industry assets have risen to $1.2 trillion—a 500-fold increase. Our industry's market share has risen to 25 percent. Since each percentage point of market share is today worth $48 billion, you can quickly see that, if we had maintained our 1.5 percent share, industry assets would be $72 billion. At 25 percent, however, they amount to $1.2 trillion, doubtless a number that our young Princeton senior would have found almost inconceivable.

Creative Destruction within the Fund Industry

As dramatic as this change is among financial institutions, it pales by comparison with the change in the leadership of the mutual fund industry. For example, despite our industry's incredible growth and success, seven of the top twenty firms in the industry in 1951—one of every three—has ceased to exist, including some of the giants of that earlier era. To name a few of the departed: Hugh W. Long, Inc., Calvin Bullock, Incorporated Investors, Group Securities, and Chemical Fund. (I'm going to guess that most of you have never even heard these names.)

Of the remaining thirteen firms, only three managed to increase their market shares. One is Fidelity, whose assets have risen from $64 million forty years ago to $110 billion today. Next is Vanguard. In 1951, Wellington Fund had assets of $194 *million*. (In those days the typical fund was an "only child" and was known by its own name rather than by a group name.) Today assets of all of the Vanguard funds—Wellington Fund and its fifty-seven younger brothers and sisters—total $66 billion. The third gainer of share, Putnam, is less than half of our present size. Assets and market shares of the major groups are shown in the table that follows.

The giants of that day—number 1 Massachusetts Financial Services and number 2 Investors Diversified Services—have fallen in the rankings to number 7 and number 8, as their combined share of industry assets has declined from a dominant 27 percent to a mediocre 7 percent. The bigger they are, the harder they fall! And, of course, in this microeconomic analysis of the process of creative destruction, some small firms rose to take their places. Back in 1951, the assets of Franklin were $2.5 million; T. Rowe Price, $1.2 million; and Dreyfus, a paltry $800,000. Think of that! A combined total of $4 million—and

The Mutual Fund Industry in 1951 and Forty Years Later

	1951 ASSETS, MILLIONS	1991 ASSETS, BILLIONS	1951 MARKET SHARE	1991 MARKET SHARE*
THE BIG 10				
1. Massachusetts Financial Services	$472	$22.2	15.0%	3.4%
2. Investors Diversified Services	379	22.4	12.1	3.4
3. Fundamental (Hugh W. Long)	223	—	7.1	—
4. Keystone Custodian Funds	213	7.6	6.8	1.2
5. Affiliated (Lord Abbett)	208	6.6	6.7	1.0
6. Seligman (Broad Street)	208	4.7	6.7	0.7
7. **Vanguard** (Wellington Fund)	194	55.9	6.2	8.6
8. Calvin Bullock	178	—	5.7	—
9. Incorporated Investors	112	—	3.6	—
10. Eaton & Howard	90	—	2.9	—
Group total	$2,277	$119.4	72.8%	18.3%
THE NEXT 10				
11. National Securities	$88	$1.7	2.8%	0.3%
12. Group Securities	80	—	2.6	—
13. Scudder, Stevens & Clark	78	14.5	2.5	2.2
14. Eaton Vance (Vance Sanders)	77	6.0	2.5	0.9
15. United Funds	72	—	2.3	—
16. Fidelity Funds	64	110.2	2.0	16.9
17. Putnam Funds	52	30.2	1.7	4.6
18. Chemical Fund	51	—	1.6	—
19. Axe-Houghton Funds	50	0.1	1.6	NM
20. Commonwealth Investment	42	—	1.3	—
Group total	$6.54	$162.7	20.9%	24.9%
ALSO-RANS				
21. Capital Group	$26.0	$35.1	0.8%	5.4%
22. Kemper (TV-Electronics)	11.1	38.8	0.4	5.9
23. Franklin	2.4	45.9	NM	7.1
24. T. Rowe Price	1.2	17.3	NM	2.7
25. Dreyfus	0.8	56.7	NM	8.7
Group total	$41.5	$193.8	0.8%	23.9%
Grand total	$2,972.5	$475.9	95.1%	72.9%

*Market share excludes broker-dealer and bank management segments.

an aggregate market share of ⅒ of 1 percent. Today, these three firms account for $120 billion of our industry's asset base, an 18 percent share.

This brief glance at "ancient history" presents a sort of Darwinian survival-of-the-fittest thesis—and a paradox. The thesis is that those fund complexes (even those with but one fund, and forty years ago, few had more than two) that perceived a turn in the tide would prosper. The key lay in foreseeing the move from the sales-power-driven, broker-dealer distribution system that dominated the field from the industry's inception in 1924 to the late 1970s, to the intelligent-client-driven, no-load, direct marketing system that has become, in little more than a decade, the industry's most potent distribution channel.

One Radical Decision: Going No Load

The paradox is that the fund groups that were *already* no-load in 1951 were not in the vanguard of industry growth. Rather, the growth would be spearheaded by three newcomers who converted, by and large, from dealer distribution to direct marketing—Vanguard first, at "one fell swoop" in 1977, then Fidelity, and finally Dreyfus. I should note that neither Fidelity nor Dreyfus is fully committed to no-load even today. It is the dominant sector of their business, but they still retain an amalgam of low-load and even dealer-sold funds.

An amusing anecdote: The mere whisper of no-load in the early 1970s was so appalling and contentious to broker-dealers that it had strong competitive implications in the marketplace. When Vanguard converted to no-load on February 9, 1977, not only did our dealer sales vanish—literally overnight—but Dreyfus felt compelled to run full-page advertisements with their lion roaring "No Load? No Way!" (I'm not sure that the accuracy of their ads has gotten much better over the years since then.)

What judgments were required to make this dramatic transition, thereby to be among the creative destroyers rather than the creatively destroyed? Essentially only these four:

- First, recognition of the obvious fact that in a maturing industry with growing public recognition, in an expanding economy with larger personal wealth, and in a better-educated marketplace with the self-evident logic of lower costs, the elements of change were firmly in place.

- Second, postulating not only that these elements of change would not abate but that they would accelerate.
- Third, carefully calculating the interim risks of near-zero sales volume and soaring redemptions and then to guess how long it would be before the tide would turn.
- Fourth, having made these reasoned judgments, having the courage—*and persuading others to have the courage*—to do the deed. It took us about six months to lay the groundwork, and our recommendation was finally approved by our directors—by a vote of seven to four at about 1:30 A.M. on the morning of February 9, 1977. It was an exhausting meeting!

Our decision to change our distribution status was so fundamental, so basic, and so complete that few major strategic changes remained to be made. Since the no-load decision included a determination to shift the responsibility for distribution from Wellington Management Company to Vanguard, only two other major decisions were required. The first, under the aegis of our new distribution responsibility, was to radically expand the diversity of the mutual funds offered by Vanguard. Only seven of today's Vanguard portfolios predate Vanguard's formation in 1975; by 1980 there were twenty; by 1985, thirty-seven; and today there are fifty-eight members of the Vanguard family.

Another Radical Decision: Internalizing Management

The second was our 1981 decision to internalize the management of the Vanguard municipal bond and money market funds, using our own staff rather than an external adviser. Vanguard, then, having begun as a mutual fund administrator in 1975 and having then taken on the responsibility for distribution and marketing in 1977, would take direct responsibility for investment management in 1981. (The board vote was eight to two. We're making progress!) It is impossible to overstate the importance of this decision in the growth that followed. Suffice it to say that our Fixed Income Group—which came into existence less than a decade ago—now manages $33 billion of our assets, or more than one-half of the Vanguard total assets. Our people do so with consummate professionalism, which, combined with our extraordinarily low cost expense ratios, has enabled us to emerge as *the* leader in the fixed-income segment of the industry.

There are three important reasons that I have taken you on this long walk down memory lane. First, I want to remind you of the powerful force of creative destruction, even in this burgeoning industry. Second, I want to emphasize how very few truly critical decisions were required to position us for our industry leadership role. (If they seem obvious today, let me assure you that they were also obvious then. It is fair, I think, to describe our success as importantly derived from the uncanny ability to recognize the obvious.*) And third, I want to lay out the history of our past in order to discuss what we must focus on to assure our future. It is to this point that I now turn.

In my view, we require no comparable sea-change decisions today. Rather, what is required is the perhaps less glamorous but equally vital task of measuring up to—and indeed exceeding—the expectations of those who have entrusted their assets to us. We have a sound foundation; if we are to maintain our leadership in the years to come, we must now build a magnificent mansion atop it. All that is required is that we deliver on *performance* and that we rely on *people.*

Performance

Let me say it straight out: Good investment performance is the sine qua non of our future success. Of course, we all know it instinctively. So it is reassuring to see that fact confirmed by our recent survey of client needs and expectations. In the survey, 55 percent of shareholders rated performance as "the most critical" service that we provide, and 88 percent rated it among the most important five. Second was cost-effectiveness, with 84 percent of clients rating it among the most important five services, at least tacitly recognizing the close link that exists between lower costs and higher returns.

Can Vanguard deliver top performance? We have thus far, and our performance excellence is recognized by independent analysts. *Financial World* says that Vanguard "runs more top funds than anyone else." *Fortune,* in an article dated this very day, states that, in terms of performance, "The clear winner is The Vanguard Group." We can—and we shall—deliver such performance in the future too. I need hardly emphasize that in money market funds—35 percent of our asset base—performance, that is, the highest available yields, is captured by the

---

* I am told that it was the eminent mathematician Alfred North Whitehead who said, "It takes an unusual mind to undertake the analysis of the obvious."

lowest-cost funds. That is the position we hold today, and for the success of this enterprise, it is our responsibility to hold it tomorrow as well.

In bond funds—25 percent of our assets—the same principle applies, most particularly where the policies of the funds are stated with clarity and specificity, as in *insured long-term municipal bonds,* or *GNMAs,* or *intermediate-term U.S. Treasury bonds.* Under these circumstances, the margin for management error is modest, and the commensurate margin for management success is nicely enhanced by our substantial cost advantage.

In stock funds, of course, performance is much less predictable, and therefore it is much less cost dependent. For our equity and balanced funds—which make up the remaining 40 percent of Vanguard's assets—we must rely on common sense, judgment, and experience in selecting our outside managers, and wisdom and patience in evaluating them. To say the very least, these practices are fraught with fallibility in the case of relatively undiversified funds that have high portfolio concentration or aggressive investment objectives. But at Vanguard, much of this business risk is being squeezed out with each passing day, as we rely more heavily on index funds, with relative predictability that is absolutely assured. We still have almost a proprietary franchise in this arena, where low cost, again, is absolutely critical to our success.

Service Quality

Before I describe the link between performance and people, let me talk about our service. While the client survey that I mentioned earlier gave preeminence to investment results and cost-effectiveness, please make no mistake about the fact that the service tasks that nearly all of us at Vanguard undertake must be performed at the highest quality levels—and, ultimately, with zero defects—if we are to avoid being the victim of creative destruction over the coming decades.

To be sure, in the survey, one client doubtless was speaking for many when he said, "Let's not forget what we are all about. I have invested in Vanguard to make money. Give me an additional return of 3 percent and I don't care if you fire the staff, close your buildings, and work out of the back of a used Studebaker." In a sense, this kind of comment is the ultimate accolade, and it can be read to mean that our service quality is invisible—that we are ably meeting our clients' service expectations. The survey shows that, by and large, we are doing just that. So what is "convenience" to a buy-and-hold investor? What is "accuracy" to an investor who has never received an inaccurate statement? What do "courtesy" and "personalized service" mean to an investor who is consistently accorded both? What is timeliness to an investor whose only transactions are the reinvestment of twelve dividends each year? My point is that one of the marks of service quality is its very transparency.

A more satisfying, and less subtle, evaluation of our service excellence is revealed by two extensive surveys—one independent, one in-house. On February 27, 1991, *USA Today* captioned its story on mutual fund service quality, "Living Up to Its Name, Vanguard Group Leads Mutual Fund Industry in Service to Investors." The story described the *Financial World* 1991 survey, which ranked Vanguard as number 1 in service quality—the elite of the elite group—for the second straight year. This independent survey confirms the results of our recent in-house client survey, which shows that 57 percent of our shareholders regard our services as better than those of our competitors, and only 3 percent as worse. (Our service was regarded as "about the same" as the others by 40 percent.) Since one of every three Vanguard shareholders also owns Fidelity funds and one of every six owns T. Rowe Price or Dreyfus, these ratings effectively reaffirm our leadership.

People—Human Dignity and Compensation

In the final analysis, service is provided by people—those of us who talk on the telephone with our clients, those who answer correspondence, those who process transactions, those who price our funds at the close of each day, those who provide computer and technical expertise, and those who are involved in the administration of this enterprise. *You are our people, and we are your company.* We want you to understand our policies. So I'd like to discuss two issues—controversial though they may be—in response to the results of our recent *Crew's Views* survey. In both issues—human dignity and compensation—Vanguard's values come sharply into focus.

I assure you that we are utterly committed to a policy that puts a premium on human dignity. *We shall succeed by example—from the very top down—and violations will simply not be tolerated.* For I am absolutely positive that no enterprise can succeed without the support and enthusiasm of its people and that the first place to earn that support and enthusiasm is by treating people with respect and fairness.

The *Crew's Views* survey makes it clear that you agree. You rate "respect and fairness" as the most important factors in any job, far ahead of "type of work," "knowing the job," "opportunity to advance," "recognition for performance," and, yes, even "compensation."

Nonetheless, at Vanguard there is a concern among some crew members—actually about one of every four of you—that compensation is less than it might be relative to other financial services organizations. That this attitude is prevalent among the people of most other enterprises is not, for me, a satisfactory answer. So we shall be carefully studying our compensation program to assure both that it is fair and that the balance among current compensation, deferred compensation, and benefits is optimal.

As you know, our compensation program consists of four principal elements. Here are our objectives in each:

1. Our current compensation (salary) should be marginally above competitive norms, which I will define as *par plus*.
2. Our fringe benefits (largely medical and life insurance) should be *par plus plus*.
3. Our thrift and retirement plans should be *par plus plus plus*.
4. And our Vanguard Partnership Plan should be at *par plus plus plus plus*.

I am convinced—and our survey suggests that the vast majority of you agree—that we are meeting the last three of these objectives. Most of the dissatisfaction appears to center on the first component—salary—so that is where we will focus our study, as we evaluate competitive compensation in each of our job grades.

The Partnership Plan

Let me now turn to the Vanguard Partnership Plan. At this celebration, as our 1990 earnings are distributed, I want to call your attention to two of its most important aspects: first, the huge increase in its financial dimension, both in the aggregate and to each one of you as partners, and second, the sources of the earnings in which we are all sharing today.

On the financial side, we are about to distribute something like $6 million to you. This compares with $3.9 million in 1989, $1.8 million in 1987, and just $500,000 in 1985. This steady growth reflects many factors: The number of our crew members has increased enormously; the number of years each of you has served here increases like clockwork, every year; over time, many of you earn promotions in job grades; and, most importantly, our earnings per unit have grown tremendously.

Obviously, it is not possible to illustrate these factors in a simple case that fits each one of you. But let me give just one example: Assume that you joined us five years ago at a job grade of seven, and you are now at grade ten. Your units have therefore grown from 25 to 380. The earnings per unit have grown from $7.29 in 1986 to (using last year's payout—we'll keep you in suspense about this year's for a few additional moments) $12.96. Your total cash payout in this example, then, would have increased from $182 to $4,925! (I hope that I'm not tipping my hand by assuring you that it will in fact be more than $5,000.*)

To be sure, only about 500 of you have been here for more than five years, but that is not the point. Rather, the point is that in each year ahead (up until ten years of service) and with each promotion, your number of units will increase. All that remains for the continued growth in your distribution is that our earnings continue to grow.

Where Do Our Earnings Originate?

Let me now turn to the source of these earnings. (This exercise may seem tedious, but it is important!) They are derived from: (1) our low-cost advantage (that is, our fund expense ratios relative to those of our major competitors); (2) the extent to which our fund performance exceeds or falls short of the returns of our competitors; and (3) the size of our asset base. Of course, each factor interacts with each other factor. Low cost, for example, helps us to achieve high performance, which in turn is a major factor in the growth of our asset base. Together, these three elements control the checks you will soon have added to your bank account.

In reading your comments in the *Crew's Views* survey (a mere 5,000 of them!), I was stung by the fact that some of you believe that your compensation is less because of our determination to maintain our low-cost provider status. It is not so. The fact is completely the reverse: *Our low-cost advantage is the root cause of the payments you are*

---

*Earnings of $14.58 per unit were announced later. The crew member in the example will receive a gross payment of $5,540.

about to receive. It is this advantage that serves as the basis for our unique partnership arrangement and that is among the principal forces in our enormous asset growth.

From whence, then, is our low-cost advantage derived? Well, last year we operated at an expense ratio (expenses as a percentage of assets) of 0.35 percent, compared to 0.85 percent for our main competitors. However, this incredible 50-basis-point difference (up from 21 basis points in 1985 and but 4 basis points in 1980) does not "come out of the hides" of our crew (as one survey respondent put it) or indeed even relate to it. Rather, it comes principally from these three sources:

First, our truly mutual form of organization, in which profits go to our clients rather than to an outside management company. We estimate this advantage at about 30 basis points—more than one-half of the 50-point total.

Second, our internal fixed-income management, plus our fee negotiation at arm's length with external advisers, plus substantial economies of scale in money management, may well provide another 10 basis points.

Third, our unwillingness to undertake the mammoth advertising and marketing expenses incurred by our competitors—based on our conviction that market share must be earned and not bought—might account for another 10 basis points.

Note that not a single one of the major factors contributing to our low-cost-provider status is based on our operating expenses or our compensation. The point is that our low-cost achievement—in fact, one of the wonders of the financial world—is derived not from inadequate compensation but from the very structure of Vanguard's organizational form and from our investment advisory and marketing policies. This being the case, I am unabashedly proud of our achievement in putting our competitors' expense ratios utterly to shame—importantly, a fact noted over and over again by the press.

I have taken you through this tortuous path of compensation and partnership to ensure that each of you understands what we are doing and how we are doing it. I want you to be "onboard" with respect to our compensation philosophy and to be confident that—in a world of limited resources but unlimited claims upon them—our policies are enlightened and, certainly with regard to the Vanguard Partnership Plan, singularly generous. I am not saying that you have not earned the distribution you are about to receive. You *have* earned it, and you *deserve* it. With your continued support, I have no doubt that together we will provide with excellence the *people* half of the *people-plus-performance* equation that is our goal, and I thank each one of you for being part of the best crew that this industry has ever seen.

Our tasks for tomorrow are clear: working together in harmony; doing our very best to live up to our mission; making every effort to avoid the bureaucracy that too often diminishes respect and fairness to individual human beings; and continuing to earn the signal honors bestowed by independent evaluators of our performance (*Fortune:* "The clear winner is Vanguard") and our people (*USA Today:* "Vanguard Leads Industry in Service"). I hardly need to tell you this, my fellow members of the crew, but that is one dynamite combination!

Struggling with the Challenge of Growth

What remains is struggling with the challenge of rapid, almost exponential growth—successfully dealing with the tyranny of compounding—to ensure that we continue to earn top honors by remaining number 1 in the two overwhelmingly dominant determinants of our future success: people and performance. But if size has its bane, it also has its blessing: We gain the luxury of staying the course, continuing to run this enterprise our way, doing not what is expedient and expensive but what is right for us, and for those who have entrusted their money to us.

Despite the turbulence in our industry's leadership during the past forty years, so much has remained unchanged. Then, our Princeton senior waxed enthusiastic about the prospects of this business. Now a bit older, he is even more enthusiastic than ever.

Then, he called for mutual fund management "to serve investors . . . in the most efficient, honest, and economical way possible." Now he sees Vanguard as setting the industry standards in these areas, with an unparalleled reputation for integrity.

Let me sum up: Since our founding, Vanguard has been the agent of creative destruction. Many of our major competitors have been its victims. We are among a handful of firms that have been, not the destroyed, but the destroyers. Thanks to our people and our performance—accompanied by some major, if obvious, strategic decisions—we have brought the highest levels of client services and investment returns in this industry to investors who seek no more than what they deserve: *better investment programs, and better service, at better prices.* We must continue to meet those standards over the next forty years—and beyond.

DARING AND CARING

December 11, 1991

W HEN LORD Horatio Nelson, aboard the HMS *Vanguard,* caught the French armada anchored in Egypt's Abu Qir Bay on August 1, 1798, he was operating under a compelling disadvantage: The British had no charts of the anchorage. Nor did they have experienced pilots with knowledge of that shoal-studded bay. But they did have a war-tested and experienced admiral with insight and daring.

Nelson's insight was that the French ships had to be able to swing 360 degrees on their moorings. Thus, they had to have sea room all around them. With the wind coming from the north, there would almost certainly be a navigable corridor between the column of seventeen French ships and the southwestern shoreline, which lay close by. Nelson's daring was to send six of his ships of battle down the east—or open—side of the French column, where they were expected, and to send the other seven down the narrow and risky, but ill-guarded, western corridor.

The rest, of course, is history. The British fell with a fury on the surprised and overconfident French fleet. The great fight was over in scarcely six hours, the British fleet intact, the French fleet destroyed. The Battle of the Nile, to this day regarded as "the most complete victory ever recorded in naval history," was over.

That battle—and that flagship—were the inspiration for choosing the name of our enterprise. This modern-day Vanguard—the ship on which we all sail together—has also had its share of daring maneuvers. Until we began operations on May 1, 1975, there was no "Vanguard" in the mutual fund industry, nor anything like it, nor any company ever before organized in the way that we chose. We designed a truly mutual structure in which the mutual funds would control the management company—the diametrical opposite of the traditional industry form in which the management company controls the mutual funds.

And in that daring stroke—we called it "The Vanguard Experiment"—came a new, and I think far better, way of doing business in this hidebound industry.

Breaking with Tradition

Let me be clear that our daring break with tradition hardly compared with that of the British fleet at the Battle of the Nile nearly 200 years ago. But in our own mundane way, we fought a tough battle and won a major victory—indeed one without which two subsequent daring changes in Vanguard's course would not have been possible. First, it encouraged us to abandon, in 1977, our traditional distribution system—the brokerage community and its potent sales force—for a then–virtually-untested no-load distribution system based on client pull rather than sales push. This daring and highly risky decision was virtually unprecedented in financial marketing. In essence, we staked our existence on a new distribution strategy, which required independent investors to make intelligent choices. It was a good decision. Our $90 million *outflow* of shareholder investments in 1977 turned positive the very next year, steadily rising to an *inflow* of $15 *billion* in 1991. That is quite a turnaround!

In 1981, we took another daring step: Vanguard, for the first time, assumed responsibility for directly providing investment management services to the funds, the third leg of the administration-distribution-management stool on which every mutual fund complex exists. Some $1.6 billion of Vanguard money market and municipal bond fund assets were moved from external to internal portfolio managers just ten years ago. Today, our Fixed Income Group manages twenty-seven Vanguard portfolios with assets of $37 billion—just over one-half of our total asset base. This twentyfold increase in the assets that we manage directly, if not quite as dramatic as the increase in Vanguard fund cash flow, is surely awesome by any other standard.

Indexing Catches Hold

This year, we also celebrate the fifteenth anniversary of our formation of the industry's first index investment fund, Vanguard Index Trust. Our daring decision to put to the test the proposition that no management could outperform traditional management was not greeted with enthusiasm by our competitors. They described it as "un-American" or "the acceptance of mediocrity," and even as "tulipmania" (a reference to the great tulip bulb boom—and subsequent bust—in sixteenth-century Holland). The initial acceptance of Vanguard Index Trust in the mutual fund marketplace could be compared—unfavorably—with the proverbial lead balloon. Our assets were but $14 million at the close of 1976, ranking us as number 220 among 352 equity funds.

But progress, at first slow, began to accelerate. The asset rank of our Index 500 Stock Portfolio rose to number 109 at the end of 1981, to number 72 in 1986, and to number 10 (among 841 equity funds) currently. With net assets totaling $3.75 billion, this portfolio is now one of the ten largest equity funds in the world. Indeed, this comparison sharply *understates* our success since the 500 Portfolio is but one element in Vanguard's burgeoning indexing component. We now have $6 billion in index assets, spread among seven funds that span the gamut—the giant corporations in the Standard & Poor's 500 Stock Index, the remainder of the stock market, small companies, European and Pacific stocks, and even the bond market. Our daring indexing strategy, an artistic success from the outset (we succeeded in our objective of "matching the market") has become a commercial success as well. The 500 Portfolio alone could well be one of the world's *five* largest mutual funds a year from now.

Candor As a Business Strategy

Further, although it doesn't sound very novel any more, our strategy of full disclosure—call it "candor," or "honesty," or just "plain talk"—was an equally daring move for its day. When I wrote my 1974 chairman's letter to the Ivest Fund (now Vanguard World Fund) shareholders, I boldly stated, "We regard the fund's performance as unsatisfactory." While it might have even been unduly generous to describe the fund's return of –44 percent (in a –31 percent stock market) as unsatisfactory, one fund director was infuriated and appalled and in fact was soon to resign from the board. One can only imagine what he would have thought of our warning letters calling attention to the risks inherent in Windsor Fund, junk bonds, health care stocks, and GNMAs!

But there is no mystery about the benefits of candor. Making investors aware of risk is not only ethically essential but it is essential to wise shareholder relations and good public relations. In short, miracle of miracles, candor has proven to be a sensational business strategy, and Vanguard is, I think without challenge, its greatest proponent within the mutual fund industry. We have turned candor into an art form, and we distinguish ourselves by being straightforward rather than strident, understating rather than overstating, using litotes rather than hyperbole. While a television commentator recently stated that "some people in the industry think Bogle's lost his marbles," there are worse things than having Vanguard known for (as a shareholder said in a letter to me just last week) "honesty and integrity, Mr. Bogle, honesty and integrity."

I should acknowledge that there is nothing inherently advantageous about daring as such. Rather, what has earned us our credentials is daring to depart from the crowd—for common-sense reasons, and with sound judgment—and succeeding in the ensuing competitive battle, just as Nelson did at the Nile. It is *that* kind of daring—daring with a purpose—that, having sustained us throughout Vanguard's history, must sustain us in the years ahead as well. I pray that it will.

But daring won't do much good unless it is accompanied by caring. And caring *about* our clients—to say nothing about caring *for* the assets that they have entrusted to Vanguard—must continue to be accepted here as an article of faith. If you think about it, each of the five daring decisions I outlined earlier was driven by a philosophy of caring about our clients. Our initial Vanguard experiment put the shareholders in the driver's seat of fund governance, and it was to return to them staggering amounts of profits in the form of lower costs. Our no-load decision has saved them literally hundreds of millions of dollars in sales commissions. Our internal portfolio management structure now saves them something approaching $50 million in annual advisory fees. Index investing offers the market's return, and, given our minimal costs, we can be virtually certain of earning a performance premium over the average mutual fund and never be embarrassed by a bottom-of-the-deck ranking. As for candor, I guess it means neither more nor less than caring enough to give the intelligent investor the peace of mind that comes with an unquestioned spirit of honesty and fair dealing.

Caring about our clients, I should add, calls for *personal* service. We must go out of our way to empathize with their needs and concerns, accord them the courtesy that they deserve, provide them with accurate and timely information, and handle their needs with flexibility and individuality. Too often in this late-twentieth-century environment, rules and procedures have replaced judgment, recorded voices have crowded out human responses, and interminable "elevator music" has taken the place of a prompt answer. To be sure, we need some of this modern-day efficiency, but if we let our humanity go, all too soon our clients will follow. And that would be that for Vanguard.

Caring, it should go without saying at this festive celebration tonight, must also be accorded to our crew. And it is not merely a matter of salaries, or of retirement and thrift plans, or of Flexcare, or of the Vanguard Partnership Plan, as important as all of these benefits are to the kind of caring enterprise we want for our crew. It is also how we work with one another, demanding of ourselves the same mutual courtesy and respect that we provide to our clients.

In the tiny company Vanguard was when we began in 1975, I could say to our 27 crew members, "I want every one of you to treat everyone here with fairness. If you don't understand what that means, stop by my office." Now, with 2,600 crew members—a near 100-fold increase—we have a five-page memorandum entitled "Human Resource Policies and Procedures. Subject: Fair Treatment. Number: C1." While I am not sure that this is progress, I will concede that it is, in this day and age, a necessity. And our principles of fair treatment, our policies against harassment, and our practices under our long-standing open-door program, and our new open-channel program will hardly suffer from being clearly articulated. Nonetheless, all the policy manuals in the world will never replace our own selves as the ultimate source of a caring attitude.

We soon close another year of astonishing success and growth for Vanguard, so we approach yet another milestone of $75 billion in assets, less than two years after reaching $50 billion, and only a few years after reaching $25 billion. (The last "billion-dollar party" took place in 1984.) With all these boxcar numbers, however, let us never forget that it was both *daring*—daring to use our wit and daring to travel the road less traveled by—and *caring*—caring about our shareholders, to whom we owe a sacred trust, and caring about our crew, our partners together on the modern-day HMS *Vanguard*—that got us to where we are today.

Giants Can Lose Their Way

But a word of caution: Even as we have the right to be justly proud of what we have done so well, we also have the responsibility to be fully aware of what we need to do better, and indeed of what we have failed to do at all. If we do not engage in self-examination and self-criticism as our assets and crew soar, we will become just one more dinosaur on its way to extinction. Consider if you will, these three giants who have lost their way:

- *IBM, the consummate growth company of the early post–World War II era:* The price of its stock rose from a low of $1⅛ in 1952 to a high of $85 in 1972. But now, after another two decades of history, it still reposes at—you guessed it—$85 per share. Surrounded by more imaginative and mobile competitors, IBM is a troubled enterprise, a fact vividly illustrated by its announcement last week that its layoff total would reach 85,000 employees.
- *Citicorp, the largest bank in the world as recently as 1984, but now number 19:* Its stock price is down 66 percent from its 1973 high. As it struggles to recover from massive write-downs of commercial real estate, it is fighting not to recapture its past leadership but for its very life.
- *American Express, considered the nation's premier financial services enterprise just a few years ago:* Its earnings and stock price are approximately one-half of their 1987 levels. It faces tough competition in its basic credit card business, and it is awash in bad debts on its Optima card. Significantly for us, American Express recently decided to throw in the towel in its attempt to enter the mutual fund business. After three years of marketing and promotion, fund assets were but $80 million. (Who says this is an easy business?)

These are but three examples of the decline and fall of the exalted, and we will be well repaid if we learn from these lessons of business history. And we might well remind ourselves (frequently!) that "there but for the grace of God go we."

The business of investing takes place on a sea of uncertainty, so we must be ever alert to change. I have often reminded our clients that anything can happen in the securities markets. And it often does. Certainly the plunge in the bond market in the spring of 1987 is one example. The great crash in stock prices on October 19, 1987, is another. The astonishing decline in Windsor Fund's net asset value during its 1990 fiscal year is yet another. The surprises are not always negative: Consider the sharp rise in the stock market in 1991 (at least through October!), coming as it did in the face of war in the Middle East, weak economies around the world, a sharp drop in corporate earnings, a near depression in commercial real estate, and yet one more record-setting federal budget deficit ($265 billion, and counting!). How long the financial markets will ignore these problems, I do not know. But we can be certain that the voyage before us holds its full share of risks and surprises.

The Judgments of History

But when history renders its judgment, the recession of 1990 to 1991 (and perhaps 1992 as well) is not very likely to loom large. The major event that will forever distinguish 1991 will be the collapse and dismemberment of the Soviet Union. The decline and fall of one of the world's two "superpowers" is not yet over, and its consequences are completely unpredictable. Only time will tell us whether this second Russian revolution is the harbinger of peace or of war, of worldwide prosperity or of depression, of environmental cleanup or of catastrophe. But whatever the outcome, 1991 will be recorded as one of the most memorable years in all human history.

Surely that is also how we would categorize 1941. Fifty years ago, on December 7, 1941, Pearl Harbor was attacked, and I think it is fair to say that the fate of western civilization hung in the balance. Had it not been for a pair of subsequent naval battles—the Coral Sea and Midway—which, at great cost in human lives, narrowly turned World War II to America's advantage, we would certainly not be here tonight. And if these two battles resulted in victories far less complete than Nelson's at the Nile, they were equally daring, and far more crucial to the outcome of the war.

I present these grand lessons of history in 1941 and 1991 to remind us all that our impact on the world—however important to us and to our enterprise—is small. Despite Vanguard's remarkable success, we are but a dot of paint on the huge canvas of human history. All we can do to shape the world is to make sure that our long voyage—whatever the winds and seas and tides and storms of history hold—is the best that it can possibly be. For just as even one person can make a difference, so even one enterprise can make a difference. If we continue our daring—in ways large and ways small—and maintain our caring—for our clients and for one another—we shall surely achieve victory in the challenging battle that lies before us.

PRESS ON REGARDLESS

June 15, 1992

SINCE OUR partnership celebration one year ago, Vanguard has performed above and beyond my very highest expectations. I want to begin my remarks by thanking and congratulating you, each and every one of you. Together, you—the crew—represent why and how Vanguard works. We will shortly report another remarkable increase in our earnings, and in your share of these earnings, as we endeavor to recognize and to salute your vital role in our growth.

This growth has been stupendous. Our asset base has soared by $20 billion since our celebration last June, rising from the incredible sum of $66 billion to the even more incredible sum of $86 billion. And our level of business activity has been simply extraordinary. Just contemplate some of our volumes during these past twelve months:

- We have answered more than six *million* phone calls from clients and prospective clients.
- We have processed more than four *million* additional fund purchases by our shareholders.
- We have opened more than *800,000* new client accounts. That is 3,200 each business day, or 400 each working hour!
- And we have provided these services at levels that have ranked us *first* in this entire industry in service quality—for the third year in a row (the 1992 *Financial World* survey of mutual fund investors). Thank you and congratulations, *again!*

I guess that it is fair to say "We lead," once again, because of our proven strengths: Not only preeminent quality of service but fine investment returns, low cost, disciplined marketing, and common-sense values such as candor and integrity. But in the past year, I sense something new: a burgeoning acceptance of the fact that we have won acceptance as the champion of the individual investor. The financial media describe Vanguard as "the mutual fund investor's best friend," "crusader for the small shareholder," "the table-pounding advocate of low fees that doesn't sacrifice service or return," "a breath of fresh air of integrity and concern," "a maverick, with straight-to-the-point views."

But enough of all that! My purpose this evening is not to dwell on the successes of the past year nor to rest on our laurels, however broadly Vanguard has been acclaimed by industry analysts, the financial press, and certainly by the investing public. Rather, my purpose is to deliver a message to you—to sound a *certain* trumpet—about what single principle must be foremost in our minds as we look to the future:

My message is: "Press On Regardless."

Press On Regardless. It has been a familiar phrase to me almost as long as I can remember. Nonetheless, even as I pride myself as an amateur lexicographer, I am unable to cite a precise source for the phrase. The closest I could come was this quotation from Calvin Coolidge, that taciturn president of the United States who meant what he said, and said what he meant. And he did so with very few words, doubtless because he wrote his own speeches. Please listen to his words:

> **Nothing in the world can take the place of persistence. Talent will not; nothing is more common than unsuccessful men with talent. Genius will not; unrewarded genius is almost a proverb. Education will not; the world is full of educated derelicts. Persistence and determination alone are omnipotent. The slogan "Press on" has solved, and always will solve, the problems of the human race.**

Two Impostors—Triumph and Disaster

Adding "regardless" is simply a reminder that we must press on under *all* circumstances. While it is commonplace to assume that *regardless* means something like "regardless of stormy seas, failure, or even disaster," I suggest to you tonight that it also means "regardless of smooth sailing, success, or even triumph." Kipling reminded us of both in this excerpt from his stirring poem, "If":

If you can dream, and not make dreams your master,
If you can think, and not make thoughts your aim,
If you can meet both Triumph and Disaster,
And treat those two impostors just the same.

The challenge, then, is to persevere in times *thick* and times *thin* alike. Just as Vanguard pressed on to avoid disaster—our very survival was at stake during the tough, dark days following our founding in 1974 through the early 1980s—so all of us at Vanguard must press on—*perhaps even more passionately*—with our mission in these seemingly easy, bright days, and despite what can be fairly termed as our "triumph."

In a sense, then, I return to the theme that I have presented to you on several occasions over the years: the strong tendency of so many great U.S. corporations (I call them "dinosaurs") to fail to press on during their halcyon days of growth and success, indeed at the moment of their greatest success.

Perhaps it was a bit premature when I first raised this issue. As far as I can tell, that was in my remarks at our celebration of crossing the $8 billion asset milestone, way back on March 21, 1984. (Yes, in that long-ago and perhaps forgotten era, we celebrated each $1 billion dollar increase in assets.) My title was "Which Axiom?" and I contrasted the conventional wisdom of "nothing *succeeds* like success" with the more provocative concept, "nothing *fails* like success." "Which will apply to Vanguard?" I asked, and concluded, "It is up to us."

There were then just 450 of us, crowded into the lobby of our first and, then, only Vanguard building. And I am pleased to say that, despite this ever-changing world, more than half of that crew—240 of you—remains with us today. In any event, we—all of us, then and now—responded to that challenge. Surely we proved that nothing would succeed like success. At that time, Vanguard, with assets of $8 billion, was the thirteenth-largest mutual fund complex. Today, with assets of $86 billion—up more than tenfold—we rank third. To be sure, we remain behind Fidelity and Merrill Lynch in terms of total assets, although our 35 percent annual growth rate since 1984 far surpasses their respective rates of 24 and 13 percent. And, with respect to our other principal direct marketing competitors, we have, figuratively speaking, left them in the dust. For example:

- T. Rowe Price mutual fund assets then totaled $9 billion. Now, they total $24 billion. Thus, they have moved from $1 billion *ahead* of Vanguard to $60 billion *behind.*

- Dreyfus mutual fund assets then totaled $18 billion. Now they total $52 billion. Thus, they have moved from $10 billion *ahead* of Vanguard to $34 billion *behind*.

One can only imagine (with considerable delight, I must say) how T. Rowe Price and Dreyfus regard the taste of dust and what they think about this upstart of an enterprise that puts them on their mettle every single day and challenges their long-term business strategies.

The Icarus Paradox

We are not here tonight to brag about the past, however, but to challenge ourselves about the future. So I would rather talk about quite another mythological figure, Icarus. Icarus, you may recall, was given a set of waxen wings by his father, Daedalus. Despite his father's warnings not to do so, Icarus soared so high, and so close to the sun, that his wings melted. He plunged into the sea and vanished forever.

I expropriate this metaphor from *The Icarus Paradox*, a recently published book subtitled *How Exceptional Companies Bring About Their Own Downfall*. The book talks about how the trajectories of once great companies change as a result of the very success they have won. A few illustrations of these trajectories will suffice:

Strategy: From quality leadership to technological tinkering, from building to overexpansion, and from brilliant marketing to blind proliferation

Structure: From orderly to rigid, and from decentralized to oppressively bureaucratic

Culture: From entrepreneurial to insipid and political

Goals: From growth to grandeur

If you recognize here at Vanguard the incipient vestiges of some of these trajectories, it would not surprise me. And the message becomes, I think, even more pointed when *The Icarus Paradox* warns that organizations that soar so close to the sun—only to have their wings melt as they become extreme, monolithic, and insular—are most likely enterprises with these three characteristics:

1. They have been highly successful.
2. They have a strong and clearly defined culture and strategy.
3. Their leader has been in charge for a long time.

If Vanguard does not represent the most obvious manifestation of each one of those three qualities in all of American business today, surely we have few peers!

Responding to the Icarus Challenge

But it is not enough to *realize* that the waxen wings that have enabled us to soar so high may melt. *We must do something about it.* We must challenge ourselves in at least three major areas. First, *we must maintain our competitive edge.* On the offensive side, we must fire a shot across the bow of our competitors who are temporarily waiving fees and will ultimately offer reduced fees (albeit fees that are much higher than ours). Fidelity and Dreyfus are simply following a conventional price segmentation strategy that will almost surely become rife in the industry. Vanguard is introducing lower-cost funds, known as *Admiral funds,* for our larger investors. We must teach them a lesson in *real* price competition!

On the defensive side, *we must be ready for whatever challenges the markets hurl at us.* Never forget—please!—that this business is highly sensitive to the market environment, and our growth has come, in truth, during an era in which financial assets gave, I believe, the best account of themselves in all U.S. history. This environment is highly unlikely to repeat itself. Further, our business depends on providing liquidity on demand for our shareholders, but we must recognize the perversity that the more shareholders who want their money, the more difficult for us to meet their needs. Many here are amused at what I have described as the "Route 202 Scenario"—a wide line of investors from our lobby all the way out to, well, Route 202—but when the laughter reaches at its peak, danger is usually nearest. Our communications facilities, and our investment portfolios, must stand in maximum readiness for such a squeeze.

Killing the Sacred Cows

Our second challenge is to engage in profound examination of our business. As I emphasized at a meeting of our senior officers two weeks ago, we must challenge our own sacred cows, every icon of our past success. If they are no longer appropriate, we must do away with them. I listed a dozen at our meeting, but a handful will make the point here:

- The sacred cow that "we do not need to be a technology leader"
- The sacred cow that "we will not provide our clients with investment advice and asset allocation guidance"
- The sacred cow that "we will not engage in active money management"
- The sacred cow that "we do not need to meet price competition because the operating expense ratios on our funds are already so low"

Those are the sacred cows that we must kill. Our other sacred cows—which so far should remain sacred—include eschewing distribution of our fund shares by banks, holding our advertising expenditures to maintenance levels, and being unwilling to undertake major international affiliations. So it is not that all of our sacred cows should lose their sanctity (many, in my deeply held view, should continue sacrosanct) but that they all must be continually examined and challenged.

Introspection

Our third challenge is to examine ourselves, and it is a critical challenge to each one of us. Do we realize that we must press on, *regardless* of our success? Are we capable of doing so? Do we have the necessary willpower? These great questions result in a lot of smaller questions, which I ask each of you to consider with me now:

- Have we lost our sense of urgency?
- Do we work as hard as we should, and with the same old dedication?
- Are we too tolerant of inferior work, too willing to accept C and B work, too flaccid to demand A?
- Are we giving enough career development opportunities to the members of our crew?
- Do we rely too much on towering stacks of data, and not enough on common sense?
- Are we creating so much process that judgment has taken a back seat?
- And are our senior officers, including me, visible enough? Are all other officers, managers, and supervisors visible enough? Do we get out on the floor with our sleeves rolled up? Do we see and understand and, above all, respect our crew?

Truth told, it is all of you on our crew who have brought success to the Vanguard Experiment that began in 1974. If we respond, with urgency, to these challenges, Vanguard will continue to be "the mutual fund investor's best friend," and, in the years ahead, even gain force in that mission.

You Can Help

Let me read a brief quotation to you:

If Vanguard's success causes us to lose the very qualities that were responsible for that success, surely our future is not very bright. So we must maintain our strength in innovation, and not sacrifice our decisiveness, our flexibility, our entrepreneurial spirit. We must hone our competitive edge and not relinquish our willingness to work hard, our enthusiasm for what we do, our fighting spirit.

Above all, we must work together cooperatively, and simply not accept the stranglehold of red tape, the curse of corporate politics, and the impersonality of technology. We must not relax, nor think that we have some divine right to succeed or some magic formula that guarantees our success. We must not engage in self-praise about our accomplishments while ignoring our problems. In short, there is a danger when a company is doing as well as we are, and that is to think we can do no wrong.

The more things change, the more they remain the same! For that quotation comes from my "Which Axiom?" talk at our $8 billion celebration eight long years ago, which I referred to earlier. Well, a lot has happened since then, and certainly, from the vantage of 1992, it is fair to say that here at Vanguard "nothing *has* succeeded like success." Sad to say, however—as the mutual fund performance comparisons reiterate—"past performance cannot guarantee future results."

Put another way, and paraphrasing a quotation from John W. Gardner that I incorporated into my remarks when I gave the commencement address at Vanderbilt's Owen School of Management early in May:

The test for Vanguard is whether in all the confusion and clash of interests, all the distracting conflicts and cross-purposes, all the temptations to self-indulgence and self-exoneration, we have the strength of purpose, the guts, the conviction, the spiri-

tual staying power to build a future worthy of our past. You can help.

And indeed you can help, each and every one of you. If that doesn't say it all, surely Saint Paul does in his letter to the Philippians:

This one thing I do, forgetting those things which are behind, and reaching forth unto those things which are before . . . I press toward the mark.

So, press!
Press on!
Press on, regardless!
Press On Regardless!

BATTLES: A WILLING
FOE AND SEA ROOM

December 11, 1992

*T*HE SUBJECT of battle often arises amid the noble causes of human history:

- Ecclesiastes (in my favorite Old Testament passage) tells us that "the race is not to the swift nor the battle to the strong . . . but time and chance happeneth to them all" (Eccl 9:11).
- Martin Luther leads the Reformation with "A mighty fortress is our God, a fortress never failing."
- Patrick Henry, centuries later, says before the Virginia legislature that "the battle, sir, is not to the strong alone, it is to the vigilant, to the active, to the brave." (Which he shortly followed with "Give me liberty or give me death!")
- In our national anthem, Francis Scott Key describes a battle tableau in which "the broad stripes and bright stars, through the perilous fight . . . gave proof through the night that our flag was still there."
- With "The Battle Hymn of the Republic," Julia Ward Howe urges the Union to press on in the Civil War.

To all of these inspiring words, I can only add that Lord Horatio Nelson, always looking for a good battle, asked only for "a willing foe and sea room"—for an enemy ship that wants to fight, and plenty of room to do so. That is a proper metaphor for my talk tonight because I want to talk about some of the battles taking place in the mutual fund industry, how Vanguard should fight them, and why Vanguard will win them.

Five years ago, almost to this very day, soon after the Great Stock Market Crash of 1987, I stated to you that Vanguard is "like a rock," ready for whatever the future throws at it. Then, our assets were $27 billion; tonight our assets total $97 billion. That is an increase of 260 percent, a compound annual rate of 21 percent per year, and a staggering rate of growth for an institution that could have been described as mature five years ago. (I hasten to add that I mean "mature" only in the business sense and certainly not in the sense that we have lost our *joie de vivre* or our delight in celebration.)

To be sure, we are in a booming segment of a booming industry, amid booming financial markets. But we are growing far faster than our major direct marketing (no-load) competitors. Indeed, among our major foes (who may not be all that willing), Vanguard *alone* is building market share. Of our $70 billion asset *increase* over these past five years, some $30 billion—more than 40 percent—of our growth has come as a result of our increased market share. Put another way, we may be said to have wrested $30 billion in fund assets away from our competitors.

Conspicuous by Its Absence: The Invisible Hand

They are not amused. They have decided they are "mad as h____ and not going to take it anymore" (in the memorable phrase from the film *Network*). They want that money back, and they are striving to become more competitive with us. Now normally, the invisible hand of competition would drive rival firms to become more efficient, to provide better service, to reduce prices, and (in mutual fund parlance) to provide better investment performance. Alas, Adam Smith's invisible hand is conspicuous by its absence in the mutual fund industry.

Let me give you a few examples. First, our competitors are not reducing management fees. Rather, they are often *raising* fees in a major way—sometimes by as much as 50 percent or even 100 percent. But they then bury the increases by waiving all or a portion of fees for some unspecified temporary period. As an article in the *New York Times* noted, they "eventually begin to pass along expenses again, often with little fanfare." Is this a major industry trend? Indeed it is! Some 1,800 of the 3,800 mutual funds in the industry are, as the article's headline noted, "Enticing Investors by Waiving Fees." One out of every four stock funds is engaging in this subterfuge, four out of every ten bond funds is engaging in this subterfuge, and more than one-half of all money market funds are engaging in this subterfuge. What a shoddy way to compete!

Sooner or later, however, the higher advisory fee rates and additional 12b-1 distribution fees they receive combine to provide enough resources to engage in blockbuster advertising campaigns. Our largest competitor is now spending at a rate of $100 million per year in print and television, some 20 *times* Vanguard's level. Most advertising takes the thrust that a particular fund is "first in performance" and is therefore a good investment. They know, of course, as well as you and I know, that today's "first" may be tomorrow's "last," and that the odds strongly favor a future return that is more or less average. But the advertising apparently succeeds in drawing large amounts of assets into the funds. And so it continues.

Next, of course, there are the new "products." It seems that even the hint that an untested new product can be sold causes a rush of funds into the marketplace. We have seen it in short-term global funds, adjustable rate mortgage funds, and prime rate funds. Each purports to offer higher yields (in giant headlines), all the while disclaiming any comparison with money market funds (in tiny footnotes). In my judgment, when demand that is created by the illusion of performance miracles gives rise to a supply of new products offered under dubious premises and inadequate disclosure, and at a high price, then something is wrong. It may be competition, but it is not the kind of competition that Adam Smith envisioned.

All of this *should* make life difficult for any firm that is actually reducing costs, spending *less* on marketing, and having the discipline to *stand back* for at least a moment to see if the so-called new products add value (and really do offer more reward with less risk). Alas for our rivals, Vanguard's advantages—in public reputation, low costs, modest advertising that shuns hyperbole, and discipline in creating new funds—are simply too great, and our share of market continues to grow, and at a healthy rate.

Appealing to the SEC

So, the largest of our competitors—one of the great advertising, promotion, and marketing enterprises of our age—stung by the loss of its market share, decides to compete not in a free and open marketplace but by appealing for help from the U.S. Securities and Exchange Commission. No "willing foe" this one, and certainly no search for "sea room."

No, *their* firm—the name I dare not say—alleges it wants to protect *our* shareholders by derailing our building plans and our proxy process, all in the name of calling for a regulatory hearing on a so-called creative and innovative proposal that in fact has been in place at Vanguard for seventeen years. I don't know how this particular battle will end, but I can say with some confidence that this firm appears to have (in military parlance) "shot itself in the foot."

The news articles reporting on our competitor's request for an SEC hearing have elicited a blistering response—not against Vanguard but against our foe. I've received a remarkable number of letters from shareholders who own both their funds and ours, letters that are addressed to *their* chairman, copy to me. Please forgive my relish if I read you one of them, in its entirety. (Here, to be faithful to the writer's words, I must read the firm's name):

> **Fidelity's request for an SEC hearing regarding Vanguard's construction application is, for me, another reason for my growing dislike of Fidelity.**
>
> **There are many reasons, but it is your general approach to the mutual fund business that has driven me off. Fidelity has become, in my view, a conglomeration of low-load, high-expense, 12b-1 junk funds, many with little reason for being other than huckster marketing. And you squander shareholders' money on junk ads, junk mail, and junk publications.**
>
> **Moreover, I have yet to see a word in the general financial press from Fidelity regarding its concern for its investors' interests; John Bogle goes to bat for us publicly all the time.**
>
> **These and many other things have created in me an impression of Fidelity as an organization of promotion-minded profiteers and aroused in me a general sense of mistrust. Consequently, I have been moving my family's funds from Fidelity to Vanguard at every opportunity for the past several years.**
>
> **You have the stature and resources to become a highly positive influence on behalf of the industry and the investor. Unfortunately, your high public profile appears concerned only with the interests of FMR. But not with my money.**

What Should This Skirmish Mean to You?

As you can probably sense, this whole sorry affair has got me a bit more feisty and competitive than usual. And you have the right to ask: Is this just a nasty skirmish between the captains of two heavily armed warships that you should shrug off? I do not think so. First, it is all of you on the crew of the HMS *Vanguard* who have brought us to a position of such strength in the first place that a competitor must stoop to these tactics. It is your dedication to superior investor service that has brought us the industry championship in service excellence for three years in a row, truly a major force in our growth.

Second, it is all of you who have worked long and hard and productively to make us one of the most efficient—if not *the* most efficient—firms in this industry. This efficiency has made an important contribution to the cost advantage that has become our hallmark. Indeed, the use of "low cost" and "Vanguard" in the same phrase by the press has become almost a redundancy.

Third, you have stayed the course with Vanguard in your careers, gaining experience in our business and understanding of our mission. I am truly impressed with the stability of our crew, manifested in the fact that nearly 900 of you here tonight have been a part of Vanguard for at least five years. (I hope that most of you heard, even if you don't quite remember, my "Like a Rock" talk at this celebration five years ago.) There is, whether in war or in business, no substitute for the experience of battle.

You might well be concerned about how this street fight—if such it be—will affect Vanguard as an organization and affect your own careers. I would urge you not to worry. The best-built ship with the most sensible battle plan and the finest crew *will* triumph. [While Ecclesiastes noted that "the race is not (always) to the swift nor the battle to the strong," Damon Runyon retorted: "However, that's usually the best way to bet."] And I would bet that we shall be "leading the way" in this industry for a long while.

A Good Fight—Strength to the Soul, Strength to the Spirit

Let's face it: In the long run the investing public will not be denied. If it is true that our largest competitor is focused on "junk funds . . . junk ads, junk mail, and junk publications," it is hard to believe it can win a battle with a firm that is known, among other things, as being "*none* of the above." Illusory low fees, intense advertising, and hot new products all create perceptions. The reality is that none of these ploys represents durable value. And, as I have noted often in the past, "*when there is a gap between perception and reality, it is only a matter of time until the gap is resolved in favor of reality.*"

Thus, I assume that as long as we continue to stay the course, concentrate on what we do best, and deliver solid shareholder services at a parsimonious price, both our asset base and the partnership profits in which you share will continue to grow apace.

As a firm, we remain totally dedicated to what I have come to believe are the important realities of investing in mutual funds: clear objectives and precise policies; competent portfolio management; low costs that put the wind at our back in achieving our performance goals. And the willingness to be honest and direct—candor, if you will—about potential future returns and actual past returns, good and bad alike.

This summer Harvard Business School did an extensive case study on The Vanguard Group. The study was a delight to read. (We will soon be making copies available to you.) It is comprehensive, interesting, and extremely complimentary. Happily, the classes studying the case (I sat in on several) were quite willing to challenge us. One student said: "Just another PeopleExpress, cutting costs for a while, then to disappear." Another said: "Not aggressive enough in marketing; it will kill them." And a third, referring to our cost discipline and a Puritan ethic that permits no compromise, said: "They've painted themselves into a corner."

Well, if we are in a corner, it's surely the corner in which I am most comfortable—and I pray that you are comfortable in it too. And if our competitors will finally compete on lower price and higher value, rather than on higher spending and dubious marketing, they will make the mutual fund world even more competitive. Indeed, as I told the Harvard Business School class, the first sign that Vanguard's mission has created a better world for the investor will be when our market share begins to erode. By that I meant that true, honest price competition will begin to *erode* our cost advantage and make our work all the more challenging. And, if we are to draw on our highest abilities, that is the way it must be!

As you consider my words tonight, I guess you could call this a fighting speech about the battle we fight each day. But I take the liberty of being so blunt with you in the spirit of Saint Paul, who asked in his first letter to the Corinthians, "If the trumpet give an uncertain sound, who shall prepare himself for battle?" So, this is my trumpet call to you—clear and certain—to urge that you be prepared, that you continue to work so effectively and enthusiastically, and with such good humor, and that you bask in the joy of competition.

As for me, I can only echo the words of Gutson Borglum, the sculptor of George Washington, Thomas Jefferson, Abraham Lincoln, and Theodore Roosevelt on Mount Rushmore. Here's what he said:

Life is a kind of campaign. People have no idea what strength comes to one's soul and spirit through a good fight.

CHARACTER

June 14, 1993

*C*haracter IS not a word I see used very often, at least in the sense of what I regard as its most important meaning. Paraphrasing the *Oxford English Dictionary*, Second Edition (OED II), *character* is defined as "the sum of the moral and mental qualities of an individual or a nation," and, I would add, "an enterprise." The OED II then includes a lovely citation in which *character* is described as "the intellectual and moral texture into which all our life long we have been weaving up the inward life that is in us."

Character is central to Vanguard's mission. So this evening I want to speak to you about character and the role that it has played in Vanguard's development. To this end, let me set the stage by bringing you up to date on the remarkable strides we have taken so far in 1993:

- Early in the year, our assets crossed the $100 billion mark, the third fund group to reach this milestone. The breakthrough came on January 18, which we designated as "Majestic Milestone Day." But I say to you now what I wrote to you then: "This staggering sum, in and of itself, is only money, and in the final analysis, it is not especially significant. But the fact that it is *other people's money*, entrusted to our stewardship, is of surpassing importance."
- Late in March, we became the second-largest fund complex in the world, passing the Merrill Lynch funds. It too was hardly a monumental event. Since our assets have been growing at a rate of +34 percent annually since 1980 compared to +14 percent for Merrill Lynch, it was only a matter of time until the lines on the chart would cross.

- In February, we won the *Financial World* award as the highest-quality provider of investment services in the mutual fund industry. While the construction of the survey leaves a bit to be desired, it was good to receive this recognition. That said, I would rather be a high-quality company by meeting *our own standards* than win an award for being a high-quality company by meeting *someone else's standards.*
- As the year began, we provided our individual shareholders, for the first time, with a consolidated portfolio summary, listing the holdings of all of their Vanguard Funds in a single statement. With this enhancement, we expect to provide even better service at an ever better price. This forward step, while overdue, was made possible by the round-the-clock efforts of a team comprising, at one time or another, more than fifty crew members. It was one of the most complex projects in our history, and it is a tribute to teamwork at Vanguard.
- We have made great progress on our Information Technology (IT) Voyage. Our objective is not merely to make Vanguard *the* technology leader of our industry but to integrate sophisticated information technology into *every aspect* of our burgeoning operations. We have high hopes that the new technology will not only create substantial efficiencies but enrich the quality of our jobs.
- Finally, to anticipate just a bit, the move to our new campus will soon begin. The first two buildings should be occupied in September, with one more occupied by the end of the year. The idea of the new campus is, simply put, to bring us all together. (Again!)

In one way or another, each of these events is a manifestation of Vanguard's character. It is this character, and, I think, our attitude toward growth, that makes us stand out above all of the other firms in this booming industry. Consider the asset growth in these various segments since 1987:

Percent Change in Assets, December 31, 1987, through March 31, 1993

Brokerage firm channel	+85%
Direct marketing (no-load) channel	+174
The Vanguard Group	+298

That our growth comes with neither a huge nationwide sales force to compete with the brokers, nor with a huge advertising budget to compete with the free-spending direct marketers, speaks volumes about Vanguard. We are content to provide the very best mutual funds, at the very lowest costs, with the very highest service quality, and then rely on the good sense of intelligent investors to beat the proverbial path to our door. Or, as I said in my year-end talk in 1991, "If we build it, they will come."

The Character of the Enterprise

We are blessed by the fact that Vanguard, which began operations on May 1, 1975, is such a young company. It has, therefore, been relatively easy to have dedicated "all our life long [to] weaving up our inward life into the intellectual and moral texture" that gives us the character that distinguishes us today. What is the character of Vanguard? It rests on three basic elements, and it is not very complicated:

1. *We shall manage the Vanguard Funds solely in the interests of our shareholders.* This principle goes to the heart of our low-cost, high-quality service strategy.
2. *We shall provide adequate, accurate, and explicit information to investors.* This principle defines our strategy for communicating with shareholders, prospective investors, and the media.
3. *We shall ensure that the Vanguard Funds are subjected to adequate independent scrutiny.* This principle is a manifestation of our belief that a fund organization should manage its own affairs, with the careful oversight of strong and independent directors.

Michael Porter Speaks

These elemental principles, set forth in our 1992 annual reports under the title "Where We Stand," carry over to our corporate strategy. Here, however, I shall rely, not on my subjective view but on the objective view of America's preeminent academic expert on global corporate strategy, Professor Michael E. Porter of Harvard Business School. In his keynote speech at the recent general membership meeting of the Investment Company Institute, Dr. Porter read the audience of industry executives the proverbial riot act, telling them that the industry has grown fat and lazy and that it is in danger of losing its competitive edge. It has become a "me-too" industry, he said, with most companies undifferentiated from one another and "stuck in the middle."

Then, to the horror of our rivals in the crowded hall, Dr. Porter said that only a single firm in the entire industry had differentiated itself from the pack. It was, he said, Vanguard, and he cited us as having a "genuine, unique, sustainable competitive advantage." He told our competitors that they will soon learn from the Vanguard challenge what rivalry is all about and that they "haven't seen anything yet."

I wish that I could fully express to you my delight, seated as I was in the audience, at Dr. Porter's insights and his recognition of what Vanguard is all about. You have heard my words about our strengths before, so let me give you his words:

1. Steady and consistent fund performance . . . if not always the best, highly predictable
2. Sole focus on the direct distribution channel
3. Limited advertising . . . highly effective word of mouth
4. Good, but not exceptional, service [I think he was misinformed here.]
5. Strict control of costs . . . no perquisites
6. Tough bargaining power with outside advisers

Still addressing himself to Vanguard (the only firm he named during his ninety-minute presentation), he accused us of being a "measured, careful, gentlemanly competitor," but he warned industry executives to get ready for the intense competition that lies ahead. He pointed out that price competition (he called it "the price war") in the money market field will soon expand into bond funds and then into stock funds. Dr. Porter recognized a fact that our competitors insist on ignoring: Blockbuster competition is on the way. While it will be detrimental to fund managers (at least initially), it will be beneficial to fund shareholders. This is called "poetic justice"!

In trying to visualize why the cost of mutual fund investing is so important, my forthcoming book, *Bogle on Mutual Funds*, abandons the threadbare premise that "risk and return go hand in hand" and replaces it with "the eternal triangle: risk, return, and cost." Simply put, other things held equal, lower cost means higher return. Or, more circuitously, each additional increment to cost erodes the risk premium to which an investor is entitled. It is that principle—and Vanguard's willingness to build a business on it—that will ultimately make this industry a better place for investors.

The Character of the Crew

So far, I have discussed character in the *corporate* sense. But we must never lose sight of the fact that, in the final analysis, it is character in the *individual* sense that drives Vanguard. It is you and those seated around you—at your jobs and under this tent—crew members, petty officers, officers, the whole gang. Every day that you arise and come to work, you collectively determine Vanguard's future. I am consistently struck by my personal observations of your work ethic, your diligence, your commitment, your loyalty, your team spirit, and your sense of humor.

These characteristics are evident in those crew members to whom our Awards for Excellence will shortly be presented. The letters I get from our clients every day, the fabled Bogle barometer, also evidences them. To be sure, many letters are legitimate complaints about service problems, and some are rather mean-spirited. But there are enough generous comments to make me preen with pride. These excerpts from a few recent letters from all over America will give you the idea:

> *From Anchorage, Alaska:* **Each year during May I write my letter of homage and thanks to people who have made a positive good in my life. . . . Your people are gracious, knowledgeable, and helpful, the result of good management and training. I heap blessings upon you.**
>
> *From Pittsburgh, Pennsylvania:* **Your organization reflects integrity and credibility every single time.**
>
> *From Apple Valley, Minnesota:* **Vanguard's no-loads, low operating costs, outstanding shareholder reports, investment alternatives, and good returns are ideal for us.**
>
> *From Milville, New York:* **I would like to tell you how pleased I am with every member of your staff. As a new investor, I had tons of questions and many moments of hesitation. But whenever I called to get information, there was total cooperation from every person I spoke to at Vanguard. They were all helpful, polite, and encouraging. I never heard a harsh word, or a telephone that was always busy or never answered or just total indifference as I have experienced with other mutual fund groups.**

From San Ramon, California: With Vanguard I always got to talk to a representative immediately. I was never put on hold, never rushed, and never made to feel like the representative enjoyed anything more than talking to me. With each call my trust in Vanguard grew. Here were *people.* And I think this is the finest compliment I can give your telephone representatives: They brought the cold, distant *organization* down to a personal one-on-one level.

I'm sure I need remind no one here tonight that creating this good-will, making this difference—whether you are on the firing line of client services or investor information, or closing out the fund's asset value for the day, or working around the clock to fix a bug in the computer system, or mailing out some of the 20 million statements we'll provide to investors this year—is why we are able not just to have this celebration tonight but to give you *your* share of the profits you have helped us earn for our Vanguard shareholders.

In a few moments, we will report to you on our earnings per unit for 1992. The growth is substantial, with earnings reaching another all-time high. That said, however, I want to candidly report to you that our earnings increase has been moderated a bit by some changes we have made in the competitive group of funds against which we measure ourselves in terms of comparative costs, the most important factor in our earnings calculation. Some of our once-strong rivals are fading away; new rivals have emerged to test our mettle. The former have been removed from our group, replaced by the latter. Thus, our substantial earnings growth comes in the face of a sterner and more realistic standard—a higher hurdle rate—against which to compare our results. Setting higher standards is, as you will read tomorrow in my annual Vanguard Partnership Plan message, emblematic of what Vanguard must do in every aspect of our operations: *Measure ourselves against our toughest competition.*

The Revolution in Financial Services

While the competition will intensify—sooner or later, our competitors will tire of being whipped in the marketplace—we remain very favorably situated. As it happens, part by luck and part by design, Vanguard is in the vanguard of the competitive revolution now taking place in American marketing. *Forbes* magazine calls it "the death of the salesman . . . with more Americans shopping by computer, television, or telephone, buying what they want quickly and efficiently." It is taking place in the financial services field as well, using *Forbes'* specific example, with "the customer's man at the local office of Merrill Lynch threatened by a far more efficient way of distributing financial products [their word!], through a computer operated by The Vanguard Group out of Valley Forge, Pennsylvania."

At almost the same moment, this theme was echoed in the *Wall Street Journal* in an op-ed article by Charles R. Morris: "The restructuring of the mutual fund industry is being led by direct marketers like . . . Vanguard, which offer the most modern technology, much lower loads and costs, and excellent round-the-clock service by capable representatives. . . . Portfolios offered by Vanguard, the low-cost leader, have no up-front charges, and annual fees of only about 0.25 percent. . . . As customers slowly catch on, there is extreme pressure on fees throughout the industry . . . with increasing use of indexed funds at a fraction of a typical fund's management cost. . . . The industry that is emerging will be completely computerized, almost entirely without paper transaction records, much less labor intensive, and with much tighter cost constraints."

In such an environment—and I have no reason to doubt that it will prevail—even more will be required of each one of you in our crew. It will make demands on our corporate character and our individual character, and, I believe, ultimately make virtually every task we perform at Vanguard more interesting and more challenging. Yet it is paradoxical that the more we grow, the tougher the challenge is to maintain our own character. Encouraging and satisfying as our growth is, each further stage calls for more vigilance against the perils of bureaucracy. I urge you once again to join with me in assuring, as best we can, *the triumph of judgment over process.* Vanguard didn't get where we are today merely by rules and regulations, manuals and meetings, planning and budgeting, necessary as they all may have become as our crew has grown from 28 in 1975 to 3,200 today. We got here together because of our *character:* integrity, judgment, imagination, intuition, diligence, and common sense, all seasoned with a little foresight and a lot of luck.

A Search for Chaos?

A recent article in *Chief Executive Officer* magazine was right on point, noting that "the larger and more mature a company grows, the less entrepreneurial it is likely to become." It begins to focus upward (to satisfy each higher level of management) and inward (to the structure of the organization itself), rather than focusing downward (giving more responsibilities to the people in the organization) and outward (servicing the client). As the company grows, in the words of the article describing the value of a "down-and-out" strategy, "requests seem to multiply. Budgets, personnel forecasts and performance reviews must be filled out on a regular basis according to policies and procedures. In addition, there are ongoing requests for updates, reviews, special projects, and committees, . . . and soon special customer needs are viewed as an inconvenience, not an opportunity."

The article then presents this wonderful anecdote about Ross Perot during his brief association with General Motors:

> **He saw something that needed to be done and directed a manager to do it. The man replied that it was not part of his job description. Perot responded, "You need a job description, I'll give you one: Use your head!" The manager snapped back, "If everybody around here did that, we'd have chaos."**

You can put me on the Ross Perot side of that anecdote. But before any members of our management team faint, I want to make it clear that I am not calling for chaos at Vanguard. Rather, I am asking each one of you here today to use your head, to bring more judgment to your work, and to assume more responsibility for what you do. I think that "character" is a fair way to describe what I have in mind.

Endurance and Courage, Faith and Hope

Of course we shall do what we must in the rigor and discipline of our daily duties. But let us never forget this: *What defines Vanguard is not our process but our character—our mental and moral constitution.* Reviewing Paul Kennedy's book, *The Rise and Fall of the Great Powers,* James Kurth used these fine words, and the last words I shall use tonight:

> **The best way—for a nation and a person [and for an enterprise]—to prepare for the twenty-first century will be what has always been the best way to prepare for uncertainty. That is to rely not so much upon the outer supports of plans, programs, and policies but upon the inner strengths of character—resiliency and resourcefulness, discipline and cooperation, endurance and courage, and, perhaps above all, faith and hope.**

WHEN BREEZES AT OUR BACK TURN TO HEADWINDS AT OUR BOW

September 17, 1993

ON SEPTEMBER 18, 1983, I had the privilege of dedicating the Vanguard Financial Center, down the road in Chesterbrook, our previous home. Now, ten years later, almost to the day, the dedication of this magnificent new 200-acre campus—ten *times* the size of our earlier office space—is a symbol of how far we have come and how fast we have arrived here and how much we have proved in the space of but a single decade.

Many of us working at Vanguard, day after day, accept growth as a kind of given, something that we take for granted, something that hardly seems remarkable. But comparing our enterprise from point to point in time is certainly enough to make us sit back and take notice. For example:

- A decade ago, our mutual fund assets totaled $7 billion. Today, Vanguard's assets total $121 billion, a seventeenfold increase.
- Then, we offered twenty-six separate fund portfolios. Now, we offer sixty-nine portfolios, six of which, on their own, exceed our $7 billion initial asset base.
- Then, our crew numbered 430 members. Now, including 140 members who have been with us the entire decade, it numbers 3,400.
- Then, we were receiving 2,000 telephone calls from investors on a typical day. Now, we receive more than 40,000 each day, about

half of which are handled by our automated phone exchange service.

- Then, some 500,000 shareholders had entrusted us with their assets. Now, shareholders number nearly 4 million, a staggering total—and a staggering trust.

It would be nice to be able to say "We did it all ourselves." And I would not gainsay that we did much of it ourselves. Surely our central and defining concept that we exist to serve only one master—our body of mutual fund shareholders—combined with our no-sales-commission distribution philosophy together provided our investors with extraordinary cost savings, in an industry in which cost-effectiveness becomes, day by day, an ever more powerful idea. The new concepts and innovations—market indexing is but one, if by far the most radical, example—that we have pioneered have played a major role. And the investment returns we have achieved in our fund portfolios have met the highest professional standards.

If our *macroprinciples* and *macroaccomplishments* have been central, surely they alone would not have engendered the growth we have enjoyed. Enterprise is a *microaffair*, for no idea is so good that it alone can carry a company to the pinnacle. Thousands of crew members, making thousands of decisions, day after day, provide Vanguard with the necessary microframework of "resiliency and resourcefulness, discipline and cooperation, endurance and courage, and, perhaps above all, faith and hope." Taken together, these are the qualities I described in my remarks to our crew at our partnership picnic this past summer as "the inner strengths of character" we required. *Character*, then, is the watchword of our success.

A Burgeoning Industry

But much of our growth results from the simple happenstance that we at Vanguard have plied our trade in a burgeoning industry. (Happily, as I've often noted, doing so also gives the chief executives of firms in those industries far more credit than they deserve.) And our industry has grown not only because its A-B-C principles—investment diversification, professional management, and convenience—came to win their long-overdue endorsement by the marketplace but because we have enjoyed the most salutary, productive, profitable decade for financial assets in the entire recorded history of the United States of

America. (It began with a huge market upsurge just one year before our building dedication of ten years ago.) Add to this a favorable tax environment—punctuated by the dawning of an era of sharply lower federal tax rates, the individual retirement account, and the 401(k) thrift plan for corporate employees—and we had it our way to an extent unimaginable on September 18, 1983.

But, at the risk of "raining on the parade" of this wonderful occasion of celebration, I must say that it is just as unimaginable that the next decade will be the equal of the past. We have enjoyed a decade with the breezes at our back almost unremittingly. In this ever-market-sensitive field, it is a question not of *whether* but of *when* the tailwinds will turn on us and become headwinds. In my 1983 dedication speech, I quoted these stirring words:

> Sailors know what some citizens have forgot in this latter day: that no purpose is achieved, nor any course made good upon God's ocean, until first you have trimmed your sails and set the helm to fit His winds and the set of His tide upon the deep.
>
> Keen is the mariner's eye to discern those telling signs upon the clouds, at the line 'twixt sky and water, or on the crest of waves where the spindrift blows, by which he might foretell the bluster or the calm, the weather God has in store for him.
>
> And if he is so fortunate as to find a wind that blows from Heaven exactly in the direction he would go on earth, then easy and gay the skipper who can barrel down before that wind, all canvas set, rolling along upon the bosom of the blast.
>
> This has been America in these latter times; affluent and easy, not having to work very hard to run out her log: just cruising wing and wing, tide and breeze at her back, and the men lolling upon the deck. . . .
>
> But more often in this world it is a headwind that we face. Then, although the bearing of your destination be precisely the same, you have to tack back and forth, back and forth; close-hauled; wind in your face, spray on your legs; fingers white upon the sheet; body tense against the bucking tiller; fine-tuning your lively lade to the majestic forces of splendid Creation; and so wresting from that opposing wind the destiny of your desire.
>
> That's when your boat must need be staunch and true, well braced and put together, and lithe like a living thing. And that is when the sailor too is on his mettle, no less in command for all his reverences in the presence of a power mightier than his own.

This evocative passage was part of a sermon given on July 4, 1976, by the Very Reverend Francis B. Sayre, Jr., dean of Washington Cathedral, to mark the occasion on July 4, 1976, when a parade of tall ships arrived in Newport in honor of our nation's birthday. Surely those words symbolize the decade we have enjoyed: a wind that has blown from Heaven exactly in the direction that we would go on earth, a climate affluent and easy, an environment for our industry that could not conceivably have been more salutary.

Yesterday's Tailwinds, Tomorrow's Headwinds?

But, as we dedicate this campus, we must, more than ever before, be ready for the headwinds we will surely face one day. Then, we'll be tacking, close-hauled, wind in our faces, wresting from that opposing wind the destiny of our desire. The signs are everywhere: High valuations in the U.S. equity markets; interest rates that seem far more likely to rise than decline; price inflation that will not be kept in rein forever; the emergence of the mutual fund industry as the dominant investment choice for individuals; an industry that, while promising liquidity to all investors, is now of a size that limits liquidity, by definition, to only some; an industry whose traditional focus on long-term investors has been, to an important degree, subordinated to the whims of short-term traders; an industry suffused with cash flows that have dwarfed anything ever seen before. These are all signs that risk is high, and we ignore them at our peril.

We all must be ready to face these challenges. Our ship must be staunch and true, well braced and put together, with sailors on their mettle, no less in command for all their reverences in the presence of a power mightier than their own. Believe me, each one of us can make a difference, as we surmount the challenges before us just as we have surmounted them since Vanguard took the road less traveled by— indeed, never traveled before, or since, by our competitors—when we were incorporated in September 1974.

My First Building Dedication

It is another curious accident of the calendar that almost exactly *twenty* years ago, on August 24, 1973, I dedicated Wellington Management Company's new building at Glenhardie, just a few miles from here, and adjacent to our nation's historic Valley Forge National Park. Within months, Wellington Management Company and I would reach a parting of the ways, and the door leading to Vanguard's creation would miraculously open. At that dedication, I tried to express some ideas that would endure. I repeated them in my next dedication speech on September 18, 1983, and today, on September 17, 1993, in what is doubtless my final opportunity to dedicate a Vanguard headquarters, I repeat them here:

> **Some 200 years ago, and perhaps only 2,000 yards away, America went through her first crisis. The winter in Valley Forge, history books tell us, was a rugged, bitter test for a tiny army, which not only survived but went on to earn the independence too many of us take for granted today. Now, two centuries later, America is again being tested, and it is hardly an exaggeration to say that every institution in our society, from the White House on down the line, is being challenged—challenged to reassess its goals, its values, its contributions to society.**
>
> **The challenges are profound, and they affect overwhelmingly the environment in which we do our work. In addition, the challenges are directed to those institutions which we refer to as "financial institutions"—including our own. Despite the billions of dollars entrusted to us, our company is small and fragile, and perhaps even unimportant in the vast context of space and time. Nonetheless, by doing our work as best we can, we can be better and stronger as individuals, and we can make this ambitious and interesting organization better and stronger too. Each of us, then, can in a small way be a positive force in helping to make this land just a little bit better.**
>
> **I believe that even one person can make a difference. Thus, I dedicate this building to the individuals in our company—the individuals who got us started with the founding of Wellington Fund sixty-five years ago, the individuals who work with us today, and the individuals who, God willing, will come forth to assure our future.**

So it comes down to us. If we each do our share, and if our sails are trimmed and our helm is set, we can indeed follow "a course made good upon God's ocean" in the years ahead. It may well be a harder course, but it will be a good course and a winning course. Of that I am supremely confident.

We are an enterprise with a heritage that comes from a naval battle fought by Great Britain nearly 200 years ago. But we are also an enterprise that never could have come as far as fast had we not existed in the

United States of America. So I'd like to close this dedication with the great bell atop our Majestic building tolling the cadences of Katharine Lee Bates's "America the Beautiful" as I read three of its verses:

> **O beautiful for spacious skies,**
> **For amber waves of grain,**
> **For purple mountain majesties**
> **Above the fruited plain!**
> **America! America!**
> **God shed his grace on thee**
> **And crown thy good with brotherhood**
> **From sea to shining sea!**
>
> **O beautiful for Pilgrim feet**
> **Whose stern impassioned stress**
> **A thoroughfare for freedom beat**
> **Across the wilderness!**
> **America! America!**
> **God mend thine every flaw,**
> **Confirm thy soul in self-control,**
> **Thy liberty in law!**
>
> **O beautiful for patriot dream**
> **That sees beyond the years**
> **Thine alabaster cities gleam**
> **Undimmed by human tears!**
> **America! America!**
> **God shed his grace on thee**
> **And crown thy good with brotherhood**
> **From sea to shining sea!**

May God bless you, each and every one, always.

COUNTING OUR BLESSINGS

December 15, 1993

I HOPE YOU will forgive me for not beginning this message for Christmas and the Holy Days in today's more conventional terms such as "Season's Greetings" or "Happy Holidays." But I have chosen a title that seems to me to better give us the opportunity, whatever faith we may hold, to reflect on who we are as individuals, families, and shipmates, and to express our gratitude to the Almighty, and to count our blessings.

Certainly, after surviving yet another adventure with my failing heart, I'm counting my own blessings. My recuperation is coming along splendidly, but, alas, I'm in no position to deliver my remarks in person, nor was I able to attend "the circus that came to town" for our Holy Day party several weeks ago. But I do want to thank each one of you for your good wishes in the Christmas card that you signed for me at the party, which had 6,000 signatures on it! The boost you gave to my morale sent my spirit skyward, and my heart promptly followed its beneficent example.

The Blessings of a Revolution

One of the great blessings we all share, of course, is that Vanguard has been a part of a revolution in the financial industry of the United States. *It is history that did this, and not we ourselves.* Mutual funds have now surpassed banks as the investment of choice for America's households. Our industry assets now exceed $2 trillion ($2,000,000,000,000!), approaching the $2.4 trillion total for our competitors in the nation's banking institutions, which have been in the savings business for—give or take a few years—a century and one-half longer than we have. Just think of it:

- Twenty years ago, our industry had just $11 in assets for each $100 in bank assets.
- Ten years ago, we managed $18 per $100.
- As recently as five years ago, in 1988, our share had risen to $32 per $100.
- And today, of course, the number is something like $80 of mutual fund assets per $100 in bank assets.

These may seem, in the abstract, like dry statistics. But they are presented here for a reason: so that we all (especially I!) maintain a sense of humility and balance and not take our remarkable success for granted. *It is almost impossible to stay dry while swimming in such an ocean.* Although, come to think of it, a fair number of our earlier competitors of the 1950s and 1960s no longer exist, and even a great many strong firms have participated only marginally in the industry's growth. Indeed, Vanguard has achieved since 1987 the largest growth in share of market of any firm—bar none—in this industry.

The banks, not being stupid, have watched our industry's growth, first with curiosity and skepticism, and then with envy and even panic. They are now in the game, having started by selling the mutual funds of many of our competitors. (But only if they receive sales commissions for doing so!) They are just beginning to start their own mutual funds, with assets presently about $95 billion in the aggregate. Two-thirds of this total is in money market funds, suggesting that the banks are still struggling to become "full-service" providers. But while their assets are approaching the $100 billion mark that we crossed on Majestic Milestone Day, January 18, 1993 (I hope that each of you takes as much pride in our celebratory Tiffany bowls as I do!), their progress has been slow. Nonetheless, banks as a group will surpass even Vanguard's present $125 billion asset total, sooner rather than later. Not to worry!

Several weeks ago, to much hoopla and fanfare, the first takeover of a major fund group (Dreyfus) by a major bank (Mellon) occurred. My own insight is that it is destined for failure, at least in terms of either firm's solving the other's not-inconsequential problems. But it is big (Dreyfus, with $74 billion in assets, is, after all, the sixth-largest fund complex), and it is brazen. But it *looks* important only because the press—in its stereotypical and often superficial way—makes it *seem* important. The press calls this acquisition "the wave of the future," and doubtless some mutual fund magnates will not only read it but believe it. So more bank acquisitions of today's independent fund complexes may lie ahead.

The Blessings of Independence

Being acquired by a bank does not lie ahead for Vanguard. (I'm told that I have little difficulty in making my points with clarity!) Our independence—something that I think we all take too much for granted—should be one of our most treasured values. Not just in the abstract but as the key to almost everything we do. We are not subject to the power (or even whim) of public stockholders (or even private). We do not rely on a giant retail (here, I mean "retail") sales force, which calls the shots for so many of our rivals. We start new funds that make sense to us, and we need never pander to an investor marketplace that—all too often—wants just the wrong funds at just the wrong time. (Government-plus bond funds, adjustable rate mortgage funds, and short-term global income funds come to mind.)

With independence, we act solely in the best interest of our Vanguard shareholder-owners, as best that we can see it. And we accept the consequences of our actions. But don't forget that we've made lots of errors in timing and judgment. Notably, our record in selecting advisers for our new funds and our multimanager funds and in terminating existing adviser contracts suggests not only what a tough business this is but how fallible we all (again, especially I) can be.

It is, I pray, our independence that will help us solve Vanguard's major current challenge: trying to retain a warm, personal environment in which *judgment* rules rather than a cold, bureaucratic organization in which *process* is king. We are well on the way toward having a crew of 4,000, and it is difficult to see not growing well beyond that number. Every one of us—from me, to our senior officers, and right down the line—needs to do our best to surmount the monumental challenge in which bigness equals bureaucracy. I am hardly discouraged by the fact that I cannot think of a single American corporation that has succeeded in this crusade. *After all, we are Vanguard.* And we have the independence to make our own crusade succeed.

On that note, I wish I could tell you how proud I am of our information technology group in playing such a vital role in meeting this challenge of growth. With the truly incredible advances in interactive video and computerization, we have the opportunity to capitalize on this crescendo of electronic communication, operating with greater efficiency and providing more meaningful jobs and careers in a more humane environment.

The Bane of Bureaucracy

Today, it seems to me that the risks of overmanagement are often far too close to the realities. We have grown to a size (and exist in a world) in which we need an extensive, complex manual of practices and standards of conduct—a rule book—for our crew members. I know it's necessary, but I don't love it. And I hope we can continue to be guided by *Bogle's rule:* "Do what's right. If you're not sure, ask your boss."

I've learned something about our rules through our Open Channel communication program, whereby crew members can express their concerns anonymously, receive a response from the senior officer running the appropriate division, and then critique the response. It has provided a remarkable means of enabling our management to give full consideration to the *real* issues that affect our crew members' work lives daily. Through an Open Channel that I received a few weeks ago, I learned that our Policy D-2 on absence by reason of illness requires that (1) crew members (no spouses allowed!) (2) inform their supervisors (3) preferably within an hour prior to the beginning of their workday. Furthermore, (4) voicemail messages don't qualify. Now, I know that, as a company that prides itself on high service quality, we need to know when a crew member is going to be absent. But we should enable our managers to administer Policy D-2, and other rules too, with one eye toward the policy and the other eye toward using their own judgment. *Justice, as it were, should be tempered with flexibility, understanding, and compassion.* Otherwise, we shall all wake up to the eternal verity expressed by Pogo: "We have met the enemy, and he is us."

I hope these comments make clear my view that it is the enemy *within* (bureaucracy) rather than the enemy *without* (among many others, the banking industry) that is of the most concern to us today. My recently published book, *Bogle on Mutual Funds*, I hope, will help

deal with the enemy *without,* and I cannot tell you how much pride
having the book published has already given me.

Three Generous Comments about My Book

I have received scores of wonderful letters from readers, and I thought
you might enjoy these excerpts from three of those letters:

> *From New York:* **After studying your fine book, I get this feel-
> ing: that you look at this whole thing in a very honest, responsi-
> ble-to-the-public spirit, a spirit of wanting to help people. . . .
> Thanks for your moving book—an unusual accolade for a book
> on finance. This is more than a book on finance. It's almost
> poetic.**
>
> > *From Healdsburg, California:* **This is probably one of thou-
> > sands [of letters] you'll receive complimenting you for your
> > recent honest book. That Warren Buffett made that very point is
> > a reflection of his own integrity. . . . It is an inspiration to many
> > of us that there are still business executives who care enough
> > about their character and their fellow man to reject demeaning
> > behavior. . . . I've bought copies for my daughters with the
> > advice that they "read, mark, learn, and inwardly digest" your
> > book.**
>
> *From the former president of the Association of Investment
> Management and Research, which represents the financial ana-
> lyst profession:* **Jack, you hit a home run! History will record its
> immeasurable value to the investing public, and to those who
> are counseling both personal and pension money. For your life-
> time of wisdom, wit, and experience to have gone unrecorded
> would have been a tragedy. From one small corner of the
> world—Thanks! Forget being humble, and take great pride in
> the enormous contribution you have made.**

Please forgive me for accepting the urging of the writer of the
final excerpt to "forget being humble," if only for a moment. I know
it is bad form. But the intelligent understanding of mutual funds,
especially now that funds approach banks as the principal custodian
of the savings of American households, makes any worthwhile contribution important. I hope the book meets at least that standard.
And I hope that, over the years, it will serve as a symbol of intelligent
investing not just for my reputation but for the very core of our Vanguard character.

Three Final Blessings

This message gives me an opportunity to reaffirm—in this burgeoning, changing industry—that the "star we steer her by" remains as unchanged as any constellation, and it will remain ever so as long as we protect Vanguard's cherished independence. It also gives me an opportunity to wish, during Christmas and this Holy season, the blessings of life, love, and hope for each of you and your families.

THE ROAD LESS
TRAVELED BY . . .

June 14, 1994

W ELCOME TO the ninth celebra-
tion of our partnership—our mutually constructive partnership with
one another, and with our clients. Traditionally, this is my moment to
thank you for who you are and for what you do, and to formally provide
you with your fair share of the extra rewards you have helped us to earn
for those who have entrusted their assets to our stewardship.

Since I missed my customary talk with you last December, I'm
especially happy to be here. Counting the year-end written message I
sent to you then, this is the twenty-eighth time—at parties celebrating
various billion-dollar, ten-billion-dollar, and one-hundred-billion-
dollar milestones, building dedications, holiday celebrations, and partnership meetings—I've had the opportunity to share directly with you
my thoughts about Vanguard, the mutual fund industry, competition,
people, history, and philosophy.

It's been a long voyage, with some long speeches, a fact brought
home to my by this note one crew member sent me a while ago: "If I
had but twenty minutes left on earth, I should like to spend it listening
to one of your marvelous partnership speeches—honest, enlightening,
philosophical, sonorous, and powerful." Of course, I reveled in it.
However, the note instructed me to turn the page over. I did so and
read this: "It would seem like an eternity!" Despite the advice suggested by this apocryphal story, I'll probably be pretty true to form and
time this evening. I have an important message I'd like to share with
you, so please sit back, relax, and enjoy the moment.

The theme I have chosen will be familiar to many of you. It is an excerpt from "The Road Not Taken" by Robert Frost:

I shall be telling this with a sigh
Somewhere ages and ages hence:
Two roads diverged in a wood, and I—
I took the one less traveled by,
And that has made all the difference.

Those words, of course, describe our journey as well in that we also took the road less traveled by when we began the Vanguard venture nearly two decades ago. The idea of managing mutual funds solely in the interest of the shareholder was a revolutionary concept. (I still wonder why.) *That powerful idea was then and is now Vanguard's greatest strength.* We've had a wonderful and productive trip down this long and lonely road, a trip that has yet to be taken by any other firm in this entire industry.

The Early Challenges: 1974 through 1981

As far as I can recall, the first time that I used the theme of "the road less traveled" was in a Vanguard memorandum dated February 1977, after we had made our second revolutionary decision: to go no-load, to eliminate all sales charges, and to abandon the broker distribution system that had supported our predecessor company, one way or another, since Wellington Fund began operations in 1929. We take what we now call "direct marketing" for granted today, but when we made our decision, no-load funds accounted for but $4 billion of industry assets—less then one-thirtieth of the assets of Vanguard alone today.

The 1977 no-load decision was notable for two reasons: First, we had experienced net cash outflow from our funds every month since our founding. Nautically speaking, we were "in irons," sailing backward—a pattern that was to persist in each of the first thirty-nine months of our existence (it seemed like an eternity)—and a bold move was needed. Two, our concept was unique—so novel, in fact, that the Securities and Exchange Commission had to hold a hearing to determine whether Vanguard could finance its marketing costs with a modest expenditure of fund income. When the positive decision finally came down in 1981, it came with these wonderful words from the commission's unanimous opinion:

Vanguard's distribution plan is consistent with, and actually furthers, the objectives of the Investment Company Act of 1940. The plan fosters improved disclosure, benefits each fund within a reasonable range of fairness, enhances the funds' independence, and promotes a healthy and viable mutual fund complex in which each fund can better prosper.

After four long years of being held in suspense with the sword of Damocles hanging over us, we all found these words music to our ears.

The Challenge of Tough Financial Markets

I mention these early challenges because, as I know you are aware, Vanguard is again being challenged—challenged by the tough environment of the financial markets (more so the bond market than the stock market) and, to be candid, by some of our own performance shortcomings; challenged by our industry (most notably, the big Boston Bruin); and challenged by the self-imposed constraints of our corporate philosophy.

The net result is that, for the first time in memory, our market share—our share of the assets and cash flows of all direct marketing funds—has turned *downward.* For Vanguard, market share (I hope you haven't forgotten this) is a measure, not an objective. The decline in our share of direct marketing assets has been, so far, modest. After rising from 9 percent of assets in 1980 to 21 percent in 1992, it has eased off to 20 percent in 1994. It seems a small dip, but you should know that *any* change in trend is cause for concern. What is more, our share of industry cash flows—a far more sensitive indicator of investor sentiment—has dipped from 30 percent in 1991, to 20 percent in 1993, to about 10 percent during the first half of 1994. Again, hardly fatal, even remaining impressive, but it is a warning sign we ignore at our peril. What this means, simply put, is that while three out of ten new investors preferred Vanguard three years ago, one out of ten prefers us today.

We know—quite precisely, I think—why. The first challenge has been tough financial markets. While what has transpired in the stock market is, so far at least, little more than a blip, all of our competitors have faced the same environment. But our relative standing has been impaired by the poor 1993 performance of our two largest growth funds and by the absence of aggressive, high-risk, often specialized (for example, emerging market) funds among our offerings, together resulting in the (I think, inaccurate) perception that, somehow, Vanguard can't manage equities.

More significant has been the plunge in the bond market—the worst decline since 1987. (In that year, "April was the cruelest month"; this year, it has been January, February, March, *and* April.) Again, to be sure, all of our competitors have faced the same environment. But our relative standing has been impaired, paradoxically, because bond funds are our "strong suit," more important in our asset mix than in most of our competitors'. And our strong entries in the long-term bond and GNMA arenas have been hit the hardest in the marketplace, despite the fact that our *relative* investment performance has been perfectly satisfactory.

The Challenge of Competition

The second challenge has been mounted by our competitors, overpoweringly dominated by Fidelity. In the first quarter of 1994, Fidelity garnered 55 percent—$16 billion of the $30 billion total—of net cash flow into the direct marketing funds. While our $3.8 billion cash flow was second largest in the group, it was far less than our accustomed pace, and it was *only* (if that's the word) about $2 billion above the $1.7 billion gathered by T. Rowe Price, the third-place fund group.

Fidelity's success was born largely of its success in equity management. The large risks they assumed in most of their funds paid off with 20 percent gains in 1993—a year in which the market as a whole achieved its long-term par of 10 percent. Add to that figure their huge ($300 billion) asset size and their market importance. They account for 10 percent of all U.S. equity trading, and they are not hesitant to flex their sheer power in the stock market. Further buttressed by their $70 million advertising budget and their formidable technology powerhouse, they are truly a force to be reckoned with.

The Challenge from Within

The third challenge comes not from outside Vanguard but from within. We are a conservative, disciplined, thrifty enterprise. We believe that conservative funds, while less glamorous in speculative markets, will recoup their shortfall in less heady times. We have tried to avoid, with some degree of success, the curse of the mutual fund industry: huge cash inflows from investors *after* spectacular performance gains have been achieved, and huge outflows *after* commensurate losses have been incurred. (This is not a good way for investors to make money!) We are disciplined, endeavoring to assure that our investment policies are clearly stated and not tinkered with. An index fund's job is to match the market index. A growth fund's job is to compete—successfully we hope—with a comparable peer group. A money market fund's job is to own the highest-quality investments, with very limited maturities. A long-term U.S. Treasury fund's job is to parallel the returns on long-term treasuries. In short, we hope to perform to our standards, without the assumption of extra risk.

Finally, of course, we are thrifty, keeping operating expenses at the lowest reasonable levels. Not only out of our concern for the prudent use of our shareholder's dollars but also with our conviction that, in an investment world where most factors equalize over time (reversion to the mean), the performance returns achieved by our funds will be enhanced over time by as much as 0.5 to 2 percent annually relative to our higher-cost competitors. Through the magic of compounding, a 10 percent rate of return dwarfs an 8 percent rate over the long term.

In short, and I really believe this, our loss of market share is measuring something more subtle than our problems in the financial markets, our few serious equity performance shortfalls (without enough "long-falls" to offset them), and championship results by our largest competitor. *It is measuring the impact of the fact that we hold to a long-term philosophy in a marketplace in which, for the moment, short-term results are the name of the game.* Certainly the rapid growth of the Charles Schwab OneSource service for providing a simple, convenient statement and facilitating ease of trading funds among different fund families is one of many manifestations of this short-term focus. The growing pervasiveness of this "quick-buck" philosophy poses, for the moment, a major challenge to Vanguard.

Responding to the Challenges

If these are the challenges, what must we do to respond? First, we must look ahead to more rational stock and bond markets, in which our funds will shine whether the trends are up or down. This has always been a cyclical, market-sensitive business; it remains so today. But sooner or later the investment pendulum, having swung to the speculative extreme, swings back to the defensive extreme, finally coming to repose in the conservative center, before repeating the cycle again. (I see evidence that this is happening already.) Given this cyclicality, it is best to hold our course and sail on. In the words of Joaquin Miller's poem about the voyage of Columbus:

This mad sea shows his teeth tonight,
What shall we do when hope is gone?
The words leaped as a leaping sword:
Sail on! Sail on! And on!

Second, we must (and are) taking steps to repair the chinks in our equity fund armor. We must do a better job of the selection and evaluation of equity advisers and prepare to make tough decisions. We must capitalize on the success of our index strategy, which now accounts for one-half of investor purchases of our equity funds. In the wide range of stock and bond index funds we now offer, our results have been peerless. And we must develop an active equity management group *within Vanguard* both to manage allocations of existing fund assets and to manage new, and in some cases more aggressive, funds. By taking major steps to enhance our quantitative, computer-driven management capacity, we are already well on the way to accomplishing these goals.

Third, we must take further advantage of our role as the low-cost provider of services in the mutual fund industry. Our competitive advantage versus our major peers has risen to a record level. That is, our expense ratio of 0.30 percent is fully 66 percent *below* the 0.89 percent average expense ratio of our prime competitors. (You will recall that we have toughened our standards a bit, lowering the expense ratio we use for the calculations of our partnership plan earnings, thus making earnings increases harder to come by. But I am confident that you will not be disappointed in the record-high earnings that we will report to you a few minutes hence.) Many of our competitors are raising fees. Many are temporarily waiving fees that will ultimately translate into higher real expenses for their funds. None—so far at least—have introduced *low-cost* funds, which are even vaguely competitive with our *normal* cost structure. Nonetheless, the competition will surely heat up, and we must do everything in our power to preserve and protect our traditional pricing advantage. The four low-priced, high-minimum-balance Admiral Funds we began in 1992 are just the beginning.

Fourth, we must add to public awareness of who we are and how we serve investors. Today we receive an astonishing amount of favorable press recognition. A recent *Wall Street Journal* article ("Boggled by Fund Picking?"), for example, provided ten investment pointers that included investing in index funds, sticking with large fund groups for consistent results, using no-load funds, and favoring low-cost funds. It described Vanguard to perfection, without even mentioning our name. ("Boggled" may have been an inside joke!) But we must reconsider our deliberately timid (both in amount and content) advertising strategy, which sought to build—forcefully, tastefully, candidly—the power of the Vanguard name.

Ignore the message of most mutual fund advertisements. *Good advertising need not be strident, obfuscatory, and deceptive; it can be informative, straightforward, and candid.* In my view, it is time to reconsider our conservative policies and undertake modest additional expenditures to assure that the investing public learns more about Vanguard's values and understands the special virtues of some of our funds offering major, obvious competitive advantages—for example, our money market and our variable annuity funds—and our promising new fund introductions: the Emerging Markets Portfolio, the three new defined maturity segments of our Bond Index Fund, our pioneering series of unique Tax-Managed Funds (which can materially enhance after-tax relative returns to investors), and our four new LifeStrategy Portfolios, each allocating assets in accordance with the risk-reward profile of the investor.

What Can WE Do?

Inevitably, many of us here tonight will not play a major role in developing these responses. Most are corporate decisions rather than operating decisions. Thus, the question for each crew member is: What can I do? What can each one of us do to help Vanguard through this rough patch? Well, to state the obvious, if several of our sails are a bit tattered, we must make sure that the other sails are taut, strong, and rightly set—prepared to capture a little more of the wind.

In short, each of us can—and must—do our job well. We must work smart, hard, and with maximum effectiveness. We must strive to meet ever-higher standards of processing efficiency, telephone service, and fund share pricing accuracy. The pace of our technology voyage must quicken: We must provide better training, better supervision, and better leadership. We must continue our unremitting fight against bureaucracy, the better to assure the triumph of judgment over process. The Pennsylvania Dutch call this "giving good weight"—serving our clients with excellence, and at a fair price.

This seemingly simple prescription reminds me of Aesop's fable, "Hercules and the Wagoner":

> **A wagoner was driving his team along a muddy lane when the wheels of his wagon sank so deep in the mire that no efforts of his horses could move them. As he stood there, looking helplessly on, and calling loudly at intervals upon Hercules for assistance, the god himself appeared and said to him, "Put your shoulder to the wheel, man, and goad on your horses, and then you may call on Hercules to assist you. If you won't lift a finger to help yourself, you can't expect Hercules or any one else to come to your aid."**

Put another way, *God helps those who help themselves.*

I would rather tell you candidly about the problems Vanguard faces today than make an inevitably futile attempt to keep you in the dark. Many of you see the numbers every day in terms of lower telephone volumes, lower transaction volumes, fewer new households investing with Vanguard, more IRA asset transfers going out than coming in, and so on, and, as partners, you have every right to be informed about our responses.

While *hope* is usually a weak reed to rely upon in the financial markets, *expectation, experience,* and *history* all suggest a return, sooner or later, to rationality, which is all we need ask. While good results are never guaranteed, playing a larger direct role in the management of particular Vanguard equity funds breaks new ground for us. While our timing in forming several more aggressive funds is surely late from a market *selling* standpoint, it may prove timely from a market *level* standpoint. In any event, these funds will be offered with full disclosure of the extra risks they entail. More advertising—and more sensible advertising than we see from our peers—may also lie in prospect. *But not a single one of these changes will violate one of our most fundamental principles: Vanguard is designed to serve the needs of the long-term investor.*

245

A Broader Perspective

I do not want to leave you with a negative perception of where we stand. We remain the second-largest firm in this vibrant industry. Our assets are at a near record high of $131 billion, nearly $20 billion higher than one year ago. We have fine funds, a loyal crew, and a durable strategy. These are hardly trivial advantages. Nonetheless, 1994 marks a rough patch in Vanguard's history, a year in which we have faced—and continue to face—tides that swell against us and winds at our face. But, put into perspective—which I hope you all will do—the tides and winds are far from disabling, and they have been relatively mild storms at that. The seas could have been far, far tougher. If this is the first real rough patch we have faced since 1981, I can assure you it will be by no means the last—nor, in all likelihood, the worst—challenge we will ever face.

But conquer them all—large or small, near or distant—we will, if only we hold fast to the character of our charter. We can resolve each challenge and honor our founding principles by basing each business judgment on these three standards:

One, what is best for our clients?

Two, what is best for our crew?

Three, what is the best way to manifest the tradition and character symbolized by our flagship?

If we meet these three standards, there are no markets, no foes, no internal dissension, no winds, no tides, no circumstance that could ever deter us from ultimately raising our flag and signaling victory.

I close on a timely, if paradoxical, note: As we honor our ship's flag—the British Union Jack—we also honor America's flag—Old Glory—on this, our nation's Flag Day. The stars and stripes symbolize the fact that in no other nation in the world could The Vanguard Group of Investment Companies have come into being and risen so quickly to a position of industry leadership. Let us not forget that this remains, for all its flaws, the nation of opportunity for newcomers (Vanguard was just that twenty years ago), of free enterprise (we are truly that today), and of creative and competitive capitalism (we are, I think, the most *sensibly* innovative and cost-competitive firm in this industry). We have taken the road less traveled by, and that has made all the difference for Vanguard.

Thank you very much for traveling that road with me.

❉   ❉   ❉

Note: The flags of the United States and The Vanguard Group were featured on the covers of the 1993 annual reports of our Vanguard mutual funds. At the end of our celebration tonight, I hope you will join me in a brief moment of contemplation as we hear from our bell tower the music of "America the Beautiful," by Katharine Lee Bates, just as we did at the dedication of this magnificent new campus last September.

❉   ❉   ❉

Note: The Book of Virtues, by William J. Bennett, has been the source of some of the thoughts in this speech. It includes the quotes from Robert Frost on the virtue of courage, Aesop on the virtue of work, Katharine Lee Bates on the virtue of loyalty, and Joaquin Miller on the virtue of perseverance. I recommend that you acquire a copy and read more wonderful writing about ten key virtues that also include responsibility, compassion, and faith.

CELEBRATION

December 10, 1994

*T*HE THEME I have chosen for my year-end comments is "celebration."

"Celebration" is the title we chose for our beautiful new woven tapestry, hanging high and proud in our galley. This tapestry celebrates two themes: One is new—the magnificent new campus we now occupy—and is reflected in the perspectives of some of our buildings and our bell tower; the other is old—the flags to which we ascribe our Vanguard heritage.

The American flag, Old Glory, of course, represents this land of opportunity where an entrepreneurial upstart of an enterprise like this one can rise like a phoenix from the ashes to become, in but two short decades, the second-largest mutual fund complex in the world. The Union Jack of Great Britain represents the nautical heritage of the HMS *Vanguard* that has given us a seemingly infinite supply of ships' names—(*Victory, Majestic, Goliath, Audacious, Zealous, Swiftsure,* and the like for our buildings)—concepts (*winds and tides, shipshape, trim the sails,* and so on), and organizational values—(*crew member,* never *employee*).

Celebrating the End of a Tough Year

But my meaning is deeper than the celebration of new buildings and old flags. For this is also a time to celebrate our making it through a tough year—in a real sense, the toughest year that Vanguard has faced since our incorporation on September 23, 1974—with professional skill, camaraderie, and panache, and with our heads held high.

To be sure, our asset growth of a mere billion (to $132 billion—just think of that!) is well below our $29 billion increase in 1993. But a tripling of our asset base from $46 billion in late 1989 over the past five years is no trivial accomplishment. Indeed, it is the highest growth rate of any major fund complex in our industry.

And, even as I describe 1994 as a tough year, I emphasize the paradox of simultaneously celebrating a welcome—perhaps even overdue—reminder that the business we are in is "market sensitive" and often volatile. It is truly a reminder worth not only receiving but celebrating. For the financial markets have not given a very good account of themselves in 1994. The bond market is experiencing its second-worst performance in more than 120 years: That's right, since 1872. The stock market so far is also down, for only the fourth year in Vanguard's twenty-year history. Overall, this past year was a poor environment for the mutual fund industry. So, let's celebrate the reminder, even as we celebrate our resiliency in dealing with tougher times.

Celebrating Our Crew

This is a time too to celebrate what each of you here today do to make Vanguard the best enterprise that it can be, and to celebrate having your families with us to share these brief impressions of where Vanguard has been and where we are going. So I extend special thanks to all of your spouses and children, for without their support, none of us could work with our customary enthusiasm, energy, and professional skill. It is all of us, working together, who give Vanguard the strength of character that is our greatest asset and our greatest blessing.

Thanks to a fine crew, we came through with flying colors in 1994 despite bad markets. In a sense, 1994 was a landmark year for Vanguard, a year in which the innate conservatism and rigid discipline of our investment philosophy stood us in good stead. It was a year in which the managers of a dozen or more money market funds—mostly those run by bankers, who are supposed to know *something* about cash management—had to ante up tens of millions of dollars to protect the asset value of their money market funds from falling below $1.00 per share.

It was a year in which many otherwise professional managers of bond funds also reached out too far for yield and were lured into exotic derivative securities, many of which plummeted in price, resulting in staggering losses to the shareholders of their mutual funds, to say nothing of the multi-billion-dollar loss suffered by a pooled fund investing the resources of the second-largest county in California.

It was a year in which the managers of many mutual funds speculating in risky equities lost significant money for their shareholders, while most quality-oriented equity funds—including market index funds, the crux of one of Vanguard's major strategies, one that our competitors avoid like the plague—enjoyed a fine relative return, even if the absolute stock market returns were little to write home about. At this moment, it looks like our unmanaged Standard & Poor's 500 Index Fund may outpace 85 out of every 100 professionally managed equity funds!

I also want to stress how proud I am of our operational excellence in 1994. We conducted our business virtually without flaw. That may not sound like much, but it does contrast with our major competitor, who stumbled at least twice: first, deliberately releasing incorrect fund net asset values to the press, and second, making a "manual error" that overstated one of their fund's realized capital gains by $2.4 billion dollars (yes, billion). Nonetheless, let's learn from our competitor's errors (it's cheaper that way!), avoid complacency, and never, never smirk at others' mistakes. "There but for the Grace of God go we" is the attitude I would suggest. Or, as a World War II song went, "Praise the Lord but pass the ammunition."

A Word from Our Ship's Bell

I'm pleased and proud of where we stand today—even as I know we must look ahead to distant horizons with, yes, even more new Vanguard funds, with new ideas for our Information Technology Voyage, with greater operating efficiencies, and with ever better service to our clients—individual and institutional alike. These continuing improvements at Vanguard are the structures that we must build, year after year. *They must be built on a sound foundation of corporate and human character.* Each person here must be a part of it, for it is character, I reemphasize on this wonderful day of celebration, that will assure our continuing leadership in our industry.

Finally, I'd like to celebrate a personal first. Of all of the thousands of letters I've received over the years—mostly wonderful to read—I received just a few weeks ago my first letter from an inanimate object. Here is the letter:

I tolled at a beautiful old church in Chicago before moving to your magnificent campus in Malvern. I am your one-and-a-half-ton bronze Ship's Bell.

Think how wonderful it would be to hear "America the Beautiful" on a warm and glorious autumn day. Or on a day that the snow is falling softly upon the limbs of the tree, or a day that the rains and winds are blowing too hard against the windowpanes as crew members are rushing from building to building to make that scheduled meeting.

I am here to remind my Vanguard family of our unique duty: faithful stewardship of our clients' assets. But please let me ring more often; let me be heard more frequently in celebration of what this great company is today.

I am proud to be at Vanguard. I am your landmark. I am your Ship's Bell.

Well, like the Ship's Bell that apparently signed that letter, I am proud to be at Vanguard; I hope that you are too. I may be the captain who sets the course, but it is the crew who sets the sails. It is the crew who fires the cannons and swabs the decks. It is the crew who is ultimately responsible for the success of the long voyage. I thank you all for getting us through a difficult year, one of many, I am sure, that we shall face again—perhaps in 1995; perhaps beyond some longer time horizon—in shipshape fashion.

So let's have our celebration; let's ring the bell and sing the carols as I wish you Merry Christmas, happy Holy Days, and the greetings of this wonderful season of love and hope.

VANGUARD SCORES
AGAIN—TWICE

May 18, 1995

As you know from one of my earlier speeches, *score* began its career in the English language as meaning a mark on a measuring stick. Since the stick came to have twenty marks, it was only a matter of time until *score* came to mean twenty, and then to mean the number of points (scores) earned in a game—its most common usage today.

Tonight I have the opportunity to use *score* in both of its senses. For we celebrate not only the twentieth anniversary of the start of Vanguard's operations on May 1, 1975, but also our passing of the $150 billion asset milestone, a large score indeed in the highly competitive mutual fund game. But asset growth milestones, while a comfortable measure of competitive success, are really just a measure of the faith and trust that investors have in Vanguard. So, rather than smugly brag about this astonishing milestone, I would downplay its significance. To this end, I again quote sports writer Grantland Rice:

> **When the One Great Scorer comes**
> **to write against your name—**
> **He marks—not that you won or lost**
> **—but how you played the game.**

Tonight, after twenty years of expanding assets and operations, of putting a brand-new mutual fund name on the map, of creating mutual funds, of developing a new kind of organization, of stresses and strains, of tears (not many) and laughter (a lot), we have become the second-largest mutual fund complex in the world. But the poem is right: Not winning, but how we played the game, is what matters to the Great Scorer up there in Heaven.

If I could leave you with a single thought tonight, it is not that we have played a *winning* game but that we have played a *fair* game. Indeed, we have played a game in which we have set tough rules for ourselves, and we have let our competitors play by easier rules. The Vanguard Experiment, which happened to begin on a revolutionary day, May Day—May 1, 1975—is really the story of a company that sought to be fair with its fund shareholders, who reap the rewards of its "at-cost" structure, and to be fair with its crew, who share in those rewards.

Averse to luring investors to us with hyperbolic claims and overblown advertisements, we have also sought to be fair in how we have presented ourselves, describing our funds' performance results with full and candid disclosure. As one of our rivals said a few years back, "Vanguard sets the standards by which we should measure ourselves." (I hope that he wasn't misquoted!) This is an extraordinary tribute not to *what* we have accomplished in a score of years but to *how* we have accomplished it.

The "We" in We Lead Is Crucial

As the HMS *Vanguard's* officer's badge says, we lead. The *we* is crucial. To be sure, there may in fact have been a lot of *I* in structuring and naming this enterprise, in laying out twenty years ago the simple corporate strategies and values that remain intact today, and in articulating just who we are and why. But there is no doubt in my mind about the self-evident fact that many others have made major—and surely essential—contributions to our growth, and to help us to achieve the preeminent industry status we have earned. All of you who are here tonight to celebrate our twentieth anniversary—and your predecessors—played key roles at each step of the way in our development:

- Walter Morgan, the founder of Wellington Fund, gave me my first break forty-four years ago, and has supported my work ever since.
- The board of directors, sharply divided when we began—even as it was willing to approve a new governance structure, a new concept, and a new name—is now working as a unified group in sup-

253

porting, challenging, and probing (sometimes prodding) the officers, and always demanding cogent answers to hard questions.

- The members of our senior management team have helped develop Vanguard into a solid and cohesive structure. Bringing to bear their wide range of talents and experience in an age of complex information technology, they now manage a huge corporation.

- The 3,600 dedicated and invaluable crew members are the unsung heroes and heroines who come to work day after day and undertake the hard work of handling Vanguard's enormous volumes, improving what we do with each passing day.

- The investment advisers of our fund portfolios (now eighty-two in number) have, far more often than not, delivered the kinds of returns that our shareholders demand, and indeed to which they are entitled. They are our most public face, and their achievements, coming in this business where fallibility is so rife, have been central to our growth.

- And finally, my staff assistants from years past have given so much of themselves to me and to Vanguard. Over the years, they have been both my students and my teachers, both my servants and my leaders. I am proud of each one of them, not just because of the extraordinary career success they have achieved—three are presidents of major mutual fund firms—but because of their character and integrity.

Doing It Our Way

We gather at a time in which Vanguard is winning on every front. We have had the best fund performance in our history, we are the winner of the *Financial World* service quality award for the fifth consecutive year, we have witnessed a 100 percent increase over last year in investor purchases of our funds, and our market share is at an all-time high. These important accomplishments in which we have all shared, however, are but scores in a thrilling and competitive game. What is important, I remind you, is that history will judge Vanguard not by how many tens of billions of assets we manage but how we played the game. And we have played the game the right way—our way: *The record shows we took the blows and did it our way. We faced it all, and we stood tall and did it our way.*

To which I would add, we *all* need strength to carry on. Thank you for giving it to me. Together we are accomplishing something truly worthwhile: making this industry an even better one for investors. As Nobel Laureate Paul Samuelson said in his foreword to my book: *We have changed a basic industry in the optimal direction. Of very few can this be said.* So, from the bottom of my heart, thanks to each of you who have been among those stalwart few.

LET THE WISDOM OF THE PAST ILLUMINATE OUR FUTURE

June 4, 1995

*F*IRST, AND MOST IMPORTANT, thanks to all of you on our crew for all that you do to make Vanguard what it is today. You *are* Vanguard, and I am proud of you.

I have much else to be proud of this evening too—things that are far more important than the three milestones we celebrated in May. Yet something compels me to call attention to these important events in the Vanguard timeline.

- The first milestone marks the celebration of the twentieth anniversary day of the little company that almost never was.
- The second milestone marks our crossing the incredible $150 billion level, as the assets of our once-little company have risen more than 100-fold from the $1.4 billion total of two decades ago. We have become an industry colossus, and we are now the second-largest mutual fund organization in the world.
- The third milestone, the tenth anniversary of the Vanguard Partnership Plan, not only provides each of us with a share in the financial rewards we provide to our clients but also brings us all together to work as a team. *And we work not for ourselves, not for our units, not for our departments, not for our divisions, and not even for our corporation but for our clients—the honest-to-God, down-to-earth, real-life human beings who have placed their trust in us.*

This evening also marks a poignant milestone for me: After twenty years at the helm, I have decided that it is time to turn the wheel over to a new captain. Reaching those first three milestones almost simultaneously, in a year when our funds' investment results have been the best in our history, when our status as the industry's number 1 provider of quality investor services has been reaffirmed for the fifth consecutive year, and when the flow of assets into the Vanguard Funds has more than doubled, surely I step aside with the HMS *Vanguard* at the very pinnacle of her success.

But my decision is based on factors more fundamental than those I just mentioned. First, hard as it may be for me to realize, I grow older, and it is truly a sin to overstay one's time. Second, I have a worthy successor in John J. Brennan, who personifies the qualities of leadership, intelligence, dedication, remarkable diligence, and, that most important of all qualities, integrity of character. His trick—that is, his term at the helm—will begin on January 31, 1996. Finally, as stalwart and big and brave as I hope my spiritual heart remains, I have come to realize that the increasing limitations of my *physical* heart place strong constraints on my energy. No longer does my energy erupt; it must be summoned. Obviously, that handicap limits my ability to work with the intensity that the chief executive's position demands. In short, "The spirit is willing, but the flesh is weak."

All of that said, I have no intention of simply fading away. I am not *retiring* but rather will remain as chairman of the board of the Vanguard Funds for as long as I can be productive and as long as the board will have me. In this less demanding role, I hope to take it a wee bit easier, but I will continue to watch over our crew and our clients, to do more writing and financial research, and, as you might suppose, to speak out on industry issues. So, I shall be around.

Tonight, I will not dwell on Vanguard's past accomplishments. Our past speaks for itself. Rather, I propose to speak of the future by using the voices from the past that have given me the guidance I have needed to help shape the Vanguard corporate character and ethical values that distinguish us from *nearly* all, if not *all*, enterprises today. The words uttered by these voices are eternal.

I believe that the best means for summarizing these words of wisdom is to elaborate on ten themes centered on the timeless quotations that I have most enjoyed from my earlier speeches (thirty-two of them) at asset milestones, at partnership celebrations, and at year-end gatherings for Christmas and the Holy Day season. I want these voices to speak to you tonight—to let words of wisdom from the past illuminate our future—in order to remind you of the *qualities of spirit*, not just the *quantities of numbers,* that have brought Vanguard to where it is today so as to help you prepare for the challenges we will surely face as the voyage of the HMS *Vanguard* continues toward the star that shines so brightly on the horizon.

1. The Beginning

I begin with the inspiration for the name "Vanguard," a name that came quite by accident as I was reading an old book of British naval history. I came upon these words, written nearly two centuries ago from the deck of the flagship, the HMS *Vanguard,* fresh from victory over the French at the Nile:

> **Vanguard, off the Nile, August 3, 1798: My Lord, nothing could withstand the squadron under my command. The judgment of the captains, together with the valour and high state of discipline of the officers and men of every description, was absolutely irresistible. . . . The admiral most heartily congratulates the captain, officers, seamen, and marines of the squadrons he has the honour to command on the eve of the late action; and he desires they will accept his most sincere and cordial thanks for their very gallant behaviour in this glorious battle.**

These inspiring words from our heritage—Vanguard, victory, valor, judgment, discipline, gallant behavior, respect for both officers and crew—will, I hope, continue to guide us into the twenty-first century.

2. Even One Person Can Make a Difference

I have now spoken at the dedication of three buildings—the Wellington Management Company building in August 1973, the Vanguard Chesterbrook complex in September 1983, and our magnificent new campus in November 1993. In each dedication speech, I used the identical words (but changed the number of years). This is what I said:

> **I believe that even one person *can* make a difference. Thus I dedicate this building to the individuals in our company—the individuals who got us started sixty-eight years ago, the individuals who work with us today, and the individuals who, God willing, will come forth to assure our future.**

Tonight, I illustrate the importance of "even one person" with a much more elegant quote, one that offers a far broader scope. It comes from the song "The Impossible Dream":

**And the world will be better for this
That one man, scorned and covered with scars
Still strove with his last ounce of courage
To reach the unreachable star.**

As we move into the twenty-first century, and Vanguard and its crew continue to grow, let us never forget the importance of each individual at Vanguard, and let us be ever mindful of those words—"even one person *can* make a difference"—that we have placed on our Award for Excellence. As we fight our future battles—and inevitably get scarred in some of them—give us all the courage to reach out to that ever-unreachable star.

3. Remember Vanguard's Central Principle

The brevity—just seven words—of my third quotation gives no indication of its importance. Indeed, it may well be Vanguard's central principle. It is the now-famous sentence, uttered by the spirit of a deceased father, that sets the theme of the inspiring movie, *Field of Dreams:*

If you build it, they will come.

When I used this quotation in my speech in 1990, I defined *you* as our employees, *it* as our product line, and *they* as our customers. Few of you, I suspect, were fooled by my abuse of our Vanguard lexicon, in which the appropriate words were *crew, mutual funds,* and *clients.* But it did set up the embellishment of my point that we had become a $55 billion enterprise, growing at a 28 percent annual rate, with not a single employee, nor a single product, nor a single customer. Think about it!

I hope that this theme will continue to guide us long into the future. It suggests that our prime responsibility is to build the finest group of funds in this industry, to provide full and fair disclosure, and to produce performance and service of such excellence that our growth will continue from within organically, bereft of aggressive marketing or hyperbolic advertising. I would add "no matter how painful," for there will be many temptations to ignore this theme along the road ahead.

4. Milestones

We make quite a stir over our milestones at Vanguard—$1 billion, $50 billion, $100 billion, and $150 billion asset marks; tenth and twentieth anniversaries; even this tenth partnership celebration. These milestones are not only tangible measures of our scores in this competitive industry in which we ply our trade, but they are also measures of the time and intensity of the trust we earn from investors.

And yet we must realize that, in a real sense, winning scores should not be among our highest goals. We should focus on something larger. Many of you will recall how sportswriter Grantland Rice put it:

**When the One Great Scorer comes
To write against your name—
He marks—not that you won or lost—
But how you played the game**

Of all our achievements, the one I am most proud of is that Vanguard has played not only a winning game but a fair game—fair with our shareholders, who reap the rewards of our at-cost structure; fair with our crew, who share in these rewards; fair in our disclosure of past returns and future risks; fair in every aspect of what we do. Indeed, as one of our competitors said, "Vanguard sets the standards by which we should all measure ourselves."

I know that many milestones—many scores—remain before us on our long voyage, and I urge you to continue to celebrate them with the pride and enthusiasm that they deserve. But as we do so, I also urge you to recognize that history will judge us not by these scores but by how we played the game. For Vanguard, I hope that our future will continue to reflect these familiar words:

**The record shows we took the blows
And did it our way.
We faced it all and we stood tall
And did it our way.**

5. Press On Regardless

During the past three years, this phrase has worked its way into the Vanguard lexicon. Consider this quotation from President Calvin Coolidge:

Nothing in the world can take the place of persistence. Talent will not; nothing is more common than unsuccessful men with talent. Genius will not; unrewarded genius is almost a proverb. Education will not; the world is filled with educated derelicts. Persistence and determination alone are omnipotent. The slogan "press on" has solved, and always will solve, the problems of the human race.

The lore of my own family somehow added the word *regardless* to suggest that we must press on, regardless of whether we are experiencing good times or bad, whether we are sailing in calm or turbulent waters. Hew to the task, no matter what! I have no doubt that we will face both types of challenges in the years ahead, and no matter which it is that we face, we must maintain our determination. For determination is a trait of character, not a temporal attitude that can be turned off and on at will. Two thousand years ago, Saint Paul said it beautifully:

This one thing I do, forgetting those things which are behind, and reaching forth unto those things which are before, . . . I press towards the mark.

As we now reach forth to those things which are before us in the third millennium, let us do so with the same kind of determination.

6. *Why Are We Doing This?*

Traditionally, the typical corporation is not guided by inspiration. Rather, the corporation is too often typified by indifference, idleness, and lack of imagination. In contrast, the development of Vanguard has taken a different tack. As I have experienced the thrill of starting Vanguard and then leading her for two decades, I have been inspired by these words from the economist, Joseph Schumpeter, who suggested that enduring entrepreneurial motives are primarily derived not from money alone but from three more powerful sources:

The dream and the will to found a private kingdom, a dynasty. The will to conquer: the impulse to fight, to succeed for the sake, not of the fruits of success, but of success itself. The joy of creating, getting things done, or of simply exercising one's energy and ingenuity.

It is not the humdrum of adhering to daily routines and completing tasks that has inspired the Vanguard crew. Rather, it is our dreams, our fighting impulse, our seeking of success for its own sake, our creativity, our can-do spirit, and our exercise of our energy and ingenuity that have shaped our past and will carry us through the years to come.

Maintaining this spirit is Vanguard's enduring corporate challenge to each member of our current and future crew. Of course, we must constantly question why we do our work; but if we do it to serve others, and do it with the joy that comes with creativity, getting things done, and exercising our ingenuity, this organization has no limits. I well know that this philosophy is idealistic to a fault, but it will become ever more essential as we become a far larger enterprise than we are today.

7. Nothing Fails Like Success

Success is no unmixed blessing. With it too often comes complacency, laziness, and the feeling that "we've got it made." I've been concerned about the perverse axiom "Nothing fails like success" even before I made it the theme of my speech at our $8 billion milestone. (Back in 1984 we marked every billion-dollar milestone.) I illustrated it with this quotation from Carl Sandburg:

> **When an institution goes down or a society perishes, one condition may always be found: they forgot where they came from.**

Despite a decade of astonishing growth since I used that quotation, my concerns have not yet manifested themselves at Vanguard. Yet we still run the risk of flying too close to the sun with wings of wax, only, as did the legendary Icarus, to spiral to death into the sea below. I used the theme of the book *The Icarus Paradox* to illustrate this point in a speech to you a few years ago. The book concludes:

> **The enterprises most likely to fail (1) have been highly successful; (2) have a strong and clearly defined culture and strategy; and (3) have a leader who has been in charge for a long time.**

This description, of course, is not a bad description of the enterprise you all know so well! What happens next? The author goes on to describe it:

> **In strategy, they move from quality leadership to technological tinkering, from building to overexpansion, and from brilliant marketing to blind proliferation. In structure, they move from orderly to rigid, from decentralized to oppressively bureau-**

cratic. In culture, they move from entrepreneurial to insipid and political. And in goals, they move from growth to grandeur.

So far, we have fought the good fight—with reasonable success—against those evil trends. If we fail, we, who have wreaked "creative destruction" on so many foes, run the ever-present risk of being "creatively destroyed" ourselves. To avoid this fate—*to escape the perils of technological tinkering, overexpansion, blind proliferation, rigidity, bureaucracy, insipidness, politicization, and grandeur*—we must constantly examine ourselves and engage in unvarnished self-criticism.

8. *Observe Tradition, but Remember That Change Is the Only Certainty*

Vanguard's glorious tradition can be said to be 200 years old, since the Battle of the Nile; or 67 years old, since Walter L. Morgan founded Wellington Fund; or 21 years old, since Vanguard came into being in 1974.

Honoring our traditions—the stalwart reinforcement of the heritage of our highest values—has made a major contribution to our success. During Vanguard's lifetime, we have steadfastly honored our most essential traditions: (a) balanced investing, emphasizing conservatism and discipline; (b) focusing on the long-term investor rather than the short-term speculator; (c) fair dealing with clients, most evident in our dedication to low costs; and (d) managing an organization with *integrity* as our watchword.

Now, recognize that tradition has a negative side as well. It can substitute inertia for action; it can encrust and stultify. In short, however vital in the past, tradition can cast a pall over the future. T.S. Eliot put it well when he said:

Tradition is not enough; it must be perpetually criticized and brought up to date.

We have measured up to that standard and have been willing to alter traditional business practices at the appropriate time. For example, our move to a new and enlightened governance structure and our move from a salesman-oriented, commission-driven system to a client-oriented, no-load distribution system have not only shaped Vanguard's subsequent accomplishments but have also been importantly responsible for them. And the development of our new traditions—most notably the Vanguard Partnership Plan—have also added a distinctly positive thrust.

So tradition must be honored and must continue to dominate our character. But over the years the world changes, and by the turn of the century we may see more changes than we have seen during the past two decades. Two thousand years ago Ecclesiastes told us that would be so:

> To everything there is a season, and a time to every purpose under the heaven.
> A time to keep and a time to cast away.
> A time to plant and a time to pluck up that which is planted.
> A time to cast away stones and a time to gather stones together.
> A time to keep silence and a time to speak.
> A time to weep and a time to laugh.
> A time to mourn and a time to dance.
> A time to be born and a time to die.

So let us recognize that in this life change is the only certainty. We must have the wisdom, insight, and flexibility to change when change we must, even as we preserve our founding traditions and the character that, in a sense, goes back to the Battle of the Nile 200 years ago.

9. Never Forget Who Is Really in Charge

I have often said that at Vanguard, "We are the captains of our fate." I continue to believe that today. We work in a competitive world, and what we do ourselves and how we do it will largely determine our fate. But fate bestows both bane and blessing, and we should never forget that we operate under God's mysterious will, a power far mightier than our own. You've heard this thought before in a wonderful quotation from the Very Reverend Francis B. Sayre, Jr. Without embarrassment, I repeat it again:

> Sailors know what some citizens have forgot in this latter day: that no purpose is achieved, nor any course made good upon God's ocean, until first you have trimmed your sails and set the helm to fit His winds and the set of His tide upon the deep.
>
> Keen is the mariner's eye to discern those telling signs upon the clouds, at the line 'twixt sky and water, or on the crest of waves where the spindrift blows, by which he might foretell the bluster or the calm, the weather God has in store for him.

Often in this world it is a headwind that we face. Then, though the bearing of your destination be precisely the same, you have to tack—back and forth, back and forth; close-hauled; wind in your face, spray on your legs; fingers white upon the sheet, body tense against the bucking tiller; fine-tuning your lively lade to the majestic forces of splendid Creation; and so wresting from that opposing wind the destiny of your desire.

That's when your boat must need be staunch and true, well braced and put together, and lithe like a living thing. And that is when the sailor too is on his mettle, no less in command for all his reverences in the presence of a power mightier than his own.

The continued recognition that somewhere out there is a power mightier than our own may well be my highest hope for the coming era. Indeed, I think a brass plate with that quotation deserves a visible place of honor on our splendid campus.

10. *Care for This Institution!*

Finally, I am now going to read an extensive quote on some organizational principles that also have been central to Vanguard's past success. It describes the role of leadership, of foresight, of management, and most of all, about caring for the institution of which each of us is a part:

There is always a point in time when the longer view could have been taken and a difficult crisis ahead foreseen and dealt with while a rational approach was still possible. How do we avoid extremes? What do we do when short-range competition may preclude a longer view? How can substantial growth be achieved? Only with foresight—the central ethic of leadership— for so many bad decisions are made when there are no longer good choices.

If foresight is needed to protect an institution, what are the requirements necessary to make it work? Clearly the first requirement is the sense of purpose and objective. Little can be gained without knowing where one wants to go. Second is the talent to analyze, organize, and manage the process for reaching new objectives. Second-rate talent will not suffice to meet first-rate objectives. Finally, and let me surprise you by emphasizing this third need, we need people who care about the institution. In an increasingly impersonal world, I have come to believe that a deep sense of caring for the institution is requisite for its success.

> The institution must be the object of intense human care and
> cultivation: even when it errs and stumbles, it must be cared for,
> and the burden must be borne by all who work for it, all who
> own it, all who are served by it, all who govern it.
>
> Caring, we know, is an exacting and demanding business. It
> requires not only interest and compassion and concern; it
> demands self-sacrifice, wisdom and tough-mindedness, and dis-
> cipline. Every responsible person must care, and care deeply,
> about the institutions that touch his life.

So, even as I am confident that our new generation of management
will provide leadership and foresight, I urge our crew to care, and care
deeply, for the warship on which we all sail together.

In Conclusion: Get Ready Now for the Twenty-First Century

The coming of a new century is at once a milestone, a time for reflection, a time to reassess tradition, and a time to reflect on change. We
can already sense that the main challenges to Vanguard's leadership—and to the leadership of our industry—revolve around
enhancing our information technology systems, meeting new client
needs, creating a more sophisticated approach to marketing, and,
most of all, the enormous challenge of managing an ever-growing
enterprise while battling against bureaucracy to maintain the role of
each individual crew member. We must do our best to assure the triumph of judgment over process and of personal challenge over blind
routine.

And yet, there is more. My final quotation sums up how we must
prepare:

> The best way—for a nation and a person (and an enterprise)—to
> prepare for the twenty-first century will be what has always
> been the best way to prepare for uncertainty. That is to rely not
> so much upon the outer supports of plans, programs, and poli-
> cies, but upon the inner strengths of character—resiliency and
> resourcefulness, discipline and cooperation, endurance and
> courage, and, perhaps above all, faith and hope.

I know that our directors share these ideals; I believe that our lead-
ers-to-be share them as well; and I am confident that every member of

our crew will strive to live up to them. If the HMS *Vanguard* responds as I know she will, our illustrious past will be followed by an even more illustrious future.

Thank you for all that you have done for me, and for Vanguard. Good night, and may God bless you always.

Part V

To Strive, to Seek, to Find, and Not to Yield, 1996–2001

*T*HE REMARKABLE bull market in stocks that began in 1982 not only continued in 1996, but accelerated. The Dow-Jones Industrial Average, 5,098 as 1996 began, would continue its powerful surge for the next four years, more than doubling to a high of 11,722 in early 2000. But by the time the peak was reached, the Dow was considered a stodgy representation of the "old economy." Its "new economy" cousin, the technology-stock-laden NASDAQ Index, hardly noticed when the bull market began in 1982, would rise nearly *five*fold, from 1,100 to 5,048 during the same timespan, capturing the imagination of investors in the process.

It was, however, a classic bubble, and at least in its late stages easy to recognize. As always, it was impossible to predict exactly when it would burst. For the soaring market was not only about speculation. Our economy was booming; productivity was advancing at record levels; corporate earnings were hitting one peak after another. Not even Federal Reserve Chairman Alan Greenspan's now infamous admonition against "irrational exuberance" in December 1996, a phrase that quickly found its way into the financial lexicon, could stem the bull market, as the Dow closed 1996 at 6,448, 1997 at 7,900, and 1998 at 9,181. Its final surge took place in 1999, when the index closed at 11,497. In this bountiful financial environment, Vanguard's growth continued apace. Our fund assets, $180 billion when the period began, topped the magic $500 billion threshold in June of 1999, reaching nearly $600 billion in March 2001.

Flourishing and Floundering

While the firm was flourishing, its chairman and founder was struggling. Shortly before this period began, my genetic heart disease that

	Total Net Assets[1]	Net Cash Flow[1]	% Change in Assets	Number of Funds	Crew Members	Expense Ratio (%)	% of Fund Assets in:				Annual Return (%)		
							Stock Funds	Balanced Funds	Bond Funds	Money Funds	Stocks	Bonds	Bills
1996	238,654	40,887	32.5	85	4,800	0.29	48	11	23	18	23.0	3.6	5.2
1997	325,550	49,038	36.4	85	6,400	0.28	55	11	19	15	33.4	9.6	5.2
1998	434,700	66,595	33.5	88	8,100	0.28	58	10	18	14	28.6	8.7	5.1
1999	540,384	64,094	24.3	90	10,000	0.27	63	8	15	13	21.0	–0.8	4.7
2000	563,039	7,250	4.2	95	11,000	0.27	61	8	16	15	–9.1	11.6	6.0
8/31/2001	561,870	42,414	–0.2	93	11,200	0.27e	56	8	20	16	–13.4	7.1	3.1
Cumulative		270,278	22.1								13.1	7.0	5.2

[1] Figures are in $ millions

had first manifested itself in 1960 gradually worsened, reaching the critical stage in mid-1995. By then, sixty-seven years of age, I had decided to step down as Vanguard's chief executive, remaining as chairman. In my announcement to the crew ("Standing Down," printed at the end of this section), I emphasized that my faltering heart was only one of the factors that motivated me to relinquish some of the responsibilities that I'd carried all through Vanguard's history. My decision was also based on my confidence that my vision had been firmly established and that we had built an organization fully capable of carrying on our mission. The Vanguard Experiment had met the test of time. In May 1995 I announced that I would name my long-time colleague John Brennan, whom I'd named our president in 1992, as chief executive, effective January 31, 1996.

The Tale of a Heart

In October, just five months after my announcement, I found myself in Philadelphia's Hahnemann Hospital, kept alive with intravenous fluid as I awaited a heart transplant. Day after day, week after week, month after month passed. I kept busy, in touch with the office and, just as I had done since Vanguard's inception, I wrote my year-end letters to the shareholders of our now eighty-five funds. (Some were in multiple portfolios, so there were "only" thirty-five letters to write during the September through January annual report cycle.)

Of course I was not able to give my usual speech at our year-end Christmas and Holy Day celebration. But as 1996 began, I wrote my first message of this era from my hospital bed and distributed it to the crew. Entitled "Patience, Persistence, and Courage," I described those qualities as three enduring hallmarks of Vanguard. I recounted the patience that was required to launch Vanguard and to succeed with our remarkable early initiatives into investment management, distribution, index funds, and structured bond funds, breaking new ground with each stride.

Persistence was also required. Against all odds, we had built the firm not in a single giant leap but in a step-by-step fashion. And courage was needed too, as we faced without fear dangerous and powerful competition, striving to make the Vanguard Experiment succeed. As must have been obvious to the crew members reading my message, those three qualities not only exemplified Vanguard, but also represented the patience, persistence, and courage required of any human

271

being struggling with an intractable, irreversible, and ultimately fatal disease.

Heart and Soul

I reassured our crew members that despite the imminent danger that my heart would cease to beat, I too had no fear. (Indeed, in the hospital each night my final prayer was "not *my* will, but *thy* will be done.") What pleased me most, I told them, was that it seemed "altogether possible that did (Vanguard) not exist, no one would have invented it"—a rare claim for an enterprise, but in view of the fact that our mutualized structure has yet to be copied, hardly an overstatement. Under the circumstances, my final words seemed singularly appropriate. "The past is history. The future's a mystery. Today is a gift. That's why we call it "the present."

And on February 21, 1996, I received my own very special present—a new heart. The transplant came from a twenty-six-year-old man, brain dead as a result of an accident. I had been blessed with the miracle of a second chance at life! Despite some serious setbacks during the next few months, I began to recover nicely, playing squash again in May, and hiking, biking, and sailing by summer. A miracle indeed! When I spoke once again at the partnership celebration in June, discussing both our hard-earned growth and the plight of our rivals who had fallen by the wayside, of course I talked about our character. Here for the first time I referred to the *soul* of our enterprise, imploring our crew: "Without our values, we have nothing. Please never let our values change. Please never let us lose our soul."

While I was hospital bound, hoping that the transplant would arrive before it was too late, our directors suggested it might be appropriate for a statue of me to be placed on our campus. At first I was appalled. ("Shouldn't you wait 'til I'm dead?" I thought.) But I finally agreed, explaining my reasoning in a speech when the statue was dedicated at a small ceremony on November 11, 1996. I quoted from several of the letters about our character that I had received from shareholders: "The voice of reason . . . your fundamental principles . . . your philosophy and frankness . . . you stand for something—something good and pure and true." But my favorite was this one: "I'd like to see Vanguard stick to its roots. I'm sure Bogle is a hard man to work for. People like that always are. We have one in our family, and the fact that he's been dead for fifty-three years hasn't lessened his influence much." If those voices are right, I thought, perhaps my own influence on Vanguard's character would endure for a long, long time.

Certainly most of the new funds we created during the 1996 through 2001 period were built on the character we had established in our formative years. But the pace of fund formation slowed markedly. While we had formed twenty-nine new funds from 1991 through 1995, we formed fifteen in 1996 through 2001, mostly variations on earlier themes. Included were eight index-oriented funds, the first two in 1996 when we combined our European, Pacific, and Emerging Market index funds into a single Total International Stock Index Fund, and the third an REIT (Real Estate Investment Trust) index fund. In 1998, we formed Mid-Cap, Small-Cap Growth, and Small-Cap Value index funds; in 1999, two more Tax-Managed Funds; and in 2000 a Social (Responsibility) index fund. In addition, we also formed another single-state municipal bond fund and an Inflation-Protected Bond Fund holding special U.S. Treasury bonds. Three new actively managed equity funds were offered, including Selected Value Fund in 1996 and U.S. Value Fund in 2000. Right near the market's high in March 2000, we also introduced Vanguard Growth Equity Fund, a highly aggressive fund run by a manager with a hot record. It was a smart marketing move in response to the new economy fad, but, heavily oriented to technology (65 percent of its portfolio), it was to tumble far more than the market in the sharp decline that followed.

A Pioneer Passes

On July 23, 1998, my great mentor, Walter Morgan, founder of Wellington Fund in 1928, celebrated his 100th birthday. At the partnership celebration a month earlier, we honored him with our Award for Excellence. Although he had retired seven years before Vanguard was born, he was surely a person who had made a difference to all of us. He had named me his successor at Wellington, and he had drummed into me the principles that, as I said in my speech presenting him with the award, "remain at the very core of Vanguard's character today: conservative investing, long-term focus, fair dealing, and loyalty."

We had enjoyed a wonderfully constructive relationship for nearly fifty years, and Mr. Morgan would often tell others that he thought of me as the son he never had. As he grew older, it was my great privilege to honor my predecessor, to support him, and to respect his contribution to Vanguard's foundation. When I made the award presentation, illness had confined him to his home, but when I showed him a videotape of the event, he was delighted, dazzled by the thunderous applause from the assembled crew. Six weeks after celebrating his 100th birthday, he passed into the hands of the Lord. He was my hero, but he was also my friend. I miss him terribly. One of the "Bogleheads"—those self-described contributors to Morningstar's popular Vanguard Diehards website—said the character and mettle of a man is indicated by the "unflagging loyalty and recognition" he gives to his mentor and predecessor. I was delighted to be measured by that standard.

A Changing of the Guard

In the following year, a changing of the guard was again afoot at Vanguard. When I relinquished my chief executive title in January 1996, I expected to remain as chairman for a long time to come. But the transition did not survive for very long. In August 1997, the board named my successor as chief executive to succeed me as chairman as well, granting me the title of "senior chairman." As 1999 began, the board seemed determined that I leave the board at year-end, following my seventieth birthday, a standing policy that I never imagined would apply to the firm's creator. I let the directors know of my surprise and dissatisfaction, and I awaited their decision.

In August, a journalist telephoned me to let me know that he had learned the board would allow no exceptions to the policy. When the *Wall Street Journal* ran the story, it spread like wildfire in the press and on the Internet. Many shareholders expressed disappointment over the decision, writing to our directors in protest. An Internet poll of shareholders endorsed my continuation in a landslide. The directors relented. But after all the public fuss, I decided that the greater good would be served if I put the controversy to rest, and I turned down their offer that I continue on the board. I had strived to behave as a gentleman all through my career, and this occasion seemed a singularly inappropriate one at which to abandon that practice. Not interested in an "Emeritus" title while I was still active, vigorous, and engaged, I was given the title "Founder."

While my departure from the board severed my direct connection with the day-to-day affairs of the company I had founded, I was determined to continue to throw myself energetically into my mission to serve the shareholders of Vanguard—and indeed all mutual fund shareholders—acting as ambassador, interacting with our crew, writing, and speaking. The board provided me an office on the Vanguard campus and, at my request, approved the establishment of a Vanguard unit called "Bogle Financial Markets Research Center." As its president, I pursue my activities to this day.

A Twenty-Five-Year Milestone

My successor continued my practice of speaking at our annual crew gatherings, but graciously allowed me to speak at some of the partnership celebrations. The firm was becoming enormous. Our crew, less than 4,000 when 1996 began, had more than doubled by late 1998, well on its way to its present 11,000 total. We added two more locations to our headquarters offices in Valley Forge and our off-site offices in Arizona and Australia, opening offices in Charlotte, North Carolina, in 1997 and in Waterloo, Belgium (site of the Duke of Wellington's great victory!) in 1998. While the crew had become widespread, satellite television enabled us to hold a single annual partnership meeting, truly global in scope.

When the twenty-fifth anniversary of Vanguard's founding came on September 24, 1999, my speech ("The Power of an Idea"), prepared to be delivered at a small luncheon of Vanguard veterans, looked back at Vanguard's past and ahead to Vanguard's future. In the talk I used Isaiah's words to describe what Vanguard had done: "Behold I will do a new thing; now it shall spring forth . . . I should make a way in the sea, a path in the mighty waters." I described our new thing as "stewardship"—the one great idea that flowed naturally from our mutual structure—our low costs, our index funds, our fixed-income funds, and our long-term investment focus. I urged the crew to hold the line against investment fads and fashions and to adhere to the sound investment principles and decent human values that were the essence of Vanguard's character—"the *right* principles and the *right* values, not only enduring, but eternal."

Seven months later, in May 2000 at a dinner held for officers and directors, Vanguard celebrated its completion of twenty-five years of operations. In remarks notable for their brevity, I described the firm as "a company that stands for something." I told the officers that "I do not believe it is possible—*ever*—to improve on our basic strategy of providing investors with virtually 100 percent of the long-term returns available in financial markets, simply by owning those markets at reasonable cost . . . If we remain faithful to our legacy, this enterprise—of the shareholder, by the shareholder, and for the shareholder—shall not perish from the earth."

The Burst in the Bubble

Shortly before that celebration, the great stock market bubble at last began to burst. The volatile NASDAQ Index, dominated by the so-called new economy stocks, reached its pinnacle of 5,048 in March 2000. Then, the index stumbled and then plummeted. Within a month, it had fallen to 3,400—in the blink of an eye, off by one-third. It quickly bounced back above 4,000 by late summer, only to head down again, tumbling steadily to a winter low of 1,650 in early April 2001—off 67 percent from the high—and then stabilizing for a time. The old-economy-dominated Dow, which had advanced so much less in the upswing, obliged by declining far less in the decline—from near 12,000 to about 9,000, or 25 percent. The *entire* U.S. stock market had dropped by 33 percent, from a market capitalization of $16.4 trillion in March 2000 to $11 trillion. We were experiencing the sharpest bear market since Vanguard began.

Business Never Sleeps

But irrespective of the market's fickle swings—and before, during, and after the changing of the guard—Vanguard continued to adhere to its character and values. While our fundamental thrust did not falter, the world around us was changing, and there was much to be done. A major new initiative was our 1997 creation of the Vanguard Charitable Endowment Program, an independent public charity that facilitated donations by our public-spirited shareholders. Vanguard.com was further developed, and in an increasingly electronic world continued to flourish. The number of registered users topped the one million mark in 2000. The role of information technology at Vanguard continued to grow, and it came to dominate the allocation of our resources. But as we grew, all areas of our business required additional people and additional dollars. While our assets grew at a 22 percent annual rate from the close of 1995 through the autumn of 2001, our expenditures rose at a rate of some 19 percent, rising from $350 million to nearly $1.5 billion. The long and steady decline of our expense ratio—0.73 percent when we began, 0.51 percent in 1985, and 0.29 percent in 1996—

slowed markedly, falling to 0.28 percent in 1997 and to 0.27 percent in 1999, where it remains today.

Our asset mix shifted too with the changing market tides. Stock funds, just 28 percent of assets as 1990 ended rose to 63 percent at the bull market's peak, only to return to 56 percent by the end of the period. When the going got tough, our traditional strength in conservative funds—balanced, bond, money market—stood us in good stead. In addition, our client mix continued to change. Assets of corporate pension and thrift plans, other institutional accounts, and individual retirement accounts (IRAs), rose sharply, from a bit over one-third of our fund assets in the early 1990s to more than 60 percent in 2001. Those wonderful 401(k) and IRA plans that were not even in existence when Vanguard began had come to dominate our asset base, to the great benefit of shareholders who take advantage of the miracle of compounding higher returns on a tax-deferred basis, albeit only by accepting the extra risks involved. While we did not invent these plans, we emerged as a driving force and now rank as one of two industry leaders in this arena.

Near-Tragedy Turns to Triumph— A Personal Note

When I entered the hospital in the autumn of 1995, my future existence uncertain, the acceptance of the ideas that were at the core of Vanguard's character—stock market indexing, "stand-pat" strategies for bond funds, minimal portfolio turnover, tax-efficiency, no sales loads, low costs, had moved from the fringe of heresy to the threshold of acceptance. By 2001, they were approaching dogma, if not in the mutual fund industry itself, surely in academia, in the financial journals, and in the media. It has been a thrill to have survived for the more than five extra years I've been given and to be a witness to the sea change in the way people look at investing.

Those extra years of life have given me the opportunity to continue, not only my direct contribution to Vanguard, but, through speeches, press interviews, and television appearances, to spread the word about sound investment principles and sensible human values. Following the surprising success of my best-selling *Bogle on Mutual Funds: New Perspectives for the Intelligent Investor,* published in 1993, I wrote a sequel, *Common Sense on Mutual Funds: New Imperatives for the Intelligent Investor,* published in 1999, also a best-seller. In 2000, *John*

C. Bogle on Investing: The First 50 Years was published, to astonishingly favorable reviews. The book is a collection of my speeches both on investment philosophy and human values, and included the Princeton thesis I had written a half-century earlier. The surge of attention and interest generated by these books helped to sustain Vanguard's momentum in the marketplace that dated back to our formative years.

Since I walked out of the hospital to a new life of vigor in March 1996, many honors have also come my way. Nearly all of them, it seems to me, relate to the character I had strived to instill at Vanguard—to make the firm more than just another commercial enterprise. I've been honored with six honorary degrees, enshrined in the *Wall $treet Week* Hall of Fame, named as a global financial leader by a number of journals and books, designated the "Business Leader of 2000" by the Pennsylvania Chamber of Business and Industry, presented with the prestigious Distinguished Leadership Award of the Association for Investment Management and Research, and inducted into the Hall of Fame of the Fixed-Income Analysts Society.

In 1999 I was named by *Fortune* magazine as one of the four "Giants of the Twentieth Century" in the investment field. But perhaps my greatest honor was when my alma mater, Princeton University, chose me as its Woodrow Wilson Medalist, awarded each year to the alumnus who best represents "Princeton in the Nation's Service." Among the scores of statesmen, politicians, authors, and scientists who had received the prize during its long history, I was the first businessman to be so honored. It bemuses me to think that without a medical miracle, I would not have been around to enjoy these honors, bestowed as much on the company as on the man.

A Fifty-Year Milestone

I joined Wellington Management on July 5, 1951, serving to the best of my ability for nearly twenty-three years. Then followed twenty-seven years with Vanguard, the once-tiny firm I created in 1974, now an industry giant. My completion of fifty years of combined service at Wellington and Vanguard came on July 5, 2001. In May, my tiny but wonderful staff at Bogle Financial Markets Research Center organized a dinner attended by several hundred veteran crew members. It was a splendid celebration, replete with a staggering array of tributes from leaders of the financial world. I responded with a talk in which I looked back at my career, citing what turned out to be forty-eight short phrases that the crew had come to identify with me, including "Stay the course," "Costs matter," "The majesty of simplicity," "Even one person can make a difference," and "Press on regardless."

As always, I expressed my deep appreciation to our crew members for their loyalty and support, thanking them for making me look so much better than I am. I admitted I wasn't sure how long my desire or my determination or my fate would permit me to carry on my mission as Vanguard's founder, ambassador, author, and think-tank director. But I assured them that I wasn't yet through seeking challenges, using these words from Tennyson's *Ulysses,* with which I concluded my remarks:

> **Come, my friends.**
> **'Tis not too late to seek a newer world.**
> **Push off, and sitting well in order smite**
> **The sounding furrows; for my purpose holds**
> **To sail beyond the sunset, 'til I die. . . .**
>
> **That which we are, we are;**
> **One equal temper of heroic hearts**
> **Made weak by time and fate, but strong in will**
> **To strive, to seek, to find, and not to yield.**

Vanguard in the 1996 through 2001 Era

The period from 1996 through 2001 included two distinct phases in the stock market. During the first four years, the S&P 500 Index turned in three years with gains of about 25 percent, and another year with a gain of 33 percent. Incredible! The final two years saw the index fall 9 percent in 2000, and then 13 percent through the summer of 2001. For the full period, the average return on stocks was a remarkable 13 percent per year, nicely above the market's long-term norm. While Treasury bill returns declined to about 5 percent per year, bond returns averaged 7 percent annually during the period—only a bit less than in earlier periods. Putting it all together, in the golden era in which we had flourished since 1982, the financial markets had given us more than we had any right to expect.

Our growth pattern paralleled the ebb and flow of stock prices, further proof—if such be needed—that the mutual fund business is, above all, *market-sensitive.* Annual cash inflows into the Vanguard funds averaged $55 billion in 1996 through 1999, but fell to $7 billion in 2000 before recovering vigorously in 2001, with our index, bond, and money market funds leading the way. For the full period, we amassed an astonishing $270 billion of new cash flow from investors, and our asset base rose from $180 billion as 1996 began to $562 billion as September 2001 began. While our 22 percent annual rate of asset growth was the lowest for any period since our formative years, it was nonetheless stunning in an absolute sense, and triumphant relative to our major peers. Our market share continued to grow sharply, rising from 6.4 to 8.4 percent, a 30 percent increase that compared favorably with earlier periods. As the first year of the first century in the new millennium drew to its close, HMS *Vanguard* remained shipshape, steady, and well prepared for the battles that would surely lie ahead.

Memorandum to: The Crew
Date: May 24, 1995
Subject: Standing Down

*M*ORE THAN twenty years have passed since a fledgling organization that I named "Vanguard" entered the mutual fund industry. We have since become the second-largest mutual fund complex in the world, and just last week Vanguard Fund assets crossed the $150 billion mark for the first time, a 100-fold increase from where we began in 1974. I believe it is fair to say that we are changing—and will continue to change—this industry for the better, and surely to the direct benefit of the shareholders of all mutual funds.

We have had not only a challenging and exciting run but a run that has even accelerated in 1995. A few examples:

- *In investment performance,* our funds are having—across the board—their best year ever. During the past twelve months, our bond and money market funds have exceeded the returns earned by 93 percent of their peers, and our equity funds have outpaced 84 percent of their peers. These returns bring our average decade-long returns, respectively, to the 89th and 70th percentiles, highly competitive for this challenging business.

- *In service quality,* we have just won, for the fifth straight year, first place in the *Financial World* survey, the only industrywide survey available, a remarkable winning streak in this highly competitive industry.
- *In cash flow from investors,* we have made a solid recovery from last year's industrywide slump, with average monthly cash flow up 122 percent. The Vanguard funds' monthly cash inflow averaged $506 million in 1994. This year, monthly cash inflow has averaged $1.1 billion. We are leading the way once again.

In combination, these achievements in investment management, fund administration, and distribution have lifted our market share to an all-time high estimated at nearly 21 percent of direct marketing fund assets, up from 7 percent fifteen years ago.

Chairman, President Roles to Be Separated

Crossing the two-decade milestone and the $150 billion milestone virtually at the same time and witnessing what our Vanguard crew has built, it is a small wonder that I have been tempted to relax (just a wee bit) and to consider whether, as I enter my sixty-seventh year—and, counting two years for my Princeton senior thesis, my forty-sixth year of being almost compulsively addicted to this wonderful industry—it might be a sensible time for me to alter my role at Vanguard. Temptation and good judgment triumphed. At our board of directors' meeting last Friday, I told our directors that I wished to stand down, relinquishing my title and duties as chief executive officer effective January 31, 1996, but remaining as chairman of the board thereafter. The board has agreed to this change, and I am therefore announcing it today.

I also informed the board of my intention to nominate my heir-apparent, John J. Brennan, president of Vanguard, as my successor as chief executive officer. I have discussed this proposal with the directors, and I am satisfied that they have complete trust in his ability to lead Vanguard. So I am confident that when I am reelected chairman at next January's board meeting, he will be elected to the position of chief executive officer, reporting directly to the board of directors.

The Stamp of Our Character

The facts and figures I cited at the outset—which I never could have imagined back in 1974—are not really the important testament to what Vanguard has accomplished over the past two decades. Rather, I am proudest that my vision for Vanguard has come to pass. We have built a company whose stamp includes the following:

- Offering our services to some 5 million shareholders at operating costs that are, by magnitudes, the lowest in our industry and, given our pure no-load structure, at the most favorable terms of purchase.
- Proving that conservative investing is the best long-term philosophy for most mutual fund investors. High-quality financial assets have always been our stock-in-trade; as a result, we avoided some major potholes in 1994, including the failure of exotic derivative securities and Orange County municipal bonds and several international debacles.
- Putting index mutual funds on the map, forming the industry's first index mutual fund in 1975, and now offering, *with enthusiasm,* fully twenty-five index (or quasi-index) portfolios. Today, we are witnessing the triumph of indexing as an investment strategy.
- Eschewing the mad, hyperbolic advertising approach of touting "We're number 1," a claim that even those who advertise it know has no relevance whatsoever to future performance.
- Not participating in the gimmickry of offering new so-called products just as they get hot, such as government-plus bond funds, short-term global bond funds, and adjustable rate mortgage funds.
- Articulating our funds' investment objectives and policies with precision, carefully delineating their risk and their reward potential and, equally important, reporting their results with candor to our shareholders.
- Conducting Vanguard's business with integrity and the highest standards of commercial honor, although I recognize that it falls to more objective observers to make that judgment.

So, I look back with pride—not, I hope, false pride—on having created the kind of corporate character to which Vanguard aspired from the very beginning twenty years ago, with values and standards that are firmly embedded in our culture today and that will continue to be embedded there during the next twenty years and beyond.

The Courage of My Convictions

It's nearly time, then, to turn over the helm. I do so because I have the courage to hold these convictions:

- That it is possible (even for me!) to overstay one's time, a fear that, paradoxically, seems to diminish with the passage of years. Best to sense it early, then! The fact that my faltering heart has been broken (in the literal sense) for the past thirty-five years played a supporting role in my decision, for there's no point in tempting fate.
- That Jack Brennan is the best person I could possibly have found—and I've worked closely with him since 1982—to assume my executive responsibilities. I believe him to be a man of extraordinary character, intelligence, diligence, and judgment.
- That we have built an organization, from our senior officers on down to the front-line crew, that, whether I am at the helm or not, is at least as good as any in this business and that is fully capable of continuing to move Vanguard solidly forward.
- That our unique corporate governance structure—having our fund shareholders own our management company, which we referred to at the outset as "the Vanguard Experiment"—has met the test of time.
- That our cost advantage—critical to providing excellent long-term returns—will remain overpowering to our foes. While every industry must have a low-cost provider, few—if any—of them operate at *one-third* the costs of their next lowest competitor.
- That my vision of twenty years ago has now been firmly established and that the major tasks at hand for Vanguard, if we are to remain a powerful competitor, lie in furthering our information technology systems, our sophisticated marketing programs, and our enlightened management of a large enterprise. (I've never argued that these areas were my strong point.)

So, what began as the Vanguard *Experiment*—a *mutual* mutual fund organization—is now firmly in the record as the Vanguard *Experience*. We have marched to a different drummer and the world is beginning to take note. But our impact on this industry is only at its incipient stage. Even if our corporate structure is *never* emulated, the crying need to get fund shareholders out of the back seat and into the driver's seat—where they belong—will ultimately be met. I am not sure that the mutual fund industry needed "Vanguard" (and it surely didn't want us), but mutual fund shareholders clearly needed *a* Vanguard to test the proposition that a new way of doing business could succeed in serving investors while sustaining an enterprise—a company that would say, in effect, "We see what you're doing, but we think we can do it differently and better. May the best strategy win."

We have shown—in performance, in costs, in service quality, and in growth—that there is indeed a better way. But we must prove that proposition over and over again, ever mindful that in the long run, victory is won by the firm that provides the best performance, at the lowest cost, at the highest level of service excellence. I urge you to stay the course!

PATIENCE, PERSISTENCE, AND COURAGE: THREE ENDURING HALLMARKS OF VANGUARD

January 2, 1996

ON NEW YEAR'S DAY 1996, as the world completes one more turn toward the twenty-first century, I want to continue my tradition of speaking (or in recent years, writing) to you as the year begins. I hope to emulate the vision of Janus, the Roman god who, it is said, could look forward and backward at the same time.

This is a special opportunity for me to write to you, since John J. Brennan will become Vanguard's chief executive officer at the end of this month. But, no, I am not "retiring." Indeed, I am delighted to continue as Vanguard's chairman of the board, which will entail many exciting, if less demanding, responsibilities, including (1) continuing to watch over the interests of our clients and our crew, (2) being engaged in our investment management activities, and (3) speaking out on behalf of mutual fund shareholders, whether our own or those of other mutual fund complexes. *These investors deserve a fair shake, and I intend to do my best to see that they get it.* Surely the Vanguard Experiment in mutual fund governance was the first challenge to "the old order," and, as I will note later, we are today seeing the early signs of industry response to our patience, persistence, and courage.

Patience

Patience is defined in the second edition of the *Oxford English Dictionary* (OED II) as "the enduring of pain or trouble with

calmness and composure and without discontent or complaint."

As I repose at the hospital in the fourth month of my long wait for a new heart, I am staying very busy—sending memos, making telephone calls, reading, and writing. Time flies by, one day after another. At the same time, I am disciplining myself to the quality of patience, for the end of my wait is not yet on the horizon. I hardly need to tell you that patience is not one of the qualities usually associated with me. Yet it occurs to me in retrospect that, without patience—mine with the board of directors and the slowly turning world in which we operate, and the board's with me—what we know as "Vanguard" today could never have reached full fruition.

So, now for a bit of history. It is an open secret that, following the termination of my career with Wellington Management Company in January 1974, I recommended that the mutual funds in the Wellington group assume for themselves the entire set of mutual fund responsibilities in which Wellington was engaged: administration, distribution, and investment management. The funds, I proposed, would purchase the management company—and for an unbelievably low price at the time, given that the stock market was headed toward the nadir of its 50 percent decline from the 1973 high to the 1974 low. In effect, this move would have left Wellington Management Company with the institutional investment counsel business. It would have given us a running start. However, given the unprecedented nature of such a transaction, the complex regulatory hurdles to be surmounted, and a narrowly divided board—at least five of the eleven directors were strongly opposed—it quickly became clear that such a giant step was not in the cards.

Here is where the patience comes in. Rather than starting with one giant leap, we had to be satisfied with taking one small step at a time. So it took fully *seven years* to develop the sound foundation that remains central to Vanguard's activities today:

- *August 1974:* Fund directors agree to have their own officers assume responsibility for all of the funds' administrative, legal, and financial affairs.
- *September 1974:* When it becomes clear that a core corporation is needed to handle these duties, a new company is named, and then incorporated. The name "Vanguard" is born.

- *March 1975:* Vanguard internalizes all shareholder services activities, which had previously been performed by an outside data processing firm.
- *December 1975:* Vanguard takes its initial step into the investment management arena with the formation of First Index Investment Trust (now the 500 Portfolio of Vanguard Index Trust, the world's first index mutual fund).
- *February 1977:* Vanguard abandons its then-faltering broker-dealer distribution network, and drops all sales loads. Disagreeing with this new and unprecedented move, Wellington ceases to act as distributor, and Vanguard assumes responsibility for all fund distribution, marketing, and development activities (a close board vote: seven in favor, four opposed). We immediately become the second-largest—to T. Rowe Price—no-load fund complex.
- *September 1977:* Vanguard forms the first three-portfolio municipal bond fund. All three share the characteristics of high quality and low cost; they differ only in maturity—long term, short term, and intermediate term. Within a decade, this defined asset-class structure becomes the industry norm.
- *September 1981:* Vanguard becomes a full-fledged investment advisory firm, assuming portfolio management responsibilities for our money market fund (from Wellington) and our municipal bond funds (from Citibank). The Fixed Income Group is formed and staffed.

In retrospect, these step-by-step accretions to our activities seem to have happened overnight; in fact, they were accomplished only over seven long years. Taken together, they formed the firm foundation of the modern Vanguard.

Since 1981, of course, Vanguard has become a far stronger—to say nothing of far larger!—enterprise. Our senior staff is more experienced, and we have much greater management depth. We have also taken numerous and truly marvelous forward strides in information technology, in financial controls, in investment professionalism, and in both individual and institutional marketing. [Neither the IRA nor the 401(k) plan even existed when 1981 began!] We learned first to cope with, and then to master, the complexities of rapid industry growth. The eminent reputation and industry leadership of the modern Vanguard rest at least as much on the structure we have built since 1981 as on the foundation put in place in our embryonic years.

I hope you will forgive this extensive history of how Vanguard began, an unsurpassed illustration of the value of patience, both for our enterprise and for me personally. (My own patience, as I suggested earlier, then promptly departed, only to return of necessity nearly three months ago.) But while Chaucer assured us that "patience is a high virtue," I believe that patience should not last forever and at some point must take a back seat to persistence.

Persistence

Persistence is defined by OED II as "firm or obstinate continuation of a particular course in spite of opposition." I believe that persistence is the necessary concomitant of patience and that without it, Vanguard would not exist today. I also believe that, confronted with the circumstances I face today, obstinate continuance of my own course of action is essential.

As members of the crew of the HMS *Vanguard,* all of us will no doubt have need to call on the quality of persistence in the years to come, just as we have in our past. Our future is bright indeed, but we will eventually face heavy winds, wild hurricanes, and tempest-tossed seas. Unfortunately, we just don't know *when* they will happen, *how* severe they will be, and *where* they will arise. In short, at Vanguard we must continue to achieve our objectives despite the formidable opposition of our adversaries. Clearly, in the year just ended, we did exactly that.

In that light, it hardly seems inappropriate for us to take just a moment to bask in the bright sun and sail in the favorable breezes that we enjoyed during 1995:

- Our funds, as a group, provided the best returns—that is, we made the most money for the most investors—in our history. Strong absolute performance is, well, absolutely essential to our shareholders' financial well-being. Our performance was greatly enhanced by last year's astonishing bull markets in both stocks and bonds.
- Our *relative* performance was also the best in our history. That is, the Vanguard funds achieved, nearly across the board, significantly higher returns than those of their peers. We have always been in the crucible of competition of course, but we have not

always withstood its heat. However, our 1995 returns will be regarded by friend and foe alike as far exceeding competitive norms.

- Net cash flow by investors into the Vanguard funds was the highest in our history, totaling $25 billion. Coming in a single year alone, our asset *growth*—more than the *total* assets managed by all but 23 of the 250 largest fund complexes—is a marvelous tribute to the trust that shareholders have placed in us.

- Our Information Technology Voyage made extraordinary progress, bringing us to the pinnacle of industry leadership. Our service quality, with but a few exceptions, brought us to the same pinnacle.

- Our market share reversed its 1994 decline and brought us near our all-time high of 21 percent of the assets of the direct marketing group (mostly no-load or low-load funds). Simply put, today $1 of every $5 invested in funds within this dominant industry segment is now invested here at Vanguard. What is more, in 1995 $1 of every $3 of direct marketing cash flow was invested here.

- We crossed asset milestones of $140 billion, $150 billion, $160 billion, and $170 billion, and, according to our tradition, celebrated each one with pride.

As was the case two decades ago, this progress did not come in a single giant leap. Rather, it came in step-by-step fashion. Our success in 1995 was built over a score of years, brick by brick, upon the strong foundation on which we rested. We persistently sought "to dream the impossible dream," and then realize it.

Courage

To complete my trilogy, I now turn to *courage*, which is defined in OED II as "the heart of the spirit, mind, disposition, and nature . . . the quality of facing danger without fear . . . bravery, boldness, valor." It is surely among the most important of human virtues.

Let me be clear that I make this statement at a time of my life when danger lurks close by. But, far more importantly, I claim that quality for Vanguard—past, present, and future. And, most important of all, I claim that quality for each and every one of you on our crew. I am ever mindful of the fact that each of you has doubtless faced dangers of your own—perhaps different, but surely no less challenging than my own. The point is that we, collectively, have been, are, and will continue to be "Vanguard," and that is the entity that we must consider. Vanguard will require a strong sense of caring for one another, a burden that must be borne, as I have often quoted in the past, "by all who work for it, all who own it, all who are served by it, and all who govern it."

Indeed, there can be no doubt that our enterprise faces many dangers today. To mention but four of them:

1. *Absolute returns:* Repeating our 1995 success in generating outstanding absolute returns is very unlikely. ("One-way" major bull markets in stocks and bonds are probably a once-in-a-decade long shot.) Providing excellent relative returns is our mission, but we will be hard-pressed to emulate the substantial positive margins we achieved last year. And, of course, the shadow of the bear is an ever-present danger. I can only marvel at the fact that, since the stock market's complete collapse in 1973 and 1974, the Standard & Poor's 500 Index has had but two calendar years of negative returns—a decline of 7 percent in 1977 and 5 percent in 1981—both modest to a fault. (Yes, surprising as it may sound, the 500 Index actually *rose* in 1987 and 1994.) I'm not predicting that the sky will fall, but I *am* predicting that "trees don't grow to the sky." Please never forget that this is a market-sensitive business. Forewarned is forearmed!

2. *Schwab's OneSource:* Our competitive universe appears to be changing radically. Schwab's OneSource mutual fund program has truly become a new force in the mutual fund industry. Their aim is to make the fund family concept obsolete and replace it with one-stop shopping for whichever funds are "best" in each asset class or subclass, usually—and foolishly—based on short-term performance. (Some view it as the new paradigm, but I will reserve my own judgment until I see how it stands the test of time.)

   Despite its strengths, OneSource also has its weaknesses, and they are hardly inconsequential: (a) *All* of a fund's shareholders pay for the convenience, but few actually utilize it. (b) It is designed—successfully, I might add—to attract short-term traders rather than long-term investors, of which the latter I view as the key to Vanguard's future success. (c) It capitalizes on recent fund performance. A Five Star rating in Morningstar, for example, *sells* OneSource funds, despite the fact that past fund performance has no clear relationship to future performance. But at OneSource it is easy—and cheap, at least in terms of transaction costs—to change your mind when that fact is driven home by the reality of efficient markets. (d) It magnifies the tendency of investors to purchase shares *after* high returns are achieved and to redeem shares *after* the market plunges. This cycle of greed followed by panic—or, more charitably, of hope followed by fear—is the Achilles' heel of this industry. How we ultimately respond to the risk of OneSource becoming "the way business is done" in this industry is one of the major dangers that my successors will face.

3. *Benefits administration:* The third major danger that Vanguard will face is the development of *total benefits administration*, in which a single service provider assumes responsibility not only for the administration of a corporation's defined-contribution [401(k)] plan but also its defined benefit (pension) plan and its health care plan. Leaving aside the extraordinary complexities of these additional services, particularly health care, their administration could require us to undertake a very large increase in our Vanguard crew, something that I view with considerable concern, and something that may well not be in our best long-term interests. That said, in order to maintain our position of industry leadership, competition may force us to meet this challenge—whether we wish to or not.

4. *The enemy within:* As Pogo has observed, "We have met the enemy, and they are us." That is to say, perhaps the greatest danger to Vanguard is not from without but from within. We began with few assets and few crew members. Until 1990, we could manage the organization as a medium-sized enterprise (2,000 crew members). Today, we have a crew of more than 4,000, a difference not in degree but in kind. How we deal with the challenges of future growth—of lurking potential bureaucracy, of growing impersonality, of simply putting in one's time and collecting one's paycheck, rather than maintaining a sense of service and mission—remains to be seen.

But to help my successors in dealing with these challenges, I'd like to present a few pearls of wisdom, courtesy of the recently published *The B2 Chronicles,* by former Avis CEO Lynn Townsend:

> **(a) Big companies, as such, can be a lot of fun to work in, but only if they are broken up into smaller units where individuals believe they can be heard and can make an impact. (b) There are no secrets in most companies; how the leaders spend their time sends a message. Is it to be client feedback and service, or ego trips and junkets? (c) If the employees of the company don't feel passionately about anything ("it's just a job"), something is wrong with the company. (d) Fairness is essential. (e) There is a time for engagement and a time for withdrawal. A time to walk around the job. A time to contemplate it—and a time to just laugh at it.***

These are, I think, the four major challenges facing Vanguard today. I have full confidence that our crew and our leaders will respond to them courageously.

In Summary

I didn't set out to write such a long discourse, but as always, I have learned as I have written. (You can count your lucky stars that this is a written document and not a speech!) As we together face Vanguard's future, I hope that you too will learn from the lessons of our history and will be stimulated by my articulation of the values of patience, persistence, and courage.

Until we meet again, I want to tell you all that the cards, thoughts, prayers, and letters I have received from you and from our clients have been an immense source of strength for me. I cannot help but be truly inspired by these heartwarming messages, by what they say not only about me but about you who have helped make Vanguard what it is today. In particular, I want to thank you for your thoughtful and generous contributions to the Bogle Brothers Scholarship Fund at Blair Academy. I attended Blair on a full scholarship, which I helped to earn by working each mealtime as the "captain" (it's true!) of the dining room crew.

---

* I'm indebted to Morgan Stanley for these paraphrased excerpts from Lynn Townsend's book. I have done my best to have Vanguard meet these standards.

In his "Publisher's Statement" in the first issue of the *National Review* on November 19, 1955, William F. Buckley, Jr., the magazine's thirty-year-old editor-publisher, declared:

Let's face it: Unlike Vienna, it seems altogether possible that did the *National Review* not exist, no one would have invented it. We stand athwart history, yelling Stop, at a time when no one is inclined to do so, or to have much patience with those who do.

These sentiments, it seems to me, come astonishingly close to characterizing Vanguard—from its creation to this very day. *Had we not invented it twenty years ago, this new way of mutual fund governance would still await its birth. Today, we stand athwart mutual fund history, and surely yell "Stop" to the practices of the past, which have failed to place fund shareholders first—where common sense and fiduciary duty should have placed them long ago. And if our rivals have little patience with us, our own patience, limited only by our persistence and strengthened by our courage, shall carry the day.*

Let me close by extending to each of you at Vanguard this wonderful old toast to the New Year:

Yesterday is history. Tomorrow is a mystery. Today is a gift. That's why we call it *the present*.

So, ladies and gentlemen of the Vanguard crew, seize the day. *Carpe diem!* And may God bless you all.

OR WHAT'S A HEAVEN FOR?

June 11, 1996

As I COMPLETE forty-five years in this marvelous business on July 5, 1996, I offer you not a farewell address but an inaugural address. Brimming with joy and energy after my heart transplant fourteen weeks ago, I hope you will celebrate with me my transition to a less demanding role at Vanguard, serving primarily as chairman of the board. After nearly thirty years as chief executive, the time for a change has arrived, and I look forward to continuing to serve Vanguard, our directors, all of you on our crew, our shareholders, and even the mutual fund industry. I'll still be around.

To be sure, my career began long before Vanguard was even a gleam in my eye when I joined Wellington Management Company, our predecessor organization in 1951. At the same time, my career began with Wellington Fund, created by its founder, Walter L. Morgan, in 1928, itself a remarkable institution nearly one-half a century old when Vanguard was born in 1974. Wellington Fund, then, is our link to a proud tradition now spanning nearly seventy years, virtually the entire history of the U.S. mutual fund industry.

There is a canny piece of advice, said to arise from the wisdom of Yogi Berra: "When you come to a fork in the road of life, take it." Well, that is what Wellington Fund and I did in 1974, when Vanguard came into existence. We took that fork—more, we created it—and the rest is history.

Conceived in Hell

Vanguard's early years were not easy. To say, as in the song "Bui Doi" from *Miss Saigon,* that we were "conceived in hell and born in strife" might seem a bit strong. But as we bask in the glory of this halcyon era, few of you here tonight can imagine those early days. In fact, "born in strife" is fairly accurate, for Vanguard's birth was the result more of a messy power struggle among flawed human beings than a crusade for glory. And even "conceived in hell" is close to the mark, for Vanguard's conception took place during a chapter in the history of financial markets that could hardly have been worse.

Let me visualize it with you. When Vanguard was incorporated on September 24, 1974, we were just days from the bottom of the worst stock market crash since 1929. The Dow-Jones Industrial Average had fallen from a high of 1,033 in late 1972 to 577. Even worse, the total value of *all* stocks was down 50 percent in the same time period. And the assets of our mutual funds had plummeted from $2.6 billion to $1.3 billion. We were but in the fourth year of what would be an eighty-consecutive-month (!) period of cash *outflow* from our funds that was to endure until January 1978. The accumulated outflow was $930 million, equal to 36 percent of our assets when the hemorrhaging began. "Other than that," as the saying goes, it was the perfect time to start a new enterprise.

Let me put these figures in today's context. It is as if the Dow were to drop from 5,800 to 3,300. As if our assets were to drop from $200 billion to $100 billion. As if we were to enter a period of negative capital outflow that would continue unremittingly—month after month—until it totaled $72 billion at the start of the year 2003. Could it happen again? Let me give you the only honest answer to any question about the future of any enterprise, and especially any enterprise engaged in the financial markets: *Of course it could.*

Will it happen again? I can't imagine it. But I'm sure that any complacency on our part will be hardly treated kindly by history, for Vanguard must "carry on" both when the breezes are warm and benign *and* when the seas are stormy and tempest-ridden; in times of triumph and disaster alike. I hardly need to remind you that *Press On Regardless* must be our rule of action—indeed our rule of life.

Where Are the Industry Pioneers Today?

We have measured up to this motto—first tacitly, then explicitly—over our near-seven-decade history. Consider Wellington Fund. When he founded Wellington in 1928, Walter Morgan—my mentor for fifteen years and my friend to this day—was one of the great pioneers (I would argue *the* greatest) of the mutual fund industry. It was only the fifth mutual fund to come into existence, following Massachusetts Investors Trust (MIT) and State Street Investment Trust (1924), Incorporated Investors (1925), and Scudder Stevens and Clark Fund (1928). Tiny as it was, Wellington was an industry leader almost from the start. Its assets crossed $100 million in 1950, $1 billion in 1959, and $2 billion in 1965, a truly triumphant accomplishment for those days. But near disaster was soon to follow, as assets tumbled to a low of $460 million in 1982. Some tumble! An unfortunate amalgam of poor financial markets, poor investment advice, and the—premature, to say the least—demise of the balanced fund.

But we pressed on. And we endured. In 1978, Vanguard changed the fund's strategy but not its policies and objectives. After a decade of failure, good performance returned and the fund has been distinguishing itself ever since. Today, Wellington Fund—ever since 1974 controlled by its own directors, beholden to its own shareholders—has assets of $14 billion and is one of the fifteen largest equity-based funds in the world.

And what of the others? MIT (now $2 billion in assets) and State Street ($700 million) have been left in the dust of this burgeoning industry. Worse (from my perspective), they are now run by *auschlanders*—two of the largest life insurance companies in North America, bureaucratic repositories of huge assets but bereft of mutual fund tradition. Incorporated Investors ($1 billion) has long since been acquired by another fund complex, its original name now in the dustbin of history. And, saddest of all is Scudder. The fund abandoned its balanced policy in 1977 and became a bond fund named "Scudder Income Fund." At that point, ever the contrarian, I was sure that the concept of balanced investing would return to favor, and we stayed the course. Surely, the renaissance of Wellington Fund is living proof of the power of our maxim: *Press On Regardless.*

In the past decade, The Vanguard Group has moved from the tenth-largest to the second-largest mutual fund enterprise in the world. It is no small accomplishment that we all share together. We are also prospering together; witness the record $28 million distribution—think of that!—from the Vanguard Partnership Plan that will be announced in just a few climactic moments. Without any question whatsoever—whether measured in returns earned, in value added, in service quality, in information technology advances, and in organizational effectiveness—1995 was the greatest year in our history. *Thank you.*

And what of today's *largest* firm? Well, Fidelity is, as you all know, stumbling a bit. (I remind you not to smirk: *There but for the grace of God go we.*) If they still have a lock on being the biggest, I guess we will simply have to be content in being the best. In any event, that daunting leopard is being forced to change its spots, indeed to transmute into something that looks suspiciously like an eighteenth-century British warship. The *New York Times* recently reported that "Fidelity is starting [*starting?*] to pay attention to how managers achieve their results and is trying [*trying?*] to make funds more predictable—changes driven in large part by changes in the investing public." Roughly translated, they are emulating Vanguard, adopting principles that we have maintained intact throughout our twenty-two-year history—but they are doing so without commensurately reducing the large costs they lay on their investors. In short, they seem to be ignoring another Yogi Berra truism: "If you can't imitate him, don't copy him." Ever feisty, I warn Fidelity: "If you can't imitate us, don't bother to copy us."

A final observation: Our path to industry leadership is a tribute to your efforts, to our outstanding investment performance, to our low expenses and no-load structure, to our strategy, to our extraordinary shareholder service, to our communications, to our reaching out to individual investor and institutional investor alike. Not much question about all of that! But our intangible assets—our spirits—are at least equally responsible. Reiterating my quotation from Lord Keynes at our $20 billion celebration one decade ago, almost to the day: "It is the merest pretense to suggest that enterprise is actuated by an exact calculation of benefits to come. . . . Without animal spirits, an enterprise depending solely on a mathematical expectation will wither and die." Put another way, while the *value* we are almost universally recognized as providing to investors has been critical to our success, this value is the result of our *values*—our corporate character and our spirit.

The Soul of Our Enterprise

In recent months of travail and changing responsibilities, I've received hundreds of letters (six more on this very day!). Their overpowering common theme is the honesty, integrity, and candor we have brought to this enterprise and to this industry. They know—as we know—*who we are.* Always remember that numeric values, so easy to quantify, rarely fully explain the world. *Spiritual values carry the day.* For without our values, we have nothing. Please never let our values change. Please never let us lose our soul.

My conviction about values echoes these profound words from Thomas Carlyle, in his classic book *Heroes and Hero Worship,* originally published in 1841. Carlyle said that a man's thoughts are the parents of his actions:

> **The thing a man does practically lay to heart, and know for certain; concerning his duty and destiny and this mysterious universe [is] the primary thing for him, and creatively determines all the rest. . . . Of a man or of a nation we inquire, therefore, what religion they had. Was it heathenism; mere sensuous representation of this mystery of life? Was it Christianism; faith in the invisible, as the only reality? Was it skepticism, uncertainty, and inquiry whether there was an unseen world? . . . Answering this question gives us the soul of the history of the man or nation [and, I would add, "or enterprise"]. The thoughts they had were the parents of the actions they did; their feelings were the parents of their thought; it was the unseen and spiritual in them that determined the outward and the actual.**

I conclude by humbly saying to you: Thank you, to each one of you individuals who together make up Vanguard in 1996. Thank you for sharing the responsibility of caring for this enterprise, a structure that provides *value*, yes, but one that is constructed on a solid foundation of *values*. Providence created for me a role that would demand my every strength, and would seem to ignore my every weakness. Truly, it's been a bit of heaven for me, as we have grasped the goals that were within our competence and our values, even as we reach for ever higher goals. Robert Browning's timeless words express it well:

> **Ay, but a man's reach should exceed his grasp, or what's a heaven for?**

A PERMANENT REMINDER
FROM AN IMAGE IN BRONZE

November 19, 1996

GOOD AFTERNOON. I want to begin my comments by expressing my appreciation to the Vanguard Board of Directors for deciding to commission this sculpture, and to each of you for taking the time to come out on this bright but chilly day to be with me as the statue is unveiled.

Being introduced as "this great man" is quite humbling. And were I before an audience of investors or industry titans, I might even revel in it. But *not* before you who know me, and with whom I've worked for many years. Rather, I hope you know me for the man I *really* am, a normal—if flawed—human being who had just a few good—if common-sense—ideas, along with the determination to implement them with the help of a terrific crew who believed in the mission that is Vanguard, and who gave generously of themselves in the quest to make this experiment become reality. Thanks to each of you, and 5,000 others like you, Vanguard is surely a reality today.

As you know, I've had plenty of setbacks during my life. I've faced triumph and disaster during my career; tough and enduring family challenges; hard work in making the most of a decent but hardly brilliant mind; and tests of my physical body that have made extraordinary demands on my faith and determination, both of which, I hasten to add, remain vibrant today.

The Odyssey of Our Lives

But only a fool could believe that he alone has faced the challenges of dealing with a life that has been a tempest-tossed odyssey. I am certain that all of you members of our crew are engaged in similar voyages of your own—voyages that are fraught with similar challenges, in some cases perhaps less rigorous, more often surely much tougher than mine. Finally, I suppose, although I have probably had more lucky breaks than anyone here, you are just like me and I am just like you as we struggle with life's challenges. Together, we are a crew, with each individual playing a role in Vanguard's success.

In this sense, I'm somewhat embarrassed that it is *my* image on the statue that has just been unveiled. It brings forth complex emotions, and I confess that I feel rather strange and ambivalent about seeing myself in bronze, literally larger than life. (Not to be confused with "a legend in his own mind.") When the idea was proposed to me in my hospital bed, after months of waiting and continuous intravenous fluid sustaining my fragile existence, I'm not sure that I was entirely rational. As it turned out, I had many weeks still to go before receiving my heart transplant and a second chance for life. And yet even this comment may be just an excuse for my self-indulgence in accepting such an eternal monument—and it is a "kick"!

On the one hand, we all think of a statue as a memory of the departed, a memorial. I wasn't ready for that then, and I'm surely not ready now! But at the time the possibility of a sculpture of me first arose, I was comforted by seeing a photograph of a sculpture of a very-much-alive Arnold Palmer, soon to be delivered to the Augusta National Golf Course. And since my future was uncertain, I thought "Why not?"

And so here it is, and here I am—with my new heart, and with better health and more strength and energy than I've had in years, perhaps in even a decade. It is a miracle. This recent anecdote may bear witness to my rebirth: At a celebration at Princeton University just a few weeks ago, an alumnus, observing the name on my identification badge said: "I think I recognize your name. Do you mind if I ask you a question?" "Please do," I responded. "How is *your father* doing after his heart transplant?" Almost at a loss for words, I could only respond: "I *am* my father. And you've not only made my *day*, but the rest of my *life!*"

In the Vanguard tradition, this revitalized *one man* is determined to continue to *make a difference* here in the years to come. The one-word description of me on the statue says it all: *Founder.* And that's good enough for me. From the creation of Vanguard in 1974, I've tried to give us—all of you on the crew—not only the innovative corporate strategy but the conservative investment philosophy, the concern for human values, and even the details—from timeless policies to antique naval prints—that will endure far longer than my all-too-mortal body will ever last, no matter how vibrant and alive I feel today.

Something Good and Pure and True

I hope this legacy will last longer than fifty-three years. I pick that time horizon from a letter a Vanguard shareholder wrote to one of our senior officers a few years ago, purporting to describe me:

> **I've invested with Vanguard for many years, and I would like to see it stick to its roots. I'm sure Bogle is a hard man to work for. People like that always are. I know. We have one in our family, and the fact that he's been dead for fifty-three years hasn't lessened his influence much. But people like this strike a chord in the public because they stand for something—something good and pure and true.**

Thanks to all of you for sticking with me in spite of my faults.

It doesn't take many letters like that one to give me strength to carry on. Over the years I've received perhaps 2,000 extraordinary letters from shareholders expressing incredible trust and confidence in what this place is all about. Specifically, as the subtitle of the new book *The Vanguard Experiment* suggests, I will carry on my "quest to transform the mutual fund industry" by speaking out publicly. Just in the last few weeks, for example, I've received scores of letters applauding the convictions I expressed in my recent speech in Chicago to business editors and writers, entitled "Important Principles Must Be Inflexible." Here are excerpts from just four of the letters:

> **A couple in Cataumet, Massachusetts: Thank you for still being a strong voice of reason against the excessive hype, and casino atmosphere, in the industry. Thank you also for the wonderful performance of your Vanguard funds over the years and your advice and your philosophy.**
>
> **A man in Chesterfield, Missouri: The primary reason I elected to invest my family's assets with The Vanguard Group is the fundamental principle you and management continue to**

pursue. That principle is that low-cost and sound long-term investment strategies will outperform any "quick-pick" super-market or lotto fund game of the week.

A woman in LaGeorge, Illinois: Thank you for speaking up for the individual investor like me. Thank goodness for your phi-losophy and frankness. And please be a mentor to younger men and women in the investment field.

This wonderful—but unnecessary—postscript followed:

I sprayed cologne on this to make the company think this really was personal and maybe you would really read it.

An investment adviser in Larkspur, California: Fantastic speech! I couldn't agree with you more. What I particularly like was your point, how can one person's personal principles so bla-tantly contradict one's business principles? Unfortunately, that seems to be the norm in today's business world.

Changing the World of Mutual Fund Investing

Perhaps obviously, the regard our investors expressed in the countless letters I receive testifying to the belief of thousands of investors—I'll continue to refer to them as "real human beings"—in Vanguard's val-ues is gratifying to my ego. More, it shows all of us that we're doing more than merely putting in time here. We're changing the world of mutual fund investing—and changing it for the better for millions of investors.

But enough of bragging before one's own bronze image. Let me leave you and the rest of the crew with this thought: Our success—such as it may be—in this burgeoning industry has been driven by the fact that twenty-two years ago, when two roads diverged in the woods, we took (using Robert Frost's lovely and apt analogy) "the road less traveled by." And that has made "all the difference" for Vanguard. Please remember that central fact, always.

And please, every day, *stay on that road that we have chosen.* Hav-ing once diverged, let us not begin to converge on that other road followed by our rivals in this industry, an industry so badly in need of a more principled focus—a focus not on marketing but on trustee-ship, a focus not on the interests of fund managers but on the inter-est of fund shareholders. No, that well-traveled road is not the right road for us.

We have been driven by the primacy of principle over profit. We are indeed a crew, working together with a common objective and united by principle. If this statue endures as a permanent reminder of the fact that "Important Principles Must Be Inflexible," it will have done its job, and your founder, wherever he may be, will always be proud of you.

A TRIBUTE TO
WALTER MORGAN

June 9, 1998

*T*ONIGHT, WE gather to celebrate, for the thirteenth year, the Vanguard Partnership Plan. It was designed to ensure that all of you who help to create the rewards reaped by Vanguard investors share in those rewards too. When we initiated the plan in 1985, my expectation was that it would become a Vanguard tradition. And so it has.

Only years earlier, in 1984, we had instituted another practice that I also expected to become a tradition: the Award for Excellence. Even as the partnership plan was designed as a *group* award, to recognize that we needed every single member—every human being—on our crew to contribute to the successful voyage of our HMS *Vanguard* flagship, the Award for Excellence was an *individual* award, designed to recognize that "even one person can make a difference."

Among all of the Vanguard traditions we've created, I'm especially proud of these two, designed to honor the fine human beings—all of you out there—whom we are fortunate to have aboard. Together, these two very different types of recognition express my profound conviction about the sources of our success, put into words so beautifully by Helen Keller. *"The world is moved along not only by the mighty shoves of its heroes but by the aggregate of the tiny pushes of each worker."* It is you who do the real day-to-day hard work at Vanguard that is largely responsible for our success in taking this company built on a rock—on the rock of a few simple, common-sense investment principles—to the very pinnacle of the mutual fund industry.

Tonight, we continue our tradition of honoring crew members who, by displaying qualities that have truly made a difference by offering exceptional service and professionalism, special reliability in job performance, extraordinary creativity and initiative, and singular self-motivation. While the rewards for winning this award carry less financial heft—to say the least—than those of the partnership plan, they carry a sense of individual contribution of *human beingship* that makes them special indeed.

The individual whom I will honor this evening with a special Award for Excellence is someone who meets our standards of singular self-motivation, exceptional service, and extraordinary initiative to the fullest. In truth, he is one of those that Helen Keller described as heroes, a Renaissance man who, many decades ago, gave the investment world a mighty shove. As it happens, he is eligible neither for the crew member Award for Excellence nor for the management Award for Excellence. For, paradoxically, he has never worked at Vanguard, not for even a single day of his long career. *But he is not only a person who has made a difference. He has made all the difference.* While many of you know him and many more, I hope, know *of* him, I have known him intimately for nearly fifty years. For I was first introduced to him at Princeton University in 1950, a year before my graduation.

He gave me my first break. And, without ever realizing that he had done so, he gave you, if not your first break, the opportunity to be a member of this wonderful crew. Just imagine it: If he had never been born, or if he had remained a public accountant; if he had not founded one of America's first mutual funds seventy years ago this coming December 28; if he had not taken a chance on a shy, boyish, energetic, insecure, and terribly determined young kid with a crewcut way back in 1951, Vanguard would not be here—or anywhere else—today.

Whether you're a Vanguard veteran or an entering freshman wondering just what in the name of peace is going on tonight, you might take just a moment to imagine where you'd be right now if even one of the many odd, seemingly random twists in the road that brought this enterprise into existence in 1974 had not taken place. Had I never met this great man, I wonder where *I'd* be too. (It's too long a story for tonight, but perhaps I'll tell you about it on another day. In the meanwhile, the Ship's Chandlery is restocking *John Bogle and the Vanguard Experiment,* which tells the story in some detail.)

My eternal love and respect *for* him, and my enduring loyalty *to* him, may be indicated by the fact that I'm dedicating my new book to him. (It will be called *Common Sense on Mutual Funds: New Imperatives for the Intelligent Investor,* and should be published early next year.) Here are the words I'm using:

Founder of Wellington Fund, dean of the mutual fund industry, fellow Princetonian, mentor, friend. He gave me my first break. He remained loyal through thick and thin. He gives me strength to carry on.

Principles That Endure

While he hardly could have imagined the two long traditions we celebrate tonight, I want you all to know that this fine mentor was responsible for inculcating in his young protégé many of the principles that governed *his* enterprise, where I worked for twenty-three years. Those principles remain at the very core of Vanguard's character today:

- *Investment balance:* Stocks and bonds, working together
- *Conservative investing:* Quality, quality, always quality
- *Long-term focus:* For the goals of our funds and the horizons of our shareholders alike
- *Fair dealing:* Keeping costs low for clients, and speaking to them with complete candor about risks, returns, and costs
- *Loyalty: Equitable and honorable relationships* with the human beings within our two constituencies—those we now call clients, and crew

I'm hard-pressed to think of much of Vanguard's existence that hasn't been strengthened by my mentor's tutelage. The only example that comes quickly to mind is the index fund, and my recollection is that he thought that was a pretty "wild and crazy idea." He also didn't much care for the name "Vanguard" when he first heard it ("Sounds like a troop of acrobats"). But today he's enormously proud of it, and all of you, and of what we have accomplished together.

You should know that during his years as my boss, as Wellington's chief executive and chairman, Walter Morgan and I had great times, but in candor, not always easy times. During the years after I became chief executive and he remained chairman, we also enjoyed a superb relationship. And when he stepped down and made me fund chairman in 1970—now nearly thirty years ago, before Vanguard even began—the great years continued, right up to this very day. Only last Saturday I visited him at his home, and I was once again treated to the force of his personality, the generosity of his spirit, and the warmth of his soul. No relationship in my entire life has endured so long and so powerfully.

I placed his nomination before our Awards for Excellence Committee for a very special and timely reason. And I was delighted that the committee enthusiastically endorsed my recommendation. So it is with great pride, and no small amount of emotion, that I present the Award for Excellence—*in absentia,* for he's not able to travel right now—to an extraordinary human being to whom we all owe a monumental obligation for helping to shape the high values we represent. He is indeed a hero. Tonight we honor him with our Award for Excellence, even as we prepare to celebrate not only the coming seventieth anniversary of Wellington Fund on December 28 but, on July 23, his one hundredth birthday.

Thank you, and God bless you always, Walter Morgan.

THE TYRANNY OF COMPOUNDING

June 8, 1999

*I*T IS AGAIN my special privilege to present this quarter's Awards for Excellence to some of our most loyal and dedicated crew members. Before I do, however, I want to take just a few moments to tell you all what a truly fantastic year I've had working with all of you human beings who have made me look so good for so many years. And I thank you for doing that!

When Vanguard Was Incorporated

As you may know, the twenty-fifth anniversary of my founding of Vanguard will take place just a few months from now. On September 24, 1974, we had just 28 crew members; today we number 9,200. And yet I think I've spent more time in face-to-face meetings with you in the past year than in any of the first twenty-four.

Yes, meeting, exchanging a few words with you, shaking hands with you, and signing my newest book for you helped! I think I've signed more than 3,500 copies of *Common Sense on Mutual Funds* so far, and I'm still ready, willing, and able, and with a full pen, for any more. I've also given talks about Vanguard's history and future challenges to at least ten different groups within Vanguard—something I'll also continue to do on your request—and, just to maintain a human touch, I've held thirty- to forty-five-minute meetings with each Award for Excellence winner. And, when I'm not traveling, I've also been thrilled just to hang out and see you in and around the galley at lunch hour.

But I have traveled a great deal in the past year, giving speeches and meeting with Flagship clients from coast to coast and abroad, and visiting our offices in Australia, Phoenix, and Charlotte, completing the sweep in Brussels (actually in Waterloo . . . a great Wellington place!) just a few short weeks ago. The extravagant generosity of your welcomes—here and there alike—and the opportunity to be with you have reinforced my extraordinary pride in all of you who serve on our crew with such distinction, dedication, and effectiveness. You are my legacy, and the fact that you share the human values we have held since the outset nearly a quarter century ago has made possible the rapid and widespread acceptance of our astonishingly simply investment ideas and human values.

To recall a theme I've spoken of before, we operate in an industry filled with foxes who know, oh, so many things. We are the lone hedgehog who knows one *great* thing: that financial success is based on long-term investing in highly diversified portfolios, grounded in investment fundamentals and operated at low cost. *For the wise investor who stays the course, the hedgehog strategy is the winning strategy.* For it works. *It works.*

The growth and acceptance of our ideas was so easily predictable. In fact, in a real sense, I predicted it a decade ago. At the officers' off-site meeting early in 1990, I drew a chart showing the 26 percent annual growth rate that had taken our assets from $1.4 billion in 1974 to $48 billion at the end of 1989. I pointed out that, if that rate continued—of course, I couldn't imagine that it would!—our assets would reach $435 billion at the end of 1998. Adding another half year to that to carry us to mid-1999 would bring us to $485 billion. And where do we find ourselves at this moment? At $490 billion. *A truly remarkable coincidence.*

Always concerned and sober about the challenges we would face as we grew—even at a growth rate slower than 26 percent—I titled that 1990 chart "The Tyranny of Compounding." And so it is. While I revel in our ability to effectively serve more and more shareholders, I must confess that I cringe a bit at the obvious fact that our giant size makes neither the *business* of investing nor the face-to-face *management* of human beings any easier. On the contrary. So I entreat each of you to take the responsibility to keep this great warship operating on a personal, human basis, using your energies in your own groups to ensure that we honor the contributions of each one of the near-10,000 crew members who ply the seas together on the mighty HMS *Vanguard* today. It is a sacred mission. I'll continue to do my best in the years ahead, and I trust in you to do your best too.

May God bless you all, always.

THE POWER OF AN IDEA: REFLECTIONS ON OUR TWENTY-FIFTH ANNIVERSARY

September 24, 1999

Remember ye not the former things, neither consider the things of old. Behold. I will do a new thing; now it shall spring forth; shall ye not know it? I will maketh a way in the sea, a path in the mighty waters, and the army and the power shall lie down together and they shall not rise: they are quenched; they are extinct.

*T*HESE WORDS attributed to the Lord by the prophet Isaiah strike me as eerily prophetic of the success Vanguard has enjoyed since our birth twenty-five years ago.* We did a new thing, and it sprang forth. The HMS *Vanguard* made her way in the sea; many of the industry powers then opposing us have been quenched, and, despite the extraordinary growth of this industry, a few are even extinct.

Perhaps even more to the point, the passage from Isaiah poses an interesting paradox: Even at the pinnacle of our success today, should we now forget our things of old? Before we look ahead to the next twenty-five years, let's look back to the time of our founding for some perspective.

---

* I confess that I modified the passage from Isaiah 43:15 in my ordering of the phrases, so as to enhance its relevance to Vanguard.

Like the phoenix, Vanguard sprang from the ashes of its predecessor. Just as that mythical bird of gorgeous plumage burned itself to ashes when it grew old, only to reemerge with renewed youth, so Vanguard was created out of the shift of the responsibility for the operations of the then-Wellington funds from Wellington Management Company to this new, untried enterprise. At the outset, only the administrative activities—not the investment and marketing activities—were transferred.

In 1974, the proposition that mutual funds would administer their own affairs was a novel idea. Our objective: to put the fund shareholder in the driver's seat, in effect moving the management company to the rear. In order to suggest that our idea would be in the forefront of an important new trend, I chose the name "Vanguard," hardly unaware that in the glorious sea battle at the Nile in 1798, Lord Nelson's victorious flagship was named "the HMS *Vanguard*." And so, with the naming of the new firm on September 24, 1974, our nautical tradition too began.

To get where we wanted to be—to manage all the activities of the now-Vanguard funds—it was obvious that we needed to control both our investment management and our share distribution activities. But at the outset, these responsibilities had been declared the sole responsibility of Wellington Management Company. Since they were off-limits for Vanguard, they put a roadblock in the way of our ability to control our destiny. We were able to overcome that obstacle with remarkable speed. In less than a year, I proposed that Vanguard introduce a new and hitherto-unheard-of approach to mutual fund investing: the market index fund. In a contentious board meeting, the day was carried only when, reaching for a straw that would justify this apparent breach of our limited mandate, I pointed out that such a fund required no active management. And when the world's first index mutual fund was incorporated on December 31, 1975, we had assumed our first important responsibilities.

Less than eight months later, we turned our attention to distribution. Sales commissions and stock brokers had been part of Wellington throughout its fifty-year history, but the future seemed to call for making funds available to investors on a no-load basis through the direct marketing channel. Thus, I took a deep breath and recommended that we abandon our historical dealer network and terminate Wellington's services as distributor. No, we were not becoming a distributor (or so I argued in order to justify another departure from the board's initial mandate). Rather, we were obviating the very need for a distributor. While that argument, like the index argument, may have stretched the board's credulity, the plan to go the no-load route was approved by a margin of just two votes, and sales charges on all of the funds were eliminated on February 9, 1977. In little more than two years from our founding, we had put into place the essential structure under which we operate today: a full-line mutual fund complex providing administrative, investment, and marketing services.

Stewardship—The One Great Idea

Stewardship: The one great idea that explains what Vanguard is, who it is, and what it does. Serving the shareholder first; acting as trustee, in a fiduciary capacity. Mutual funds of the investor, by the investor, for the investor.

If you reflect on this concept, you quickly come to realize that it is from this one great idea that everything else flows:

Our mutual structure: Funds owned and controlled by their shareholder-owners

Low costs: Eliminating the huge profits extracted by fund managers, and then holding operating expenses to the lowest level possible, together ensuring that the maximum portion of each fund's investment returns flows through to its owners

Market index funds: Relying on minimal cost to effectively guarantee that investors receive some 98 percent of the annual returns earned by a given financial asset category (The facts are that few fund managers can ever reach 100 percent consistently and that the typical mutual fund has provided some 75 percent.)

Long-term investment policies: Holding portfolio turnover, and hence the attendant costs and taxes, to rock-bottom levels, and allowing a seemingly modest annual cost advantage to compound the aggregate growth of an investment account at a rate that can easily *double* the wealth accumulations of a fund's long-term shareholders

Fixed-income funds: Giving low cost its optimal leverage in providing extra returns to investors by clearly defining maturity ranges, maintaining peerless quality, and providing skilled professional management

I hope you will forgive my repeating this litany of things that you already know about Vanguard. But I have presented them in order to drive home the point that it is that one great idea—*stewardship,* as I have defined it—that explains so very much of our success. These simple policies I have described may not seem very imaginative. Indeed they are not. Not only unremarkable, they are trite; they are dull; and they are obvious. In fact, they are startlingly close to the formula for fund success that I described in my Princeton senior thesis, which I began to write nearly fifty years ago this December: *Mutual funds should be run in the most honest, efficient, and economical way possible.* And it works.

Anyone else in this business could easily have thought of these policies and implemented them long before I started Vanguard. Why they *didn't* and why we *did* is a question that is surprisingly easy to answer: If a fund manager were interested in maximizing its *own* profits— inevitably at the expense of the owners of the mutual funds it manages—it would charge the *highest* fees that traffic would bear unless it was absolutely forced to charge lower fees, either by the marketplace or by government regulation. But if the firm's goal were to maximize the profits of its *fund shareholders,* it would charge the *lowest* fees possible, and minimizing fund costs would be its highest and most obvious priority.

In the direct, dollar-for-dollar trade-off between the returns earned by fund shareholders and the returns earned by fund managers, the manager who takes the least delivers the most. No matter whether a stock fund or a bond fund or a money market fund, the syllogism holds. This trade-off is not only self-evident but it is also borne out by the record: Low-cost funds as a group consistently outpace their high-cost counterparts. In some cases it takes a while; in others it is immediate—money market funds and index funds, for example. That's one reason why index funds are so unpopular with managers, and why they are so popular with investors.

Twenty-Five Years Later

Twenty-five years later, the tangible results of our one great idea are all around us. Our assets, $1 billion at the outset, are $500 billion today. With a compound annual growth rate of 27 percent, our assets have doubled every three years and with remarkable regularity. At the outset, we were an also-ran in a stagnant industry with aggregate assets in

1974 of but $40 billion, and we ranked fourteenth among mutual fund firms. The Dow-Jones Industrial Average was then at 650, near the bottom of a horrendous bear market that had slashed stock prices by 50 percent. (Never forget that it *can* happen again.) But within a year, the industry's resurgence began.

Today, the Dow stands above 10,000; the assets of the mutual fund industry exceeded $5.6 trillion; and we are one of the industry's two leaders in assets under management. What is more, we are *the* leader in cash inflow, and by a compelling margin. Vanguard alone accounts for a truly remarkable 31 percent share of the market for long-term funds: Of every $3 that flows into mutual funds, $1 presently comes through the door of the house we built all those years ago.

But it is not the tangible reflections of our leadership that rate highest with me. It is the great intangible: the leadership of our philosophies and values. And, even if ever so slowly, they are beginning to spread. *Even one company can make a difference.* The most obvious example is the index fund. We formed the Vanguard 500 Index Fund in 1975, and nearly ten years passed before a single competitor entered the fray. But today there are 341 index funds out there, 108 modeled on the Standard & Poor's 500 Index. We remain the leader by far, with 63 percent of the industry's index fund assets, including not only our two 500 funds but index funds keyed to the total U.S. stock market, mid-cap and small-cap stocks, growth and value, international, bond and balanced, virtually all Vanguard firsts.

Index funds today represent nearly $200 billion of our $500 billion asset base, and their importance is soaring. So far this year, they represent 88 percent of our stock fund cash flow, 97 percent of our balanced fund cash flow, and 40 percent of our taxable bond fund cash flow. The initial theoretical appeal of indexing has proven itself through pragmatic experience, providing superior performance relative to active professional managers.

Tax-managed funds are another example. While I'm proud of the early timing of our first index funds, I'm embarrassed by being so late to start our tax-managed funds. Not until mid-1994 did we form these funds, probably at least five years after the need for them became obvious. Yet, once again, our series of tax-managed funds was another Vanguard first. And the list hardly stops there. Our bond funds totally dominate the direct marketing arena. Only 33 of 1,200 such bond funds have topped $2 billion of assets, and 10 of them are

Vanguard funds. Many of our rivals have aped our pioneering defined-maturity strategy, but, alas for their success, without copying our quality rigor and our low costs. Our money market funds are among the very highest yielding and, hardly surprising therefore, among the largest in the field. And while the excessive costs that burden the returns of these bond and money market funds have declined but little, most observers credit our competitive posture with helping to put a ceiling on expense ratios of the funds of our peers.

Making a Difference

These examples are enough to make the point: In the areas that mean the most to investors, we are the leaders in investment policy and strategy. *We have made a difference in the marketplace.* But, most important of all to me, we have built a name and reputation that is second to none in serving investors—*stewardship* in the truest sense. And stewardship means far more than the mere mechanisms through which we deliver our services. Yes, it means funds with sound investment policies and clear investment strategies. Yes, surely, it means providing services that result in record-keeping precision, financial controls second to none, and the communication of information, accurate to a fault, that approaches the instantaneous.

But stewardship means even more than that. The human beings we serve—real, honest-to-God, down-to-earth human beings—have been at the very epicenter of every business decision we have made. Vanguard does *not* represent a throng of 14 million investors; Vanguard represents 14 million souls, all of whom with *their own* hopes and fears, *their own* financial objectives, and *their own* trust in us. And we have never let them down. This philosophy was hardly invented here. We see some of it, for example, in the film classic *It's a Wonderful Life,* now fifty-five years old. Mr. Potter (a grouchy Lionel Barrymore) tells George Bailey (integrity-laden Jimmy Stewart) that Bailey's father, who founded the local building and loan society, was no businessman. "He was a man of huge ideas . . . a starry-eyed dreamer who gave people impossible ideas" about owning their own homes. Bailey responds, "People were human beings to him, Mr. Potter, but to you, you warped, frustrated old man, they're cattle." To which a growling Potter snarls, "Sentimental hogwash."

Well, it's *not* sentimental hogwash. Even in this age of instantaneous communication, electronic commerce, and computerized investment advice—all at our fingertips and in real time—it is human beings that must be at the core of any enterprise worth its salt. And this focus on human values is one of the "former things" that, contrary to Isaiah's warning at the outset, we must remember. This grand intangible would, however, serve little use if it represented good intentions but flawed investment policies. So we must also remember the investment policies that are fundamental to almost all that we have built—our mutual structure, our dedication to low costs, our fixed-income policies, our index funds, and our implementation of long-term investment strategies for long-term investors. Truly, we need *both* our human values *and* our investment philosophy if we are to retain our leadership as stewards of the assets of investors in the future.

What, then, should we forget? Certainly any investment approach that no longer works; any organizational qualities that have proven flawed; any corporate strategies that have become inconsistent with common sense in the new world in which we exist today. That said, sometimes the changes in the world—to say nothing of the changes in the financial markets—are transitory, so we must hold the line against fads and fashions and adhere to our bedrock principles, no matter how painful in the short run. Sound investment principles and decent human values proved to be a solid bedrock upon which to build Vanguard's foundation twenty-five years ago. They will remain the *right* principles and the *right* values, not only enduring, but eternal.

Hold Fast to That Which Is Good

What then do we make of Isaiah's words? "The new thing" he described in the Holy Bible that has surely sprung forth was the Judeo-Christian ethic. It has marked its way in the sea, its path in the mighty waters of our world. So, I don't imagine that now, centuries later, old Isaiah would be looking for *another* new thing. So it is with Vanguard. Our new thing too—albeit a pale reflection of what Isaiah was talking about—has sprung forth, and we all know it and recognize it every day. The world of investing is beginning to know it too. Our version of the great flagship HMS *Vanguard* has made its way in the sea, its path in the mighty waters of the world's financial system. Yes, we must be ever alert for fundamental change, but our watchword for the next quarter century and beyond must be, as the Bible entreats us: *"Hold fast to that which is good."*

So as this anniversary day ends, I thank all of you who serve so ably on our remarkable crew, now 10,000 strong, for helping to make that vision of 1974 come to pass. Our investment ideas and human values are necessary to all we have done, but without your dedication and loyalty, your enthusiasm and spirit, and your teamwork, Vanguard today would be a mere shadow of what we have become.

A COMPANY THAT STANDS FOR SOMETHING

May 20, 2000

I STAND BEFORE YOU, my fellow crew members, to thank you for this celebration of the twenty-fifth anniversary of the company that I founded on September 24, 1974. While it is doubtless traditional for the creator of a company to make a speech on such an occasion, I put you at ease by assuring you that I have no speech to make. But I do have just a few thoughts I'd like to leave with you on this gala evening.

❊   ❊   ❊

We read much today about the need, in this decidedly new era, for what is called "business concept innovation," the need for radical, not incremental, change. As you all can recognize, that is exactly what Vanguard did a quarter century ago, radically changing, within our first three years of existence, the very way that investors look at mutual funds.

Call it "mutualization" if you will, but the idea of funds being managed with their owners' interests paramount began right then. That structure called for rock-bottom operating costs, a recognition that almost instantly led to our creation of the industry's first index fund and then to the industry's first defined-asset-class bond funds, and to the complete elimination of distributors and sales commissions. Together, these revolutionary changes have constituted the driving force that has carried us to the pinnacle of industry leadership that we enjoy today.

Putting the Shareholder First

But even our novel corporate structure and our innovative investment strategy would not serve investors as they should without something more: a sense of stewardship for the assets of, yes, those real, honest-to-God, down-to-earth human beings who have turned over to us their assets and their trust alike. "Putting the shareholder first" is not just idle talk. To do so we would need a strong, determined, and integrity-laden crew, bound together in common cause by the idea of a powerful warship whose crew forged a chain that could be no stronger than its weakest link.

To have such a crew, we've relied heavily on traditions—some venerable, such as a spirit of fair dealing dating back to Wellington and Walter L. Morgan, others going back to the earliest days of Vanguard, such as our Award for Excellence and the Vanguard Partnership Plan. Yes, *even one person can make a difference,* and yes, each crew member has earned the right to share in the fruits of our success.

Taken together, our structure-driven corporate strategy, our innovative investment ideas, and our progressive implementation of business values have made Vanguard an industry revolutionary: *a company that stands for something.* And the world knows what it is we stand for: The primacy of the shareholder. Stewardship. With the power of an idea we have flourished. I know no other firm in this industry about which that can be said with such crystal clarity.

Looking to the Future

What of the future? "The times they are a changin'." What does a revolutionary firm do? Live off the legacy that I have put my heart and soul into giving you, or build on the legacy? The answer to that question, fellow crew members, is in your hands, no longer in mine. But as you make these decisions, please remember that we will be judged not only by what we do but by what we refrain from doing. Opportunity yes, but discipline too. And confidence. And courage, always.

I do not believe it is possible—*ever*—to improve on our basic strategy of providing investors with virtually 100 percent of the long-term returns available in the financial markets, simply by owning those very markets at minimal cost. By doing so, we have stripped the mystery from the investment process. You've heard me call our structure "the majesty of simplicity in an empire of parsimony." And it works! If we remain faithful to that legacy, I assure you of this verity: *This enterprise—of the shareholder, by the shareholder, and for the shareholder—shall not perish from the earth.*

Press on regardless, and stay the course.

AT THE FIFTY-YEAR MARK: LOOKING BACK, LOOKING AHEAD

May 29, 2001

Part I. The Legacy

ON VANGUARD   We lead. Crew member, not *employee*. Client, not *customer*. Mutual funds, not *products*. *Mutual* mutual funds. Rock-bottom costs. No sales charges. "If you build it, they will come." Market share: a measure, not an objective. Put the shareholder in the driver's seat. Index funds. Three-tier bond funds. Admiral Funds. Excellence. Serving real, honest-to-God, down-to-earth human beings who have their own hopes and goals. Never forget where you came from. A company that stands for something: stewardship. *Stay the course!*

ON INVESTMENT PRINCIPLES   Common sense on mutual funds. Investing is an act of faith. Invest for the long term. The eternal triangle: risk, return, and cost. Costs matter. The *magic* of compounding. Occam's Razor. If you can't foretell the future, diversify. Buy right and hold tight. Reversion to the mean. The hedgehog and the fox. The bagel and the doughnut. "Don't look for the needle. Buy the haystack." Time is your friend. Impulse is your enemy. The majesty of simplicity. *Stay the course!*

ON HUMAN VALUES   Treat human beings—from the highest to the humblest—with respect and honor. Loyalty is a two-way street. The Vanguard Partnership Plan. The Award for Excellence. The Swiss

Army. "For God's sake, let's give judgment a fighting chance to triumph over process." Sacred cows. Nothing fails like success. The *tyranny* of compounding. "Do what's right. If you're not sure, ask your boss." Servant leadership. Even one person can make a difference. "Never give up. Never. Never. Never. Never. Never!" Press on regardless. *Stay the course!*

Part II. The Appreciation

Surely most of you have come to recognize those ideas and phrases, most of which I've repeated endlessly ever since I created Vanguard all those years ago. Taken together, they paint a clear picture of what this enterprise is all about. While I doubt that many firms have such a clear legacy, the legacy I will one day leave at Vanguard is more far-reaching than those ideas. For ideas—however noble or humble, however simple or complex, however durable or ephemeral—must be transmitted and implemented, put into action by individual human beings. And so it is all of you on our crew who represent my legacy. *Stay the course!*

In my past meetings with throngs of you, and my continuing meetings with you in small groups and individually, my sole mission is to convey our heritage to you. For it is *not* boxcar-sized numbers—billions of dollars; millions of accounts; hundreds of thousands of phone calls, mailings, and Web site impressions—but individual human beings, person by person, who are what the best and most durable businesses are all about.

I speak, of course, of those shareholder-owners whom we serve but also, especially on this occasion, of you who have served with me on the Vanguard crew—newcomers and veterans alike, with a special note of thanks to those of you who have served with me during a decade or more of Vanguard's existence, and even at Wellington before that. I thank each one of you for your dedication, your loyalty, your conviction, and your hard work in the great cause of serving as stewards for those investors who have entrusted their resources to our care. As I'll repeat to my dying day: *Thank you for making me look so very much better than I am.*

Part III. The Mission

In a short time, I'll mark the fiftieth anniversary of my joining this industry on July 5, 1951. I won't burden you tonight with the saga of my exciting odyssey. (Just read my books!) But I do want to tell you that these past five years have been in some important respects the happiest of my career. First, of course, because I *lived* through them. The miracle of my heart transplant, on February 21, 1996, has not only restored but enhanced my lifelong energy, enthusiasm, and optimism.

Second, because, after freeing myself, shortly after the transplant, of the responsibility for the day-to-day management of Vanguard's operations, I seized the moment, undertaking the research, writing, and public appearances that I so enjoy, conducting face-to-face meetings with fund shareholders from coast to coast, and with crew members in Valley Forge, Arizona, and North Carolina, and, for that matter, in Belgium and in Australia. It is by being an ambassador, an author, and a think-tank director that I can continue to best fulfill my responsibilities to you, to our shareowners, and to this enterprise that I created nearly twenty-seven years ago.

As this fifty-year milestone rushes by, I honestly don't know how long my desire or determination, or my fate, will permit me to carry on my mission. So I live my life one day at a time. As you might imagine, that maxim proved to be a marvelous secret for dealing with a heart attack at age thirty, surviving a firing at age forty-four, launching a new enterprise at age forty-five, leading it through the ups and downs of nearly a quarter century of growth and success, waiting for a heart transplant at age sixty-six, and thereafter undertaking my new responsibilities. But I want to be fair to Eve, and to my children and grandchildren too. So I struggle with powerful emotions about the meaning of life that go deep into one's soul. But in each facet of my multifaceted life, I intend to—surprise!—*stay the course!*

Part IV. After the Odyssey

What comes next in the career of this aging warrior? Tennyson answered that question with far more poignancy and articulateness than I could possibly summon. So hear now the powerful words of the poet, speaking for Ulysses as his long, sea-borne odyssey concludes. He speaks for me:

> **I cannot rest from travel: I will drink**
> **Life to the lees: All times I have enjoy'd**
> **Greatly, have suffer'd greatly, both with those**
> **That loved me, and alone, on shore . . .**
> **I am become a name;**
> **For always roaming with a hungry heart**

Much have I seen and known; cities of men
And manners, climates, councils, governments,
Myself not least, but honour'd of them all—
And drunk delight of battle with my peers.
I am a part of all that I have met.
How dull it is to pause, to make an end,
To rust unburnish'ed, not to shine in use!
As tho' to breathe were life! Life piled on life
Were all too little, and of one to me
Little remains: but every hour is saved
From that eternal silence, something more,
A bringer of new things;
And this gray spirit yearning in desire
To follow knowledge like a sinking star,
Beyond the utmost bound of human thought.

There lies the port; the vessel puffs her sail:
There gloom the dark, broad seas. My mariners,
Souls that have toil'd, and wrought, and thought with me—
That ever with a frolic welcome took
The thunder and the sunshine, and opposed
Free hearts, free foreheads—you and I are old;
Old age hath yet his honour and his toil;
Death closes all: but something ere the end,
Some work of noble note, may yet be done. . . .
Come, my friends
'Tis not too late to seek a newer world.
Push off, and sitting well in order smite
The sounding furrows; for my purpose holds
To sail beyond the sunset 'til I die. . . .
Tho' much is taken, much abides; and tho'
We are not now that strength which in old days
Moved earth and heaven, that which we are, we are;—
One equal temper of heroic hearts,
Made weak by time and fate, but strong in will
To strive, to seek, to find, and not to yield.

Thank you, good night, and may God bless you all.

Part VI

EPILOGUE

THE VANGUARD CENTURY

September 5, 2001

*T*o strive, to seek, to find, and not to yield. The closing words of my fifty-year anniversary speech provide an appropriate theme for my epilogue on the creation and building of Vanguard. We strive always for excellence, and we achieve growth as a result. We seek a better way to invest, and we find it in simplicity—indexing, structured bond portfolios, low costs, and a long-term horizon. And, despite the subtle temptation of conventionalism and the intense pressure of competition, we do not yield, either in our investment philosophy or in our human values. In short, we maintain the character that has brought us to the pinnacle of achievement in our industry.

While many things have changed—and changed radically—in the world, in the economy, and in the financial markets since Vanguard began in 1974, the words of Robinson Jeffers that I cited in my very first speech to the crew seem almost prescient today, and could well have served as the centerpiece for my final speech of the era:

> **Lend me the stone strength of the past,**
> **And I will lend you**
> **The wings of the future.**

For in Vanguard's case, it has indeed been the stone strength of our past—the character that we established for the firm in its formative years—that has provided our wings of the future, the wings that have carried us soaring above our rivals in the quest for industry leadership.

Consider the sources of our dominance in the direct marketing segment of the industry:

- Assets of our equity index funds total $192 billion, 35 percent of our asset base and its largest component. Holding a predominant 75 percent market share of the index assets of directly offered funds, we are by far the dominant factor in the field. The tiny $11 million index fund we formed in 1975 is now an $85 billion giant, the largest fund in the world.
- Assets of our structured bond funds total $110 billion—including $24 billion in bond *index* funds—and account for 20 percent of our asset base. We are the largest firm in this segment of our field too, holding a dominant market share—45 percent of the assets of all bond funds.
- Assets of our balanced funds total $44 billion, equal to a dominant 44 percent share of the assets in this category. Balanced funds constitute 8 percent of our assets. Wellington, vigorous since it was restored to health in 1978, now has assets of $24 billion, the largest balanced fund in the world.
- Assets of our money market funds total $91 billion, 16 percent of our asset base. This total represents the second largest aggregation of money funds in our field, where we enjoy a 33 percent market share.
- Our actively managed equity funds, now totaling $119 billion, represent 21 percent of our asset base. While our share of this market (11 percent) is the lowest among our five asset classes, Vanguard's managed equity fund assets exceed those of all of our rivals save one.

Strong Markets . . . But Strong Market Share Growth, Too

The strong financial markets that have prevailed during our history and the strong cash inflows that have accompanied them have given the HMS *Vanguard* a good wind at her back. Our assets have grown from $1.4 billion at the outset to $562 billion today. But the overwhelming portion of that increase has *not* come from those factors, which, after all, have blessed *all* of the firms in the ever-market-sensitive mutual fund industry. Rather the lion's share of our growth has arisen from our rising share of market. Our share of total industry assets has grown nearly fivefold, from a low of 1.7 percent in 1981 to a current 8.4 percent. Had our share remained unchanged since then, Vanguard assets today would total $115 billion. *The remaining $446 billion is accounted for by the rise in our market penetration*—an increase that has carried us from a *number 14* ranking in the industry twenty years earlier to a strong *number 2* rank today.

Our massive gain in share has been neither market driven nor event driven. Almost irrespective of the financial environment, it has been consistent and steady. Indeed, during the past two decades there has been *not a single year* in which our share of industry assets declined. Our share gains—especially in recent years—have rested largely on the shoulders of the index and indexlike funds that we had put in place by mid-1977.

Leading the way to our top-ranking industry cash inflow of $42 billion during the first eight months of 2001 were our index funds—our stone strength. The 500 Index, Total Bond Market Index, and Total Stock Market Index funds ranked among the top five funds among the industry's 6,400 mutual funds in terms of cash flow for the period. Our GNMA fund, ranking number 8, was not far behind. Our total cash inflow represented fully 20 percent of the amount invested in *all* long-term mutual funds, meaning that one dollar of every five invested in mutual funds this year has found its way to Vanguard.

Investment Performance

Of course, the performance of our funds has been a critical factor in our success. While we have been beset with our share of funds encountering periodic performance difficulties (Windsor in 1989 and 1990, Growth Equity and U.S. Growth in 2001), by and large our managed equity funds have given a good account of themselves. And since low costs afford a risk-free way to enhance returns—especially in index, bond, and money market funds—our drive to keep expenses at rock-bottom levels has played a major role in keeping these funds well ahead of their peers. Our across-the-board success has been widely recognized. In 2001 alone, Vanguard was recognized as a top fund family by the respected Morningstar organization, and our funds were top rated by *Consumer Reports, Forbes, Worth, Kiplinger Personal Finance* magazine, and many other publications, an almost universal endorsement.

Thus, it is almost indisputable that Vanguard's rise to industry leadership has come largely as a result of our character, manifested in our principles and values, and in the structure and strategies with which we were endowed at our creation. But our story would not be complete without bestowing enormous credit on our dedicated crew—now 11,000 in number—who have done the hard work and toiled the long hours required to make our founding ideas a reality.

I've often said that ideas are a dime a dozen. Even if you are lucky enough to have a good one, it can be brought to fruition only by a crew whose members believe in it and are prepared to fight for it. *Implementation is every bit as important as ideation.* Perhaps this is what Helen Keller, whom I quoted when I presented our Award of Excellence in 1998 to Wellington founder Walter Morgan, had in mind when she wrote:

The world is moved along, not only by the mighty shoves of its heroes but by the aggregate of the tiny pushes of each worker.

The notion of a warship and her crew has always struck me as one of the singular merits of the name I was lucky enough to choose for the firm all those years ago. Even as life is a sort of battle, so is business. So is investing. Any battleship requires a captain and a crew. Any battleship requires leadership as well as teamwork. Any battleship depends on a chain of sailors that can be no stronger than its weakest link. While we think of a war as having a beginning and an end, however, a company wages a war that begins with its creation, and from then on battles for survival and success. And the outcome of the war is never a certainty.

When all is said and done, however, amid the creative destruction that is an essential—and beneficial—part of our system of democratic capitalism, *no company is guaranteed eternal life.* Indeed, few American businesses have endured for even a mere century. But, ever the optimistic idealist, I believe Vanguard will still be flourishing when we reach our century milestone in 2074. Of course we have a long time to work and wait and watch. But strong today, Vanguard will remain strong tomorrow too, come what may as our organization grows, come what may in our economy, come what may in our financial markets.

John C. Bogle

Postscript: In the Aftermath—October 15, 2001

Early in September, I concluded my epilogue about Vanguard's endurance with the phrase, "come what may in our financial markets." Little did I imagine that the world of investing—indeed, the world itself—would change so soon, and so dramatically. The attack on America by terrorists on the morning of September 11, 2001—etched so powerfully in our minds by images of the attack and then the collapse of the proud towers of New York's World Trade Center—brought the U.S. financial markets to a complete standstill for nearly a week, the second longest closing of our stock market in all its history. When the markets reopened on September 17, the stock market promptly plunged by 14 percent, its largest weekly drop ever.

Right after the tragedy, almost eerily, I remembered the words that I offered in earlier speeches that I gave at our building dedications in 1973, 1983, and 1993. All of those speeches, going back to the era of the Vietnam War, talked about challenges to America's character and values. Edited only slightly and updated, here is what I said:

> **It was just 224 years ago, and perhaps only 2,000 yards away, that America went through her first crisis. The winter in Valley Forge, history books tell us, was a rugged, bitter test for a tiny army, which not only survived, but went on to earn the independence that too many of us take for granted today. Now, more than two centuries later, the American character is again being tested, and it is hardly an exaggeration to say that every institution in our society, from the White House on down the line, is being challenged—challenged to reassess its goals, its values, its contributions to our society.**
>
> **The challenges are profound, and they not only affect overwhelmingly the environment in which we do our work but also are directed to those institutions which we refer to as "financial institutions"—including our own. In the vast context of space and time, our company, even with the hundreds of billions of dollars investors have entrusted to us, is small and fragile, perhaps even unimportant. Nonetheless, we must now do our work better than we have done our work before. We must now be better and stronger as individuals; we must now make this ambitious organ-**

ization even better and stronger. In our own small way, each one of us can be a positive force in helping to make America just a little bit better. Even one person can make a difference.

As we look at our new world—and at ourselves—today, we are all asking: What does the attack on our nation mean?

It means there is life as well as death, evil as well as goodness, grief as well as joy, destruction as well as creation. These things Americans know—there is enough sorrow in life to know them— yet we do not hold that knowledge in the front of our minds. We have never done so, nor is now the time we are likely to start. No life worth living is lived in mortal fear.

I am proud to associate myself with these poignant and moving words, written by James Grant, author of numerous books on the financial history of the United States and editor of *Grant's Interest Rate Observer.* We know we've been struck by a major blow, and we know that our world has changed. But we also know that we must press on.

The Nation and the Markets

What does the terrorist attack mean for America? Now using my own words, it means war, a war against terrorism; the staggering costs of rebuilding and of defending ourselves, to the extent possible, against further horrendous acts; the deepening of the impact and the lengthening of the duration of the economic recession that we entered earlier in the year; and the loss of some of the conveniences and freedoms we have come to take for granted. But it also means, I expect, that from now on we will place a higher value on those we love; that we will treat with greater compassion all of those human beings we encounter along the road of life; that we will count again, and then again, our blessings of liberty and the values of democratic capitalism that have made us both the ideal and the envy of human beings all over the world. And it means we will—as we must—reaffirm our conviction that good will triumph over evil.

What does it mean for the financial markets? It means that, for the moment, emotions have trumped economics as the driver of the stock market; that the greed manifested at the height of the bubble in March 2000 and the hope evident in the late summer alike, have been replaced for a time by fear; that, faced with an unexpected catastrophe, market participants first respond with alarm, *just as they always have;* that corporate earnings are likely to tumble in the short term and that investors will pay less for each dollar of earnings. But we can be confident that it also means, *just as it always does,* that this advice, whether in the best of times or in the worst of times, is the right advice: *This too shall pass away.* Our American economy has always been resilient; our financial markets have always recovered and gone on to new heights. I see no reason that history will not repeat. Corporations in 2005 are more likely—and in 2010 *far* more likely—to have higher earnings than in 2001, and that's really all that's important for long-term investors.

Vanguard Weather

What does it mean for Vanguard? I am impressed and delighted with the strength of our crew and our clients in the aftermath of the terrible, terrifying events of September 11. To repeat two phrases you've seen often in this book: *We press on regardless, and we stay the course.* Since the economic and financial upheaval we have witnessed means a more acute awareness of the risks of investing, it means increased attention to *asset allocation*—a sound balance between stocks and bonds—and to broad *diversification,* owning the stock market in its entirety rather than gambling on extreme styles and on the will-o'-the-wisp of past performance. It also means paying more attention to the role of cost, even more important (if possible!) when the returns earned in the financial markets are likely to be lower than in the long halcyon era that followed Vanguard's creation all those years ago. No matter what the course of the financial markets, we are entering a climate in which Vanguard will shine even more brightly: *Vanguard weather.*

But only if we continue to prove the driving message of this book: *Character counts.*

About the Author

JOHN C. BOGLE is the founder and former chairman of The Vanguard Group, the pioneer—and world's largest—no-load mutual fund company. One of the towering business leaders of this or any generation, Bogle has also written three books on successful investing, including *John Bogle on Investing: The First 50 Years, Bogle on Mutual Funds,* and *Common Sense on Mutual Funds.*